Federalism: A Tool for Conflict Management in Multicultural Societies with Regard to the Conflicts in the Near East

PIFF

Publications de l'Institut du Fédéralisme Fribourg Suisse
Publications of the Institute of Federalism Fribourg Switzerland
Publikationen des Instituts für Föderalismus Freiburg Schweiz

Etudes et colloques, volume 50

LIT

Thomas Fleiner (ed.)

Federalism: A Tool for Conflict Management in Multicultural Societies with Regard to the Conflicts in the Near East

A la mémoire de Jean Nordmann

Jean Nordmann Colloquium
on Federal Co-Existence in the Near East
(March 14th to March 17th 2004)

Avec l'aide de la Fondation Nordmann

INSTITUTE OF FEDERALISM FRIBOURG SWITZERLAND

LIT

Bibliographic information published by the Deutsche Nationalbibliothek
The Deutsche Nationalbibliothek lists this publication in the Deutsche Nationalbibliografie; detailed bibliographic data are available in the Internet at http://dnb.d-nb.de.

ISBN 978-3-03735-254-0 (Schweiz) ISBN 978-3-8258-1442-7 (Deutschland)

A catalogue record for this book is available from the British Library

© LIT VERLAG GmbH & Co. KG Wien, Zweigniederlassung Zürich 2008
Dufourstr. 31
CH-8008 Zürich
Tel. +41 (0) 44-251 75 05
Fax +41 (0) 44-251 75 06
e-Mail: zuerich@lit-verlag.ch
http://www.lit-verlag.ch

LIT VERLAG Dr. W. Hopf
Berlin 2008
Auslieferung/Verlagskontakt:
Fresnostr. 2
D-48159 Münster
Tel. +49 (0)251–62 03 20
Fax +49 (0)251–23 19 72
e-Mail: lit@lit-verlag.de
http://www.lit-verlag.de

Auslieferung:
Schweiz/Österreich: Medienlogistik Pichler-ÖBZ GmbH & Co KG
IZ-NÖ, Süd, Straße 1, Objekt 34, A-2355 Wiener Neudorf
Tel. +43 (0) 2236/63 535 - 290, Fax +43 (0) 2236/63 535 - 243, e-Mail: mlo@medien-logistik.at
Deutschland: LIT Verlag Fresnostr. 2, D-48159 Münster
Tel. +49 (0) 2 51/620 32 - 22, Fax +49 (0) 2 51/922 60 99, e-Mail: vertrieb@lit-verlag.de

Distributed in the UK by: Global Book Marketing, 99B Wallis Rd, London, E9 5LN
Phone: +44 (0) 20 8533 5800 – Fax: +44 (0) 1600 775 663
http://www.centralbooks.co.uk/acatalog/search.html

Distributed in North America by:

Transaction Publishers
New Brunswick (U.S.A.) and London (U.K.)

Transaction Publishers
Rutgers University
35 Berrue Circle
Piscataway, NJ 08854

Phone: +1 (732) 445 - 2280
Fax: + 1 (732) 445 - 3138
for orders (U. S. only):
toll free (888) 999 - 6778
e-mail:
orders@transactionspub.com

Table of Contents

Nation, Religion and Identities in the Near East : Challenge or Opportunity for Federal Solutions ?

The Alternatives : Other Institutional and Procedural Tools for Conflict Management

From Conflict to Peace : Procedures to Enhance Peaceful Transition

Preface

The papers of this book contain the main ideas which have been presented at the colloquy on: *"Federalism : A Tool for Conflict Management in Multicultural Societies with Regard to the Conflict in the Near East."* This conference has been sponsored by the Nordmann Foundation and it was organized to the memory of the late Jean Nordmann by Prof. Claude Klein, Jerusalem and Thomas Fleiner of the Institute of Federalism Fribourg University. Since many years Jean Nordmann and his family have supported the good relationship between the University of Fribourg and the Hebrew University in Jerusalem. For this purpose the family has founded the Nordmann Foundation which contributes to the good relationship and cooperation between the Hebrew University in Jerusalem and the University of Fribourg. Jean Nordmann and his family have always contributed to the understanding of Jewish and Chrstian communities throughout Switzerland and in particular in Fribourg.

The title of the Colloquy is in many ways a symbol for Jean Nordmann and his family. The Nordmann family was and is still an open place for different generations of different religious, political and cultural background open and prepared to learn from each other through a friendly and constructive dialogue. Jean Nordmann and his wife Bluette have contributed and supported with their mind and heart young scholars and students interested to learn from other cultures, religions and countries and to contribute with their research for better common understanding. Thus the content of this colloquy did share the main ideas the family Nordmann has always tried to pursue.

Unfortunately we were not able to publish these papers short after the conference. However each of the articles and all ideas are of a general value for the better understanding of the complexity of tragic conflict but also of the high potential and values rooted within the tradition and the philosophy of the conflicting nations which may help one day to promote the common goals of peace and peaceful managing the actual violent conflict.

This edition could only be published with the help of Prof. Claude Klein, Jerusalem, the Nordmann Foundation and all my collaborators in particular Markus Kern, Claudia Josi and Christine Verdon.

Thomas FLEINER

Fribourg, in March 2008

The Authors

André ALEN

Prof. Dr., Instituut voor Constitutioneel Recht (Institut de droit constitutionnel), KU Leuven.

Lidija R. BASTA FLEINER

Research Professor, Institute of Federalism, University of Fribourg, Director of the International Research and Consulting Centre of the Institute of Federalism.

Stefano CECCANTI

Professor ; University of Bologna, Italy.

Jan CLEMENT

Dr., Instituut voor Constitutioneel Recht (Institut de droit constitutionnel), KU Leuven.

Thomas FLEINER

Professor of Public Law at the University of Fribourg, Director of the Institute of Federalism, Honorary President of the International Association of Constitutional Law.

Liah GREENFELD

University Prof. ; Director, Inst Advancement Ss, University Professorsprogramm, Dept. of Sociology, Boston University, USA.

Ilan GREILSAMMER
Professeur de science politique, Université Bar-Ilan, Israël.

Nicolas HAYSOM
Professor ; Consultant and Specialist in Mediation and Conflict Resolution, South Africa.

Julian Thomas HOTTINGER
Dr, Expert in Mediation & Facilitation, Swiss Federal Department of Foreign Affairs, Bern, Switzerland.

Michael Mousa KARAYANNI
Prof. Dr. ; Hebrew University, Jerusalem, Israël.

Claude KLEIN
Université hébraïque de Jérusalem, Doyen du Collège de droit de Ramat-Gan.

Antoine Nasri MESSARRA
Professor ; Lebanese Foundation for Permanent Civil Peace (LFPCP), Lebanon.

Dragoljub POPOVIĆ
Professor at the Business Law School of Belgrade, Ambassador of Serbia and Montenegro to Switzerland.

Matthias SCHNYDER
Research Fellow, IRCC, Institute of Federalism.

Ronald L. WATTS
Professor Emeritus and Institute Fellow ; Institute of Intergovernmental Relations, Queen's University, Kingston, Canada.

Federal Co-existence in the Near East : General Introduction

Ronald L. WATTS

INTRODUCTION

Back in 1992, Daniel Elazar presented a public lecture at the Institute of Intergovernmental Relations at Queen's University in Canada on the subject "Can Federal Arrangements Serve the Cause of Middle East Peace?" Taking the Middle East to range from Egypt, Sudan and Libya in the west, including Israel, the Palestinians and Jordan at its centre, and also to the east Arabia, Iraq, Iran and Afghanistan, he noted the dismal prospects in most of the region for federal solutions, the only stable federal example to date in the region being the United Arab Emirates (Daniel J. ELAZAR, *Federalism and the Way to Peace,* Kingston : Institute of Intergovernmental Relations, Queen's University, Reflections Paper N° 13, 1994, pp. 95-110). For this colloquium, the geographical scope is narrower. The focus will be on the "Near East", which I take to embrace primarily Israel, the Palestinians, Jordan and Lebanon, although their relations with neighbouring Syria and Arabia cannot be left totally out of consideration.

At first sight, the prospects of federalism as a tool of conflict management in the multicultural societies of the Near East region, as I have defined it, look decidedly unpromising. In fact at the current time the prospects look positively dismal. A key factor is that the region is marked by politicized religious fundamentalism. It is a region in which religious fundamentalists see their political role as a necessary and vital one. As Daniel Elazar has noted (p. 97), it is an integral part of the Islamic but also all the other near eastern religious cultures that there should be close relations between religion and politics. Indeed, where there have been efforts to have democratic elections in the Near East, the more democratic the elections, the more often the fundamentalists have won. The current intense religious-nationalist polarization has made difficult the development of any of the compromise, tolerance and mutual trust which any federal political resolution requires. Moreover, the federal idea and its effective application elsewhere have in practice been closely tied to the development of a civil society in which government plays a limited rather than a total role. But the Near East remains a region in which there seems to be little or no desire for the development of an unpoliticized civil society. If anything, the whole complex of forces seems in the Near East to be working in the opposite direction.

Nevertheless, there are reasons for examining carefully whether federalism could serve as a tool for conflict management in the Near East, and as I shall argue later, for identifying the pre-conditions that need to be established before federalism can work effectively as such a tool. For instance, there is the experience of South Africa over the past decade and a half. In the 1980s there appeared to be an inevitably looming disaster generated by apartheid. But subsequent developments there indicate that seemingly hopeless situations can, with the right leadership on all sides, be turned around. Second, over the years there have been many proposals to establish relations between the peoples in the Near East based upon federal or confederal arrangements. Indeed, the Jerusalem Centre of Public Affairs noted that in the 60 years between 1917 and 1976 over 60 proposals were made (Elazar, p.104), and there have been many more since. While the mere advancing of federal proposals does not ensure that they are workable, Daniel Elazar, writing a decade ago, did see some hopeful and realistic signs for a confederal solution of one kind or another embracing Israel, Jordan and the lands in between (Elazar, pp. 103-6). At that time he thought that the region was on the threshold of the first real opportunity for Israel-Arab peace with a narrowing in on confederal solutions, possibly a Jordanian-Palestinian federation that in turn would be confederated with Israel.

Sadly, however, in the past decade the prospects for any federal or confederal solution would seem to have declined seriously as political conflict and polarization have sharpened.

In such a context, the program of this colloquium appropriately focused on four basic issues. First, what can we learn from other cases where federalism has attempted to serve as a conflict management tool? Here the focus in the program of this colloquium was primarily on the concepts of personal federalism in the Austro-Hungrarian and Ottoman Empires, the experiences in Lebanon and elsewhere, on the combination of territorial and personal federalism in Belgium, and on lessons from the territorial multicultural federation of Switzerland. Other examples which could also further provide both positive and negative lessons are India, Malaysia, Nigeria, Ethiopia and Canada.

Second, we need to take account of the nature of the sources of conflict in the Near East and particularly the clash of nationalisms, religions and identities contributing to this conflict. This analysis will help to identify the possibilities and limits for federal solutions in the region. Hence the importance of understanding Arab, Islamic, Jewish, Israeli and Christian perceptions.

Third, alternative institutional and procedural tools for conflict management need to be considered to see if they might serve better the conditions of the Near East. In addition to the three alternatives identified in the program – the melting pot, the unitary universal citizen state, and the confederal model – consociational and hybrid models might also be included in this consideration of alternatives.

Fourth, is the issue of the procedures required to manage a transition from conflict to peace. This includes the role of the international community, the transition from negotiation to democratic legitimacy (a prime issue currently in Iraq), and the fundamental requirement of trust and compromise for any effective federal solution.

The fundamental issue before the colloquium, thus, was the challenge, not of eliminating national, religious and multicultural identities and diversity, but rather of how to accommodate, reconcile, and manage these social diversities within an overarching polity that enables peaceful co-existence. In examining the potential and limits of federal solutions for resolving deep multicultural conflicts, an important aspect may be not simply how to design an appropriate federal framework and how to negotiate agreement upon it, but first how to develop the necessary preconditions. These include an environment and conditions conducive to federal thinking and a political culture sustaining the combination of self-rule and shared rule which is the essence of federal solutions.

WHAT DO WE MEAN BY A FEDERAL SOLUTION?

Over the years there has been much scholarly debate about the definition of federalism as a form of political organization. Definitions have varied from broad inclusive ones to narrow restrictive ones. Through all these, however, runs the basic notion of federalism, i.e., the operation of two or more orders of government within a single polity combining elements of "shared-rule" for some purposes and "self-rule" of the constituent units for other purposes. Federalism as a normative idea is based on the objective of combining unity and diversity, i.e. of accommodating, preserving and indeed promoting and cherishing distinct identities within a larger political union.

This basic idea has been expressed in practice through a variety of federal institutional forms which contrast to the single source of constitutional authority in unitary systems. In federal political systems there are two (or more) levels of government enabling a combination of shared-rule through common institutions with territorial self-rule for the governments of the constituent units. The broad category of such federal systems encompasses a wide range of institutional forms from constitutionally decentralized unions to confederacies, federacies, associated states and joint functional authorities. Within this broad genus of federal political systems, *federations* represent a distinct species in which neither the federal nor the constituent unit governments are constitutionally subordinate to the other, i.e. each has sovereign powers derived from the constitution rather than from another level of government, each is empowered to deal directly with the citizens in the exercise of legislative, executive and taxing powers, and each is directly elected by its citizens (R. L. WATTS, *Comparing Federal Systems*, 2nd ed., Montreal and Kingston: McGill-Queen's University Press, 1999, pp. 6-14).

The structural characteristics generally common to federations as a specific form of political organization are the following:

- Two (or more) orders of government acting directly on their citizens (rather than indirectly through the other order);
- A formal constitutional distribution of legislative and executive authority and an allocation of revenue resources between the orders of government ensuring some areas of genuine autonomy for each order;
- Provision for the designated representation of distinct territorial views within the federal policy-making institutions, usually provided by a federal second chamber composed of representatives of the electorates, legislatures or governments of the constituent units.
- A supreme written constitution, not unilaterally amendable by one order of government, and therefore requiring the consent not only of the federal legislature, but also of a significant proportion of the constituent units through assent by their legislatures or by referendum majorities;
- An umpire, usually in the form of courts (or as in Switzerland through provision for referendums), to rule on interpretation or valid application of the constitution;
- Processes and institutions to facilitate intergovernmental collaboration in those areas where government responsibilities are shared or overlap.

What of the alternatives? One category is unitary political systems. What distinguishes them, including even unitary systems with a considerable measure of decentralization, is that in unitary systems all the other constituent units of government ultimately derive their authority from the central government and therefore are constitutionally and politically subordinate to it. Such systems tend to leave minorities with a sense of insecurity in relation to majorities controlling the central governments. Another set of alternatives to federations are confederations which, like federations, combine shared-rule and self-rule, but in which ultimately the central institutions derive their authority from the constituent units and the central institutions consist of delegates of the constituent units. This contrasts with federations in which each order of government derives its authority, not from another government or governments, but from the constitution. Confederations provide the populations of constituent units with a greater sense of security because of their veto power, but have in practice been prone to weak central governments and in the long-term to instability. Among other federal forms with similar characteristics are federacies, associated states, and joint functional authorities (Watts, pp. 8-13).

It should be noted that there are also hybrids combining characteristics of different kinds of political systems. Some which are predominantly federations in character have included a number of central powers (usually emergency powers) more typical of unitary systems. Consequently, at different stages in their development Canada, India, Pakistan, Malaysia and South Africa have been categorized as 'quasi-federations'. On the other hand, the Bundesrat in the German Federation represents a confederal element. The European Union in its current form, predominantly a confederation but with some features of a federation, represents an innovative hybrid. Hybrids have occurred because statesman are often more interested in pragmatic political solutions than in theoretical purity, a point well worth bearing in mind in dealing with the multicultural complexity of the Near East.

The extent to which 'federation' or these alternative basic models will be appropriate models to accommodate and manage multicultural conflict in the Near East will depend on the extent to which the institutional features of each model facilitate the particular national, religious and social diversity there. At the same time, I would draw attention to the fact that while federations as a group exhibit the basic common structural features and political processes which I have already outlined, within the category of federations there have been many variations in the application of the federal idea. The effectiveness of a federation may depend not just upon the adoption of federal arrangements but upon whether the particular variant of federation adopted or evolved gives adequate expression to the requirements of the particular society or region in question. Among variations found in different federations have been: the degree of cultural or national diversity which they attempt to reconcile; the number and relative size of the constituent units; the precise distribution of legislative and executive powers among governments; the allocation taxing powers and financial resources; the degree of symmetry or asymmetry in the allocation of authority to constituent units; the degree of centralization or decentralization and economic integration; the character and composition of their central institutions; the legal and political processes and institutions for resolving internal conflicts and for facilitating collaboration between interdependent governments; the specific procedures for formal and informal constitutional adaptation; and the roles of federal and constituent-unit governments in the conduct of international relations.

It is also worth noting that the effectiveness of different federations has depended not just on constitutional structures but also upon their political practices and processes. Significant characteristics of effective federal processes have included:

- A strong disposition to democratic procedures since they presume the voluntary consent of the different groups of citizens in the constituent units;
- Non-centralization as a principle expressed through multiple centres of political decision-making;
- The operation of checks and balances to avoid the concentration of political power;
- Open political bargaining as a major feature of the way in which decisions are arrived at;
- Genuine power-sharing within the central institutions for all the major groups, often involving consociational processes;
- A general respect for constitutionalism and the rule of law since each order of government derives its authority from the constitution.

In considering how some form of federal solution might serve as a tool for conflict management in the Near East, much can be learned from looking at positive and negative experiences elsewhere in the world. Indeed, in the contemporary world, federalism as a political idea has become increasingly important as a way of peacefully reconciling unity and diversity. 'Federation' as an institutional design was not originally developed specifically to deal with multinational or multicultural situations. Indeed, it origins in its modern form lie in the essentially mononational United States in the eighteenth century, and it has since been applied in other basically mononational societies such as Australia, Austria and Germany. But the logic on which 'federation' as a form of government is based, i.e. that territorially concentrated minorities are enabled to exercise autonomy or self-rule on matters crucial to their identity without fear of being overridden by a majority within the polity, and at the same time obtain the economic, social, diplomatic, security and other benefits from participating in a larger political organization, has had a particular appeal in multinational and multicultural situations.

Consequently some variant of federation has come to be employed in such multinational or multicultural countries as Switzerland, Canada, India, Malaysia, Nigeria, Ethiopia, Belgium, and Spain. Indeed, there are in the world today some 25 countries that claim to be federations or exhibit the major characteristics of federations. Some 40 percent of the world's population lives in these federations embracing about 480 constituent or federated states. Moreover, the potential effectiveness of this form of government is illustrated by a number of examples. The United States (1789), Switzerland (1848), Canada (1867) and Australia (1901) are among the longest continuously operating constitutional systems anywhere in the world today. In recent years the annual United Nations Index of Human Development, ranking some 180 countries in terms of their quality of life, has ranked four federations among the top six – Australia, Canada, Belgium, and the United States – with Switzerland and Germany close behind. Furthermore, recent empirical studies (such as those edited by Ute WACHENDORFER-SCHMIDT, 2000) have suggested that federal political systems have in practice generally outperformed unitary states in economic policy-making. It is also worth noting that in the contemporary world it has sometimes proved useful to multiply the levels of federal organization as in the case of the European Union whose membership includes four countries that are themselves federations. Another complex multi-level federal organization is that of Bosnia Herzegovina, although many might question the degree of its effectiveness.

But although the last half-century has seen the proliferation of multicultural federations, including some remarkably successful ones, the same period has also seen the failure of a number of multicultural federations (R. L. WATTS, *Lessons from the pathology of multicultural federations*, in : Mensch und Staat; L'Homme et l'Etat, Fribourg : Editions Universitaires Fribourg Suisse, 2003, pp. 222-36). Among significant examples have been the disintegration of federations in the West Indies (1962), Rhodesia and Nyasaland (1963), Yugoslavia (from 1991 on) and the USSR (1991); the splitting of Pakistan (1971) and Czechoslovakia (1992); the expulsion of Singapore from Malaysia (1965); and alternating periods of civilian and military rule in both Nigeria and Pakistan. Any assessment of the prospects for a federal solution to manage conflict in multicultural regions such as the Near East, must therefore take account not only of the successful examples but also of the failures and of the pathology of these failures, i.e. the conditions and processes leading to the breakdown of federations where this has occurred.

SIGNIFICANCE OF THE NATURE OF DIVERSITY AND CONFLICTS

Consideration of the applicability of a federal solution or a particular form of federal institutions must take account of the particular nature of the multicultural diversity and conflicts to be accommodated and managed.

Traditionally federal political systems have been viewed as better suited to accommodating territorially based diversities because such systems distribute political authority among territorially defined sub-units. Federal systems, as a territorial form of political organization, safeguard distinct groups, minorities and interests best when these are regionally concentrated in such a way that they may achieve self-government as a majority within their own territory. Where social segmentation is not territorially distributed, other non-federal solutions such as corporative organization, primarily consociational processes, and constitutional protections of basic rights or of minority rights as advocated by Professor Klein may be more appropriate alternatives. Nevertheless, it is sometimes argued that even in such situations the dispersion of political power and the checks and balances inherent in any federal system may provide some protection for non-territorially distributed minorities.

Relevant here is the notion of non-territorial 'personal federalism' as contrasted to territorial federalism, an issue raised in the references to Otto Bauer and Karl Renner in several of the papers for the first session. On the face of it this is an attractive idea. It is appropriate, therefore, that the innovative Belgian combination of regional (territorial) and community constituent units within a federation be examined in the same session, although in Belgium it would appear to have resulted in considerable complexity and to have ultimately a fundamentally territorial basis.

It should be noted that even where the primary social segmentation is territorially distributed, populations rarely in practice are distributed into neat watertight territorial compartments. Virtually all federations have had to take account for the existence of intra-unit minorities, sometimes by redrawing the boundaries of constituent units, but most commonly by embodying a set of fundamental rights in the constitution to protect intra-unit minorities (R. L. WATTS, *Federalism in Fragmented and Segmented Societies*, in : J. Kramer & H.P. Schneider, eds. Federalism and Civil Societies, Baden-Baden, Nomos Verlagsgesellschaft, 1999, pp. 149-51). Sometimes the possibility of non-territorial 'personal federalism' has been advocated for situations where significant distinct groups inhabit the same territory (see for instance Alexandre MARC and Robert ARON, *Principes du Fédéralisme*, Paris: Le Portulan, 1948). It is appropriate therefore that the innovative Belgian combination of regional (territorial) and community (personal) constituent units within a federation will be examined later in this colloquium in some depth.

Among the factors usually inducing conflict among different groups are economic differentiation, particularly economic disparities, historical grievances, and differences in prevailing ideological views. However, social segmentation and the consequent demand for political self-expression and self-rule have been particularly virile where territorially concentrated groups have been marked by differences of religion, language, race, social structure and cultural tradition. In federations this has been most marked in Switzerland, Canada, India, Malaysia, Nigeria, Belgium, Spain, South Africa, Ethiopia and Bosnia.

Generally the territorial segmentation of a society has been sharpest where the territorial distribution of the different factors causing conflict – religious, linguistic, ethnic, economic, historical and ideological – have tended to coincide, mutually reinforcing each other. On the other hand, where the territorial distribution of the different segmenting factors has varied so that instead of coinciding, they cut across each other, this may have a moderating effect upon the intensity of the conflict. Switzerland provides a classic example of the latter. There the division between Protestants and Catholics, the linguistic concentrations, and economic interests all cut across each other. Cantonal alignments on political questions have, therefore, tended to vary according to whether religious, linguistic or economic considerations were primarily at issue. Consequently, political conflict has been less polarised than that for example between Quebec and English-speaking Canada where the differences have tended more to be mutually reinforcing.

There is also a significant difference between situations where there is a distinct majority alongside a minority or minorities, and those societies composed of a number of minorities with no single distinct group in a prevailing majority. In the former there is a tendency for minority groups to feel themselves vulnerable to perpetual dominance by the permanent majority. This sharpens their defensiveness and insistence upon a clear measure of autonomous self-rule. Among federations examples of such situations have been those of Quebec within Canada, the southern regions in Nigeria when Northern Nigeria dominated a three-region Nigeria, the concerns of non-Malay groups in Malaysia, and the non-Hindi speaking groups in southern India.[1] To some extent, the impact of the majority groups in these federations, and also in Switzerland, has been moderated, however, by distributing the majority group in each case among a number of distinct provincial, state or cantonal units, none of which has a permanent overall majority in the federation, and each of which over time has tended to develop its own historical interests and identity.

One special situation worthy of note is the particular difficulties that have been experienced almost invariably by bicommunal federations. The difficulties of dyadic federations and confederations have been widely recognized (Ivo DUCHACEK, *Dyadic Federations and Confederations*", Publius: The Journal of Federalism, 18:2 (1988), pp. 5-31). Pakistan prior to the secession of East Pakistan in 1971 and Czechoslovakia prior to the segregation of its two parts in 1992 have provided eminent examples of the difficulties which have arisen in federations organized on bicommunal lines. Other current two-unit federations or confederations experiencing difficulties have been St. Kitts-Nevis and Serbia-Montenegro. The problem with two-unit federations generally has been the inevitable tendency to insist upon parity between the two units in all matters. This has proved to be a recipe for political impasses and deadlocks. These occur because there is no opportunity for shifting political alliances and coalitions among the constituent units or their representatives on different issues which is one of the ways in which problems are resolved in multi-unit federations. Instead, in a two-unit federation every policy issue becomes a zero-sum game in which one of the two units is seen as a winner and the other as the loser. Furthermore, since invariably one of the two units is less populous than the other (e.g. West Pakistan before 1971 and Slovakia before 1992) that unit has usually been particularly conscious of the need to be insistent upon equality of influence in federal policy-making, while the more populous unit has developed a sense of grievance over the apparently undemocratic constraints imposed upon it to accommodate the smaller

1 Strictly speaking the Hindi-speakers in northern India do not constitute an absolute majority, but they represent by far the largest single linguistic group among the many such groups within India.

unit. In the cases of Pakistan and Czechoslovakia, the resultant cumulatively intensifying bipolarity led ultimately to their terminal instability. Nor does resort to a confederal structure resolve the issue. The existence of mutual vetoes, a normal characteristic of confederations, has meant that where there are only two units repeated impasses and deadlocks have simply sharpened mutual frustrations cumulatively over time. These examples provide a caution about any simple dualistic approach to resolving conflict in the Near East. Interestingly, Canada and Belgium represent two other federations with fundamentally bicommunal societies. There, however, the tendency to polarization has been somewhat moderated by the establishment of a federal structure composed in each case of more than two constituent units.

Given the importance of these various factors, the consideration of whether a federal solution or a particular federal variant is appropriate as a tool for resolving multicultural conflicts in the Near East will need to take careful account of the particular underlying conditions and motivations. Among the underlying conditions to be considered are: the relative strength or weakness of national, economic and social links among the prospective constituent units; the degree to which the prospective constituent units are themselves internally homogeneous in religion, language, race and culture; the intensity of the differences among the prospective constituent units in religion, language, race, culture, level of modernisation, economic development and political ideology; the degree of disparity in relative wealth and political influence; the relative size and bargaining power of the prospective constituent units; the complementarity or competitiveness of the elites in the different prospective units; and the interests of external political powers exerting their influence within the region.

THE NECESSARY CONDITIONS FOR A FEDERAL SOLUTION

The examples of federal successes and failures in moderating multicultural conflict raise the question: what prior conditions are necessary for federal solutions to be effective in such situations? Experience suggests that without certain necessary conditions a federal solution is unlikely to be adopted and, even if adopted, is unlikely to succeed in moderating multicultural conflict.

A first precondition is the existence of a will to federate. Federal political systems depend on consensual support and therefore are unlikely to succeed as imposed solutions.

Second, since federal systems involve both self-rule and shared-rule, without some basic underlying shared values and objectives, the basis for shared-rule will in the end be impossible to achieve.

Third, trust is necessary to make federal arrangements work. An essential condition is the development of mutual faith and trust among the different groups within a federation or confederation and an emphasis upon the spirit of tolerance and compromise. This is not simply required on theoretical grounds, but as a pragmatic necessity for any federal arrangement to work.

A fourth precondition is the development of a political culture which emphasizes sharing and cooperation and which fosters respect for constitutional norms and structures and the rule of law. Federal and confederal solutions require constitutional structures, and therefore where respect for constitutional law is lacking, there is little prospect for their effectiveness. Where a political culture fostering mutual respect, tolerance and compromise is lacking, federal constitutions have often proved to be more façades beneath which authoritarianism and centralization have prevailed. Latin America has been particularly noted for such examples. The existence of a civil society with a political culture supporting federal values is therefore vital.

Fifth, another precondition whose importance should not be underestimated is the importance of supporting economic conditions. These include not only complementary economies and common economic interests among the federating units, but also moderation of economic disparities which inevitably have a highly corrosive effect upon inter-unit relations.

The above are all necessary preconditions for federal or confederal solutions to operate effectively in moderating multicultural conflict. Where these conditions exist, their effectiveness in managing political diversity and conflict will then also depend not just upon the adoption of federal arrangements, but upon the particular institutional structure and processes developed to accommodate the particular social circumstances. These include the number, relative size and character of the constituent units, the form and scope of the distribution of legislative and executive authority and of financial resources, the degree of symmetry or asymmetry in the allocation of powers to the constituent units, the nature of the common federative institutions incorporating genuine power-sharing in central policy-making, the role of courts, the establishment of fundamental constitutional rights, and the development of processes for collaborative intergovernmental relations. An important objective therefore in the design of any effective federal structure is to insure the inclusion of institutions that contribute to the continued development of a spirit of trust and compromise.

The design of such institutional structures and processes will be meaningless, however, without the development of the necessary preconditions for the effective working of any federal and confederal solution. Given the apparent current lack in the Near East of many of these preconditions, a major issue this colloquium will need to address is whether these preconditions can be established and how to go about establishing them.

The question is "how to get there?" It will almost certainly require a step-by-step process aimed at developing modest institutions and co-operative processes to develop trust among the groups involved over a period of a decade or two until the preconditions for establishing an effective federation or confederation are in place. The process will require leadership within each of the groups involved and at different stages significant real and symbolic concessions from each side. Here the papers of Nicolas Haysom and Julian Hottinger identify important steps. The process by which South Africa moved from the fundamentally conflictual apartheid regime by stages to a democratic quasi-federal regime provides one example of such a process. Nicolas Haysom's paper presents some practical wisdom learned from this experience. The step-by-step evolution of the introduction of the European Community and its continuing evolution into the European Union provides another example.

CONCLUSIONS

In the light of both the positive and negative lessons drawn from the experience of federal systems over the past century, I draw the following conclusions:

First, federal political systems *do* provide a practical way of achieving through democratic representative institutions the management of multicultural conflict, but they are not a panacea for all such conflicts.

Second, the effective application of federal political solutions is limited to those situations where the necessary preconditions exist. Where these are lacking, a *prior objective* must be the establishment of processes to develop those preconditions.

Third, as a tool for the management of multicultural conflict, federal systems (both federations and confederations) have proved most effective as territorial political organizations. Therefore, their effective application is closely related to the degree to which different groups are territorially distributed or concentrated. In view of the Belgian experience, the practicality of non-territorial personal federalism as a realistic enduring solution, needs to be examined very carefully.

Fourth, federal arrangements are more likely to succeed where there are established traditions of democracy, constitutionalism, rule of law and political culture encouraging tolerance and compromise. In practice, the degree to which federal political systems have been effective has depended not just on the design of their constitutional structures, but even more on the degree to which there has been a political culture conducive to federalism. Important elements of such political cultures have been the cherishing of diversity, and the development of mutual respect, a sense of community, respect for constitutional norms, and a prevailing spirit of tolerance and compromise.

Fifth, bicommunal institutional solutions tend to polarize and accentuate conflict and to suffer terminal instability, and therefore should be avoided.

Sixth, where the institutional design of a federal system assures minorities of security for their distinctive self-governance, this has usually reduced tension and conflict.

Seventh, institutional arrangements which involve genuine power-sharing within the federative institutions are essential in order to generate a continuing consensus which serves as the necessary glue to hold the federal system together.

Finally, it must be emphasized that the application of federal solutions may take a variety of forms. There is no single universal form of federation applicable everywhere. There have been wide variations among federal systems to fit their own particular circumstances. Ultimately, federalism is a pragmatic, prudential technique, the applicability of which often depends upon the particular form in which it is adopted or even upon the development of new innovations in its application. That is the challenge before us.

Cases of Federalism as a Conflict Management Tool

Une solution miraculeuse, le fédéralisme personnel ?

Claude KLEIN

Tous ceux qui se sont penchés sur la question des Etats et des sociétés polyethniques connaissent, au moins de nom, la référence au fédéralisme personnel. Malheureusement, celui-ci est plus souvent invoqué que véritablement étudié. Il est vrai, par ailleurs, que très paradoxalement, le fédéralisme personnel n'a fait – relativement – l'objet que de peu d'études d'envergure. A vrai dire, le monde scientifique attend encore la grande synthèse sur les solutions personnelles, c'est-à-dire non-territoriales ou plutôt a-territoriales des Etats multinationaux, alors même que souvent ce type de solution a été présenté, de manière directe ou implicite, comme une manière de nec plus ultra en la matière.

Il n'est d'ailleurs pas inintéressant de s'interroger sur les raisons pour lesquelles le fédéralisme personnel reste plus imaginé qu'étudié. De même, au sujet des réticences que l'on discerne de nos jours devant les solutions personnelles, par opposition aux solutions territoriales.

Une première raison en est évidemment que les tentatives historiques les plus connues ont, en général échoué ou sont considérées comme des échecs. C'est le cas des premiers essais dans le cadre de l'empire austro-hongrois finissant, c'est ensuite le cas des Etats baltes entre les deux guerres (notamment l'Estonie), c'est le cas du Liban et de Chypre. Quant au millet de l'empire ottoman, il semble relever aujourd'hui d'un folklore historique et, au mieux, permettraient de rêver d'un passé idéalisé. Enfin, l'autonomie juive d'Europe Orientale (dans le cadre de la grande Pologne d'avant le partage[1]), elle aussi, supprimée dès 1764, est associée au naufrage de la Pologne après le partage de 1772 et, en fin de compte à la catastrophe qui s'est abattue sur le judaïsme polonais deux siècles plus tard.

Une deuxième raison a été avancée par un des rares auteurs contemporains qui se soit penché sérieusement sur les solutions non territoriales[2] : celui-ci indique que ce modèle d'autonomie culturelle non-territoriale est souvent associé à certaines formes d'organisation politique prémodernes, parfois considérées racistes[3]. C'est le cas, plus particulièrement de certaines tendances qui se firent jour en Afrique du Sud, avant la chute du régime de l'apartheid.

Pourtant, il nous a semblé intéressant de présenter une réflexion sur le thème du fédéralisme personnel (ou de l'autonomie personnelle) dans le cadre du présent colloque. Au demeurant, je me permets de rappeler que dès 1986, j'avais suggéré le recours à ce type de solution pour proposer un modèle constitutionnel à la minorité arabe de l'Etat d'Israël (à l'exception de la question des Palestiniens dans les territoires occupés par Israël depuis 1967).[4]

Si certains des exemples historiques concernant les formules personnelles sont très anciens, la théorisation en est beaucoup plus récente. De fait, elle est surtout le fruit des travaux de ce que l'on appelle communément les austro-marxistes. C'est la raison pour laquelle je me propose

---

1 Cf Louis LEWIN, *Die Landessynode der grosspolnischen Judenschaft*, Frankfurt, 1926.

2 Cf Johan COAKLEY, *Approaches to the Resolution of Ethnic Conflict : the Strategy of Non-territorial Autonomy*, International Political Science Review (1994), Vol. 15, N° 3, 297-314 at 311.

3 Cf également la préface écrite par Ephraim J. Nimni à la première édition en anglais de l'ouvrage fondateur d'Otto Bauer (dont la publication originale remonte à 1907 !!). Cette traduction est parue en 2000, sous le titre *The Question of Nationalities and Social Democracy*, Minneapolis University of Minnesota Press, 2000, p. XXV. La traduction française de ce livre fondateur est parue sous le titre : *La question des nationalités et la social-démocratie*, Paris, 1987.

4 Etude publiée sous le titre *Israel as a Nation-State and the Question of the Arab Minority, in Search of a Status*, International Center for Peace in the Middle-East, Tel-Aviv, 1986.

de commencer par une présentation de ces thèses. Je ne manquerai pas, au passage, d'évoquer la critique théorique stalinienne. Je passerai ensuite au rappel de quelques cas concrets. Je terminerai par quelques réflexions sur les possibilités d'application de ce type d'approche a-territoriale au cas israélien.

L'AUSTROMARXISME ET LES SOLUTIONS PERSONNELLES

Il n'est pas inintéressant de rappeler les circonstances dans lesquelles les socialistes autrichiens furent amenés à se pencher sur la question de l'organisation constitutionnelle d'un Etat multinational du type de l'empire austro-hongrois (ainsi d'ailleurs que de l'empire russe). Le parti social-démocrate autrichien y consacra son célèbre congrès de Brünn (ville de Moravie connue aujourd'hui sous le nom de Brno) tenu en 1899. L'empire est déjà entré dans la période de déliquescence qui devait le conduire à la désintégration à la fin de la guerre. Cette désintégration a entraîné, comme nous le savons, la création de nombreux Etats sur les ruines de l'Empire (Pologne, Tchécoslovaquie, Hongrie, Yougoslavie). Cependant, rétrospectivement, on peut poser la question centrale de la manière suivante : faut-il favoriser les tendances centrifuges ou, au contraire, essayer de sauver l'Empire sous une forme nouvelle ? L'idée sous-jacente – j'y insiste tout particulièrement car elle me paraît déterminante – étant que l'apparition de nouveaux Etats, tout en permettant le règlement des aspirations nationales des "grandes" nations (du type les Magyars) serait de nature à provoquer l'apparition d'Etats-Nations sur le territoire desquels de petites minorités ne manqueraient pas de provoquer de nouvelles tensions. On sait d'ailleurs qu'il existe à cet égard des théories selon lesquelles les origines de la seconde guerre mondiale pourraient être imputées – par delà le nazisme et Hitler – à l'instabilité des Etats européens du fait de leurs minorités. Remarquons qu'il peut s'agir d'Etats qui ne sont pas tous nécessairement issus de la désintégration de l'empire austro-hongrois.La problématique est cependant identique. On peut aller plus loin encore, puisque certaines des tensions auxquelles nous avons assisté au cours de la période la plus récente appartiennent à la même problématique (cf la

Yougoslavie) : tout se passe un peu comme si les interrogations de la fin du 19ème siècle restaient inchangées.

Au Congrès de Brünn les deux idéologues du parti (Karl Renner et Otto Bauer) qui sont parmi les plus connus ne sont pas actifs, pour la simple raison que ceux-ci n'étaient alors âgés respectivement que de 25 ans (Renner était né en 1870) et de 18 ans (Otto Bauer était né en 1881).

Rappelons d'abord les points principaux du programme de Brünn. Il faut évidemment se situer dans le cadre du jargon socialiste de l'époque.

> *"Considérant que les querelles nationales en Autriche entravent tout progrès politique, freinent toute évolution culturelle des peuples ;*
> *que en particulier, le prolongement des querelles nationales constitue un des moyens qui assurent leur pouvoir aux classes dominantes...*
> *le Congrès déclare :*
> *Le règlement définitif de la question nationale et linguistique en Autriche dans l'esprit de l'égalité des droits et de la raison est avant tout une revendication culturelle*
>
> *1. L'Autriche doit être transformée en un Etat démocratique fédératif de nationalités (Nationalitaetenbundesstaat) ;*
> *2. A la place des pays historiques de la Couronne doivent se constituer des corporations nationales d'auto-administration dont la législation et l'administration seront l'œuvre de chambres nationales élues au suffrage universel et direct ;*
> *3. Tous les territoires auto-administrés d'une seule et même nation forment une union homogène qui règle de manière parfaitement autonome toutes les affaires nationales ;*
> *4. La sauvegarde du droit des minorités nationales est garantie par une loi spéciale que devra adopter le Parlement de l'Empire ;*
> *5. Nous ne reconnaissons aucun privilège national et rejetons par conséquent la revendication d'une langue d'Etat ; au cas où une langue de communication s'avèrerait nécessaire, le Parlement de l'Empire devra se prononcer...."*

Ce texte a fait l'objet de nombreuses divergences d'interprétation, notamment du fait des écrits de Lénine et de Staline, en 1913-14, à propos de cette même question de l'organisation de l'Empire après l'éventuelle prise de pouvoir par les socialistes. En effet, les problèmes posés à l'Empire tsariste étaient, *mutatis mutandis*, semblables à ceux existant dans la double monarchie. Les conséquences, là aussi, se font sentir depuis l'éclatement de l'URSS après 1989.

La question centrale, à propos de la résolution de Brünn est celle du principe territorial face au principe de personnalité. En réalité, il y a là une confusion entre les principes exprimés à Brünn (où nul principe a-territorial n'est exprimé) et les écrits ultérieurs d'Otto Bauer et de Karl Renner (ce dernier sous divers pseudonymes), jusqu'au début de première guerre mondiale (y compris les premières années du conflit).

Une très grande date est évidemment celle de la première publication du maître-livre d'Otto Bauer (issu de sa thèse de doctorat). Otto Bauer n'est alors âgé que de 26 ans ! Il est vrai que son travail a été précédé de quelques écrits de Renner, très préoccupé par les questions nationales dans l'Empire. C'est ainsi que dans *Staat und Nation*, publié sous le nom de Synopticus dès 1899, Renner avance :

> *"...les nations sont à constituer non en tant que corporations territoriales, mais en tant qu'associations de personnes, non pas en tant qu'Etats, mais en tant que peuples..."*[5]

Pourtant, que l'on ne s'y trompe pas, le principe territorial n'est pas écarté pour autant. Renner écrit :

> *"On n'en déclare pas pour autant que le principe territorial est faux en soi et insoutenable, au contraire. Il est la formule qui permet la création d'Etats nationaux : l'Etat national, c'est comme on l'a remarqué plus haut, l'Etat de moindre friction interne, c'est nécessairement l'idéal de chaque nation, ou du moins de ceux de ses membres auxquels on reconnaît la nationalité « active ». C'est l'une des solutions possibles de la question nationale.*
>
> *Mais ce n'est pas une formule pour résoudre la question des nationalités autrichiennes dans le cadre de l'Etat unitaire autrichien..."*[6]

Avec Renner, Bauer, de manière assez didactique et quelque peu dogmatique, insiste sur le caractère évolutif de la nation. On reconnaît ici les éléments qui ont caractérisé le darwinisme social de la fin-de siècle, mais aussi ceux qui relèvent du marxisme. En fin de compte, les deux auteurs insistent sur la nécessité de briser, plus particulièrement en Autriche, le lien absolu entre nation et territoire et parviennent ainsi à la revendication de l'autonomie culturelle nationale sur une base non-territoriale. Il faut bien voir que ce système se prête particulièrement bien à l'Empire des Habsbourg : système complexe de groupes nationaux

---

5 Cf la traduction parue en français dans l'ouvrage intitulé *Les marxistes et la question nationale 1848-1914* (édité par Georges Haupt, Michael Lowy et Claudie Weil), Paris, Maspero, 1974 pp. 222-223.

6 Ibid. 223.

mélangés, sans domination territoriale claire. Tout comme on a pu le dire du Liban, le système pouvait s'assimiler à une mosaïque de minorités. De ce fait, chaque citoyen est amené à déclarer son appartenance nationale puis à participer, dans le cadre d'un double vote, à l'élection de ses représentants dans le cadre des organes de l'autonomie.

Dans plusieurs de ses écrits, Renner se penche aussi sur la question de l'organisation municipale des entités multinationales. Pour lui, dans le cas de communes mixtes une solution fédérale locale doit aussi être mise sur pied.

Sur le plan méthodologique, une question intéressante est celle de savoir dans quelle mesure les solutions d'autonomie personnelle ainsi avancées par les austro-marxistes sont présentées comme des solutions *ad hoc*, c'est-à-dire visant une situation particulière (comme celle prévalant en Autriche-Hongrie) ou si, au contraire, il s'agit d'une approche à valeur universelle. De fait, on peut avancer que la problématique n'existe que là où, d'une part, il existe des minorités nationales, religieuses ou culturelles et ou, d'autre part, celles-ci sont dispersées et imbriquées les unes dans les autres. Cette situation est d'ailleurs relativement fréquente. On verra que dans une certaine mesure, elle s'applique aussi à Israël, y compris dans les frontières d'avant 1967.

On sait ce qu'il advint de l'Empire austro-hongrois : l'Autriche cisleithanienne (la petite Autriche) est restée presque complètement exempte de minorités (à l'exception de la minuscule minorité slovène). Sur ses ruines se sont établis une série d'Etats dont certains ne sont jamais parvenus à résoudre les problèmes posés par les rapports entre majorité et minorité (ainsi le cas de Hongrois de Slovaquie).

Le système imaginé par Renner était, à vrai dire, d'une extrême complexité. Aujourd'hui il est surtout intéressant pour la tentative intellectuelle et méthodologique qu'il représente. Comme mon titre le rappelle, le fédéralisme personnel passe souvent pour une véritable solution miracle. Il est vrai qu'elle présente bien des avantages sur lesquels je reviendrai plus loin.

A PROPOS DES BOLCHEVIQUES ET DE LA QUESTION NATIONALE ET DE LA CRITIQUE DU BUND

Avant 1917, les marxistes russes s'interrogent eux aussi sur les solutions à apporter à la question nationale. Lénine charge Staline de préparer la plate-forme du parti. C'est ainsi que naît le célèbre article "le marxisme et la question nationale" de 1913.[7] L'intérêt de ce curieux écrit n'est pas seulement historique. Il nous apprend surtout que les principaux destinataires de cet effort dogmatique sont les Juifs et plus spécifiquement les Bundistes qui apparaissent, au sein des grandes masses juives d'Europe orientale, comme étant les principaux concurrents des sociaux-démocrates russes qui viennent de se constituer en une fraction bolchévique. Précisément, le problème posé par les Juifs est bien l'absence d'assise térritoriale claire : en bref, leur dispersion (tant d'ailleurs sur le territoire de l'empire czariste qu'en Pologne...). Les bundistes avaient donc imaginé une solution a territoriale : en bref, il convenait de reconnaître une très large autonomie nationale aux Juifs, sans considération du lieu de résidence. On reconnaît l'influence des austro-marxistes...

Staline se déchaîne littéralement contre les bundistes[8] (autant que contre les austro-marxistes)[9]. Ce faisant, il fait comme si le programme de Brünn avait rejeté toute base territoriale : on sait qu'il n'en est rien.

Il reste qu'après la révolution de 1917, une certaine renaissance des nationalités de l'Empire se fit jour. On a parfois parlé, de manière sans doute exagérée, d'un (bref) âge d'or des nationalités. Quoiqu'il en soit, le principe territorial resta dominant. L'exemple juif est d'ailleurs éclatant à cet égard, puisqu'il mena à la création d'une région autonome juive (le célèbre Birobidjan) aux confins de la Chine sur le fleuve Amour ! Et pourtant, la chute du régime s'accompagna de la chute de l'Empire

---

7 En fait il s'agit d'une série d'articles rassemblés plus tard en un petit volume.

8 Lénine lui-même le suivra sur ce point quelques années plus tard, dans ses *Notes sur la question nationale* (1917).

9 Staline s'en prend tout autant aux sionistes qu'aux bundistes. Il vitupère contre la revendication bundiste qui réclame le respect du sabbat et la reconnaissance du yddisch.

russe et de sa mainmise sur de nombreuses nations. La Russie reste cependant, même après la chute du communisme,une fédération à base territoriale, comprenant de nombreuses nations d'importances diverses.

QUELQUES CAS CONCRETS D'APPLICATION DES SOLUTIONS PERSONNELLES

Comme je l'ai déjà rappelé, les exemples ne sont pas très nombreux. Pourtant, ils existent et méritent d'être rappelés.

a) le cas Estonien : Il ne fait pas de doute que le plus connu est celui de l'Estonie. Je rappelle que ce pays avait accédé à l'indépendance en 1918. On sait aussi qu'elle fut reconquise par le pouvoir soviétique en 1940 pour retrouver son indépendance en 1990 après la chute du pouvoir communiste.

L'histoire de la première Estonie indépendante est donc très brève (1918-1940). De fait, elle l'est encore davantage si l'on rappelle qu'à partir de 1934 le pays connut une dictature sévère.

En application de l'article 21 de la Constitution de 1920, une loi sur l'autonomie culturelle des minorités nationales fut adoptée le 5 février 1925. Dans la littérature spécialisée, cette loi est souvent considérée comme le véritable modèle de l'autonomie culturelle (ou du fédéralisme personnel). C'est la raison pour laquelle je m'y arrêterai plus longuement sans doute que ne le justifierai son importance historique réelle[10].

Il s'agit d'un texte qui comporte 31 articles.

Un premier point est celui de la définition d'une minorité. L'article 8 nous donne la clef :

> *"au sens de la présente loi sont considérées comme minorités le peuple allemand, russe et suédois de même que les minorités établies sur le territoire estonien dont la population totale n'est pas inférieure à 3000 personnes".*

---

10 Pour ne pas donner une présentation trop idyllique de la situation, je me dois de rappeller que le régime de protection estonien est surtout le fruit de la pression des grandes puissances. Plus particulièrement, il faut rappeler que l'admission de l'Estonie (ainsi que des autres pays baltes à la SDN) avait été conditionnée à l'adoption d'un régime de protection des minorités.

Pour comprendre la portée de ce texte, il faut rappeler les ordres de grandeur de la population d'ensemble de l'Estonie. Il s'agit évidemment d'un tout petit pays, du moins par la population. S'il est un peu plus étendu que la Suisse (45 000 km carrés contre 41 000 km carrés pour la Confédération) la population atteignait à peine 1 100 000 habitants (contre plus de 6 500 000 pour la Confédération). A l'époque, l'Estonie comportait une minorité allemande (3,7%) qui a pratiquement disparu, ainsi qu'une petite minorité russe d'environ 8% (qui aujourd'hui atteint 33% !!) De même les suédois ont-ils également disparu aujourd'hui. La disposition qui fait référence à des groupes d'au moins 3000 personnes, vise plus particulièrement les Juifs (ils représentaient 5000 personnes) qui, de ce fait, furent reconnus comme minorité. Ce chiffre de 3000 personnes représentait, à l'époque un pourcentage inférieur à 0,5% !!

Parmi les groupes minoritaires, les Russes étaient les seuls à présenter une concentration territoriale sur une portion du territoire estonien.

L'appartenance à un groupe minoritaire était liée à l'inscription des citoyens âgés de plus de 18 ans sur un registre établi à cet effet.

On remarquera évidemment qu'aucune exigence de contiguité territoriale n'est liée à la reconnaissance des droits de ces groupes. C'est précisément en cela que cette loi est un modèle d'autonomie personnelle. Il reste à examiner quelques uns des droits accordés par cette loi.

L'article 2 indique les domaines de compétence des institutions autonomes (de chacun des groupes). Ils comprennent d'abord : l'organisation, l'administration et la surveillance des institutions publiques et privées du groupe minoritaire considéré ; les autres domaines culturels et la gestion des organes créés à cet effet.

De plus, il est expressément indiqué que les organes établis disposent du pouvoir règlementaire à l'égard des membres de leur minorité. Enfin, les organes gérant l'autonomie étaient investis du pouvoir fiscal pour financer les dépenses. Les principaux organes établis sont le conseil culturel de la communauté et le conseil d'administration. Des organes locaux peuvent également être créés.

b) Le modèle lituanien : la distribution de la population lituanienne était du même ordre. Sur un total d'environ 2,1 millions de personnes, 83,9% appartenaient au groupe formant l'Etat-nation lituanien alors que l'on comptait 7,6% de Juifs, 3,2% de Polonais, 2,5% de Russes. La Constitution lituanienne de 1922 comportait des dispositions plus vagues concernant le respect des communautés minoritaires et la possibilité d'une autonomie (plus restreinte qu'en Estonie).

Dans toutes ces hypothèses, il convient de remarquer que la constitution définissait toujours la langue nationale comme étant celle de la majorité formant l'Etat-nation. Les langues minoritaires sont présentées précisément comme telles.

Il ne s'agit là que de quelques exemples. L'Europe orientale et septentrionale ont connu diverses formes d'autonomie personnelle : c'est le cas de la Lettonie, de la Pologne, mais aussi de la Tchécoslovaquie ou encore de la Finlande (qui, comme le sait, comporte une très forte minorité suédoise).

Il convient de remarquer qu'une solution personnelle n'est pas exclusive de certains aspects "territorialistes". Deux exemples sont là pour en témoigner : d'une part, le cas des Sudètes en Tchécoslovaquie et d'autre part, celui des Suédois en Finlande.

c) Les millets[11] : Je ne peux m'empêcher de faire remarquer, pour commencer, qu'une connotation très proche de celle qui accompagne l'autonomie personnelle s'attache au millet. Véritable idéalisation d'une période libérale et tolérante qui aurait prévalu dans l'Empire ottoman, au bénéfice des chrétiens et des juifs. Evidemment, on sait par ailleurs qu'il n'en est rien. Que si, effectivement, une forme d'autonomie personnelle a été accordée à ces communautés, il serait erroné d'idéaliser l'empire ottoman. Je vais essayer simplement de donner quelques indications générales.

---

11 Je renvoie, entre autres, au grand ouvrage collectif, dirigé par Benjamin BRAUDE et Bernard LEWIS, *Christians and Jews in the Ottoman Empire*, 2 volumes New York, 1982.

Le millet est un régime d'autonomie des communautés religieuses non-musulmanes (les différentes communautés chrétiennes et les Juifs) qui foisonnent dans l'immense empire ottoman.

Le point de départ est précisément celui de la réalité multi-religieuse et multi-ethnique qui est celle de l'empire ottoman. En second lieu, le statut religieux (dans l'Islam) des chrétiens et des juifs : ceux-ci appartiennent aux gens du Livre et de ce fait, ils jouissent d'une certaine protection. Le statut de *dhimmi* rend bien cette incertitude : à la fois protégés, mais aussi inférieurs. Il en résulta une reconnaissance progressive d'un statut particulier, qui permet aux membres des différents groupes une autonomie, particulièrement dans les matières religieuses et culturelles, celles-ci étant entendues dans un sens très large, puisqu'elle comprennent également la juridiction en matière de statut personnel (mariages, divorces et successions). Elles comprennent également la faculté de choisir les dirigeants de la communautés, plus particulièrement le clergé. En fait, très souvent c'est à un véritable ethnarque l'on aura à faire. Le millet désigne donc une communauté religieuse et ethnique (parfois même linguistique), largement autogérée.

Le système des millets est loin d'avoir été statique. Si ses origines sont anciennes, les transformations les plus significatives datent du 19ème siècle et accompagnent les tentatives de modernisation d'un empire en voie de décomposition. C'est ainsi qu'en 1856 fut publié le grand édit sur la restructuration des millets : les principaux groupes formés en millet furent ainsi réformés (les Arméniens, puis les Grecs et enfin les Juifs). En 1869 parut la loi sur la nationalité ottomane qui achève ce premier cycle de modernisation, avant les révolutions du 20ème siècle.

d) Chypre : on fait allusion, bien entendu, à la tentative pathétique qui fut celle de la constitution du 6 avril 1960. Signe qui ne devrait pas tromper : la constitution compte 199 articles et couvre 55 pages de texte (dans mon édition imprimée en petits caractères) !!! C'est là sans doute l'antithèse de la formule napoléonienne selon laquelle une constitution idéale devrait être courte et obscure.

La constitution de Chypre devait, entre autres, répondre au défi que représente d'une part l'existence de deux communautés et, d'autre part, leurs non concentrations territoriales. De fait, si l'on examine la solution qui a prévalu après l'invasion par la Turquie, c'est précisément celle de la répartition territoriale. A l'origine, il n'en était rien : la solution choisie fut donc celle de la reconnaissance de deux communautés sur une base non-territoriale. D'où la classification de cette constitution dans ce chapitre des solutions personnelles.

La reprise des négociations entre les deux parties de l'île achoppe précisément sur le point de savoir si la forme de réunification envisagée impliquera la maintien du statu quo, c'est-à-dire le partage territorial, ou, au contraire, impliquera le retour des "réfugiés" dans leur ville ou village d'origine, ce qui pourrait réactiver une solution personnelle. Dans le cas inverse, la solution territoriale, conséquence de l'invasion turque serait conservée.

Il convient évidemment d'ajouter ici le cas du Liban, depuis l'adoption de la constitution et surtout celle du pacte national. Mais cette question est traitée par notre collègue Messara, c'est la raison pour laquelle je ne l'aborde pas, me contentant de la signaler pour mémoire.

L'APPLICABILITE DES SOLUTIONS D'AUTONOMIE PERSONNELLE AU CAS ISRAELIEN

Cet aspect de la question a déjà été évoqué plus haut. Il convient d'abord de préciser le cadre conceptuel de manière très précise. J'entends qu'il s'agit de réfléchir ici sur un aspect de la situation prévalant en Israël qui est certes lié à l'ensemble du conflit, mais qui, néanmoins est très particulier. Je veux parler de la minorité arabe d'Israël, à l'exclusion des territoires palestiniens occupés c'est-à-dire de la Cisjordanie et de la bande de Gaza.

Pour fixer les idées, je me dois de donner les données démographiques, telles qu'elles apparaissent dans l'annuaire statistique d'Israël (le dernier volume paru étant celui de l'année 2003 qui porte le numéro 54). Je dois signaler que ce annuaire est fait avec grand soin, en particulier pour les questions démographiques. On ne sera pas étonné d'apprendre que ce soin apporté à la démographie est tout à fait caractéristique des sociétés multicommunautaires. On a vu des pays comme le Liban ou même la Belgique interdire purement et simplement les recensements de la population, à certaines époques.

L'annuaire ainsi cité donne une population totale de 6 631 100 personnes. Ce chiffre englobe la ville de Jérusalem et le plateau du Golan. La répartition de la population est la suivante :

Juifs : 5 094 200 (soit environ 78%)

Chrétiens arabes : 114 300 (soit environ 1,8 2%)

Musulmans arabes : 1 038 300 (soit environ 17%)

Druzes : 108 500[12] (soit environ 1,6%).

L'annuaire indique que 246 000 personnes sont de religion indéterminée.

L'annuaire définit également un groupe d'"autres" qui compte 26 000 personnes, définie comme Chrétiens non-Arabes.

La ville de Jérusalem compte une population totale de 680 000 personnes, dont 447 000 Juifs (soit environ 66%). Les Arabes comptent quant à eux 221 900 personnes, dont environ 14 000 chrétiens.

Pour notre propos, il est important de relever l'importance relative des chiffres. Si l'on examine ceux-ci de manière comparatiste, on se rend compte qu'il s'agit ici d'une minorité dont le poids relatif est très grand : on ne peut relever que très peu d'exemples analogues dans le monde.

A travers la littérature spécialisée j'apprends que c'est sans doute la Slovaquie qui est la plus proche de notre hypothèse. Ainsi, ce pays qui a accédé à l'indépendance en 1992 (à la suite de l'éclatement de la fédération tchécoslovaque) compte une minorité hongroise très active et revendicatrice de près de 11%.

Les problèmes posés par cette forte minorité ne sont pas loin de ceux que connaît l'Etat d'Israël dans ses rapports avec la minorité arabe. Samy Smooha, sociologue de l'Université de Haïfa a consacré de nombreuses études à ce sujet. La revendication d'autonomie est très forte,

12 Y compris les 18 000 Druzes qui habitent le plateau du Golan annexé par Israël.

ainsi que l'influence de la Hongrie voisine. La comparaison cependant a ses limites, du fait évidemment du conflit israélo-palestinien et plus largement encore israélo-arabe. Il reste que la minorité arabe d'Israël qui forme environ 20% de la population totale – avec une démographie très forte – représente un facteur qui pèse d'un poids spécifique et qui semble exiger une réflexion qui devrait déboucher sur un statut négocié. Cependant, dans la situation actuelle, ainsi que je l'ai déjà exposé, le cadre conceptuel est celui d'un Etat-nation, c'est-à-dire l'Etat-nation juif, qui se définit comme "juif et démocratique". Si les données démographiques devaient se modifier de manière substantielle, c'est le caractère d'Etat-nation d'Israël qui serait remis en cause.

Un deuxième élément qu'il convient de prendre en considération est celui de la répartition territoriale de la population arabe d'Israël. S'il existe incontestablement certaines régions à prédominance arabe (la Galilée, la région dite du triangle au centre du pays), il n'en reste pas moins que même là où cette population est majoritaire, la population juive est elle aussi très présente. Il s'ensuit qu'il paraît impossible d'envisager – j'entends à l'intérieur de l'Etat d'Israël – une solution territoriale, qui reposerait par exemple sur une autonomie ou un fédéralisme à base territoriales. Il convient d'envisager un statut non-territorial. De plus, ainsi que nous le voyons dans la problématique slovaque, il nous faut envisager une solution dans le cadre conceptuel de l'Etat-nation et non dans le cadre d'un Etat multinational ou multicommunautaire. Il n'est pas impossible de penser un statut qui serait multinational (ainsi de la célèbre formule de l'Etat bi-national en vogue dans certains milieux intellectuels avant 1948), mais il s'agit d'une solution d'un ordre différent que personnellement je ne prendrai pas en compte. Si l'on a rappelé ces différents facteurs il apparaît que la solution de l'autonomie personnelle s'impose comme d'elle même. Je voudrais essayer de brosser à très grands traits la manière dont une telle solution pourrait s'articuler.

En premier lieu, le juriste que je suis se doit de souligner qu'une solution d'autonomie sérieuse exige une véritable protection constitutionnelle. En d'autres termes, dans le cas d'Israël, il faudrait, au stade actuel de la procédure d'élaboration constitutionnelle, envisager l'adoption d'une loi fondamentale sur le statut de la minorité arabe. A vrai dire certaines tentatives ont déjà été faites dans cette direction. Elles n'ont pas abouti. Cependant, la nécessité d'une protection constitutionnelle est évidente : d'une part, il convient d'assurer la supériorité du texte instaurant l'autonomie sur les autres normes. D'autre part, il convient surtout de protéger le texte contre des amendements postérieurs qui pourraient le dénaturer. Cette protection peut se faire à l'image de certains exemples fournis par le droit comparé : ainsi de l'exigence de la double majorité en Belgique pour certaines lois à résonance culturelle ou linguistique (majorité des Chambres et majorité auprès des représentants des communautés).

En second lieu, il faut définir le champ d'application de l'autonomie ainsi envisagée.

Celle-ci devra couvrir avant tout les matières culturelles, linguistiques et probablement religieuses. En d'autres termes, il sera possible de confier aux organes éventuellement créés (examinés plus loin) toutes les matières concernant l'éducation et la culture. Il s'agit là d'un champ extrêmement vaste et de première importance pour la minorité arabe. On s'en rendra compte en comparant à la situation actuelle : en matière d'éducation, p.ex. aucune autonomie n'a été reconnue. La matière est tout entière administrée par les organes centraux. Certes, même dans un système d'autonomie, des contrôles peuvent et doivent être mis en place. C'est le cas notamment en matière de détermination minimale des programmes d'éducation. Enfin devra être résolue la question de la mise en place d'institutions d'enseignement supérieur qui jusqu'à présent n'ont pas été établi au bénéfice de la minorité arabe, qu'il s'agisse d'universités publiques ou d'institutions subventionnées par l'Etat, ou, au contraire d'établissements privés d'enseignement supérieur, comme il en existe dans la réalité israélienne. Il est probable que rien ne pourra s'opposer sérieusement à la création d'une université arabe. De même, un statut de la minorité arabe devra déterminer de manière précise le statut de la langue arabe dans le pays.

En troisième lieu, il convient de souligner les relations entre les éléments religieux et les éléments nationalitaires. La raison en est que dans la situation qui prévalait en Israël, il y avait une très grande concomitance entre l'appartenance religieuse et l'appartenance nationale, sans que toutefois cette superposition soit parfaite. Ainsi, on l'a montré à propos des rubriques démographiques, autrefois, la superposition était considérée comme parfaite : toute personne chrétienne était, en principe arabe. Désormais, en particulier depuis l'arrivée passive des immigrants en provenance de l'ex-URSS, il existe un groupe de chrétiens non-arabes. Ceux-ci appartiennent à l'église orthodoxe russe et pourraient donc bénéficier des institutions de cette communauté. La question ne se pose pas, à l'évidence pour les musulmans, lesquels sont tous arabes, encore que l'on puisse facilement imaginer des exceptions. Chez les druzes l'identité entre les deux éléments est, elle aussi, parfaite, comme chez les Juifs.[13]

En quatrième lieu, il est important d'insister sur l'une des exigences fondamentales de la mise en place d'un système d'autonomie personnelle (ou territoriale) consiste dans la mise en place d'organes élus : ainsi il faudrait établir un conseil législatif et un conseil exécutif dont les modes d'élection et les compétences seraient soigneusement définies par la loi fondamentale dont il a été question plus haut.

En cinquième lieu, il convient de mettre en place un système de financement équitable, comprenant également (à l'image du modèle estonien) la faculté de lever un impôt. Celui-ci serait probablement insuffisant et devrait être complété par un accès équitable aux richesses de la nation.

En sixième lieu, comme dans tout système d'autonomie, des système de contrôle sur les personnes comme sur les actes doivent être institués. Ce contrôle de légalité, développé, devra, pour qu'il soit considéré comme légitime, comporter une juste participation de la minorité arabe.

J'ai essayé de présenter à grands traits les possibilités d'évolution d'un statut réel de la minorité arabe, en réfléchissant sur les possibilités de

---

13 Par ailleurs, la question est posée de savoir dans quelle mesure les Druzes se distinguent des Arabes sur le plan national. Pour l'Etat d'Israël, il en va ainsi : les Druzes sont considérés comme un groupe national (Leom) distinct des Arabes. Ils forment également une communauté religieuse séparée. Cette manière de voir est souvent contestée par certains représentants druzes.

mise en place d'un système d'autonomie personnelle. Il me semble que cette voie est la seule qui permette une véritable coexistence entre les deux communautés, à partir de l'hypothèse qui est celle de la volonté de l'une telle coexistence. Je répète, évidemment, que je n'ai pas traité ici du conflit israélo-palestinien. Il s'agit là d'un problème différent : précisément, les voies que je trace ont pour but d'éviter que le statut des Arabes d'Israël ne devienne un appendice du conflit.

Principe de personnalité et principe de territorialité en fédéralisme comparé

Expérience du Liban et perspectives pour demain au Proche-Orient

Antoine Nasri MESSARRA

L'expérience historique du Liban et du Proche-Orient arabe en général en matière d'aménagements fédératifs et de régimes d'autonomie témoigne d'une profonde sagesse politique et d'un pragmatisme qui, durant plus de quatre siècles, a prouvé son efficience. Par contre, le volontarisme, inspiré par une idéologie de l'Etat-nation, a été source de conflit, de guerre civile ou intérieure et d'une impasse sanglante, notamment dans le conflit arabo-israélien qui perdure depuis 1948.

Il faut le dire crûment : Il n'y a pas au Proche-Orient arabe de tradition de fédéralisme territorial, opérant une corrélation étroite entre *espace* géographique et *identité*. Mais, par contre, de solides traditions constitutionnelles de fédéralisme personnel dont la rupture a été fort préjudiciable aux minorités, traditions qu'il s'agit aujourd'hui de revaloriser et de moderniser.

L'histoire constitutionnelle du Liban, avec tous ses prolongements ottomans et arabes, montre les effets comparés de presque toutes les variantes de la fédéralisation et le degré d'opérationnalité pratique de ces variantes quant au respect des principes de liberté, d'égalité et de participation, quant à la consolidation de la paix civile et quant à l'équilibre régional.

Dans une perspective comparative, le Liban se situe au cœur de trois grandes controverses internationales : la controverse sur l'efficience et la stabilité des systèmes de *partage du pouvoir* ; la controverse sur les chances du dialogue entre les *religions* ; et la controverse sur la place des *petites nations* dans le système international. Le Liban est l'expression et le modèle concrétisé d'un rêve de l'histoire, celui d'une coexistence inter-communautaire, conflictuelle certes comme toute réalité politique vivante et complexe, mais démocratique dans un environnement avide de liberté et régi, le plus souvent, par des théocraties, des dictatures et autrefois des coups d'Etat. L'équilibre des rapports internes de force au Liban implique acceptation mutuelle, concertation et partage. Cette cause ou ce rêve mérite d'être réhabilité, non seulement pour des raisons œcuméniques, humaines et politiques, mais aussi pour des considérations internationales. Le système international contemporain est composé d'une constellation d'Etats dont la plupart sont contraints de gérer leur pluralisme de manière à consolider l'unité et la concorde nationale.

L'impératif de coexistence, il s'agit donc de l'assumer, non en tant qu'expédient, mais en tant qu'expérience originale et cause nationale, humaine, œcuménique et à dimension internationale. Le pluralisme communautaire au Liban est une richesse à l'échelle de l'universel et de l'humain. La concordance islamo-chrétienne au Liban, d'une manière ou d'une autre, est un phénomène vivant, quotidien, inhérent à la réalité et établi sur une même terre par un même peuple uni par la même histoire, les mêmes souffrances, les mêmes us et coutumes et le même destin. L'alternative, s'il y en a, est entre une coexistence sauvage, comme celle subie en 1975-1990, et entre une coexistence rationalisée en tant que modèle de société et facteur pragmatique de stabilisation régionale et internationale. En détruisant la coexistence rationalisée et harmonieuse, l'humanité détruit au Liban l'image de son propre avenir.

1. FEDERALISME, ESPACE ET IDENTITE : UNE PROBLEMATIQUE ACTUELLE

La problématique du colloque est pertinente, novatrice, nous concerne tous et nous interpelle, dans la recherche et encore plus dans l'action.

Le passage d'Etats arabes de l'autoritarisme à la démocratie, après une longue période d'idéologie unitariste ou d'intégration forcée, pose et posera des problèmes où la référence à l'expérience libanaise est souvent évoquée. Dans le cas de l'Irak, trois problèmes épineux bloquent l'aménagement constitutionnel: la *charia* islamique, le statut personnel en ce qui concerne surtout la *femme*, et le *fédéralisme*.

Des représentants chiites ont quitté la séance du Conseil du gouvernement provisoire, le 27 février 2004, à la suite de l'abrogation du décret 137 qui porte sur l'application de la *charia* en matière de divorce, de succession et d'autres cas de statut personnel.

Les leaders kurdes réclament un régime fédéral avec extension du régime d'autonomie en y joignant Karkouk, riche en pétrole, et refusent le démantèlement de la milice kurde. Les chiites soulignent que la législation doit être "égalitaire pour tous les Irakiens et applicable partout".

Des leaders sunnites irakiens appréhendent que les chiites, qui constituent la majorité de la population, dominent le pays après des décennies de répression. Comme alternative, le Conseil supérieur de la révolution islamique propose que la présidence soit détenue par un chiite. Le Conseil a rejeté une proposition que la présidence soit rotative entre chiite, sunnite et kurde. Il faudra, selon Hamid Bayyati, du Conseil supérieur de la révolution islamique, que la présidence revienne à un chiite, avec deux vice-présidents, l'un sunnite et l'autre kurde, ou que la présidence soit rotative, au sein d'un collège de cinq comprenant trois chiites, un kurde et un sunnite[1].

---

1 *an-Nahar*, 29 fév. 2004. Dossier : al-Usûliyyûn yufajjirûn al-fidirâliyya… (Les intégristes font exploser la fédéralisation), al-Hawadess, 13-19/2/2004, pp. 16-24. KAMEL Mustapha, *Nahu ishrâq al-sunna fî rasm mustaqbal al-Irak* (Vers la participation des sunnites à la configuration de l'avenir de l'Irak, *an-Nahar*, 29/11/2003. Le débat sur le fédéralisme par les leaders Kurdes d'Irak, in : *al-Ahâlî*, n° 54,

Il ressort de ces faits que si on ne veut pas un fédéralisme territorial, il faudra trouver des aménagements qui garantissent le partage du pouvoir ou, du moins, évitent les risques d'exclusion. L'absence de tradition de fédéralisme territorial dans la région, jointe à une panique que suscite, surtout en Turquie, Syrie et Iran, tout aménagement qui associe *espace* et *identité* rend la solution difficile, parce que le régime d'autonomie en faveur des kurdes irakiens a été vécu dans l'hégémonie et la répression. Une autonomie du type décentralisée risque aussi – en l'absence de traditions démocratiques consolidées – de virer en centralisme local autoritaire. Des solutions intermédiaires à la libanaise font timidement leur chemin. Elles ne sont pas idéales, mais elles garantissent la participation dans un contexte hégémonique qui, lui aussi, est bien ancré et loin d'être idéal.

La même approche s'applique à Israël qui ne peut persister dans une idéologie originelle sioniste quand le nombre des ressortissants arabes israéliens augmente sur son territoire[2].

Une approche réellement comparative et actuelle du fédéralisme ne peut manquer de relever les risques et dysfonctions du fédéralisme territorial ou, du moins, les adaptations et variantes de la territorialité fédérale dans tous les cas où les minorités dont on entend régler l'autonomie *ne sont pas géographiquement concentrées.*

Avec la déliquescence des frontières, suite à la mondialisation des communications et au déplacement des populations à l'intérieur du même territoire national, les problèmes de la protection des droits culturels et des minorités se posent de plus en plus en termes à la fois territorial et personnel. Il faudra donc réfléchir dans les sociétés multicommunautaires à un fédéralisme non chirurgical, sans déplacement forcé de population, sans épuration ethnique, sans génocide, un fédéralisme humaniste.

---

7 janv., 55 du 14 janv. et 56 du 21 janv. 2004 (www.ahali-iraq.com). *al-Irâq tahta al-ihtilâl* (L'Irak sous occupation), *al-Mustaqbal al-arabî*, n° 298, n° 12, 2003, pp. 78-200. VERRIER Michel, *Quelle autonomie pour les Kurdes d'Irak ?*, *Le Monde diplomatique*, mars 2004, p. 10.

2 Une analyse prémonitoire en 1971 et fort actuelle : *Une pensée prémonitoire : Marcuse, Israël et les Juifs* (texte de Herbet Marcuse de 1971), *Le Monde diplomatique*, mars 2004, p. 27.

Une approche ethnocentriste occidentale a persisté à ignorer à quel point l'espace, dans des pays africains, en ex-Yougoslavie, en ex-URSS, au Sri-Lanka, au Liban durant la guerre en 1975-1989, au Proche-Orient depuis la création de l'Etat d'Israël en 1948… a été et est brutalisé, violenté, dans des stratégies identitaires souvent impossibles. La problématique de l'espace et de l'identité est, bien que naturelle et logique pour la construction "nationale" d'après l'idéologie de l'Etat-nation, est meurtrière, surtout à une époque d'échange et de communication entre des espaces mouvants, autant physiques que virtuels et symboliques.

Le fédéralisme est-il nécessairement une division du pouvoir entre des unités définies géographiquement ? Les définitions du fédéralisme impliquent l'autonomie et la délégation du pouvoir de légifération et de décision, mais aucune des définitions classiques n'implique un découpage territorial pour l'exercice de cette autonomie et de ce pouvoir. Certes toute autorité politique s'exerce sur un territoire, mais cet élément nécessaire à l'exercice de la souveraineté nationale et étatique peut ne pas l'être pour l'exercice d'une autorité à l'égard et entre des communautés ne jouissant pas d'une localisation géographique définie.

L'extension de fait du fédéralisme suivant le principe de territorialité a amené les constitutionnalistes à introduire dans la définition du fédéralisme les notions de provinces et de régions. Aussi William H. Riker définit-il le fédéralisme en tant qu'"organisation politique dans laquelle les activités du gouvernement sont divisées entre les gouvernements *régionaux* et le gouvernement central de manière que chaque forme de gouvernement jouit d'un pouvoir de décision final dans certaines activités"[3]. Ivo Duchacek considère, dans le titre de l'ouvrage comparatif sur le fédéralisme, que le fédéralisme implique une "dimension territoriale"[4]. Daniel Elazar considère cependant qu'il est "théoriquement possible de créer un système fédéral où les unités constitutives sont dé-

---

3 RIKER William H., *Federalism*, ap. Fred I. Greenstein and Nelson W. Polsby (eds.), Handbook of political science, vol. 5, 1975, p. 101. Souligné par nous dans le texte.

4 DUCHACEK Ivo D., *Comparative federalism : The territorial dimension of politics*, New York, Holt, Renehart and Winston, 1970, pp. 248-249.

terminées, mais non sur une base territoriale", mais il dénie le caractère fédéral "authentique" à tout autre fédéralisme, car "aucun système *fédéral authentique* n'a existé sans une base géographique de division fédérale"[5]. Or dans des sociétés plurales, le fédéralisme peut être appliqué sur une base territoriale, quand les clivages principaux coïncident avec les frontières géographiques, mais il *peut être* appliqué suivant le principe de personnalité quand les clivages ne coïncident pas avec des frontières définies. Le fédéralisme suivant le principe de personnalité, tel qu'il a été appliqué dans l'histoire et tel qu'il s'applique aujourd'hui, remplit toutes les conditions du fédéralisme quant à l'autonomie des unités fédérées et à leur pouvoir de légifération et de décision. La notion d'unités fédérées est ainsi plus adéquate dans la définition générale du fédéralisme que celle de "gouvernements régionaux", de provinces ou de régions.

Otto Bauer et Karl Renner avaient proposé un système de fédéralisme personnel comme solution au problème des nationalités de l'Empire austro-hongrois. Ils se sont référés dans leur projet à un fédéralisme sur la base du "principe de la personnalité", en opposition au principe territorial habituel. Chaque individu devrait pouvoir déclarer à quelle nationalité il souhaite appartenir, et ces nationalités deviendront des *Kulturgemeinschafte* autonomes. Bauer trace explicitement un parallèle entre ces communautés culturelles proposées et les communautés religieuses (catholiques, protestants et juifs) coexistant fréquemment et gérant librement leurs propres affaires religieuses et civiles[6]. Au début

---

5 ELAZAR Daniel J., *Federalism*, ap. David L. Shills (ed.), International encyclopedia of the social sciences, vol. 5, New York, Macmillan and Free Press, 1968, p. 356. Souligné par nous dans le texte.

6 BAUER Otto, *Die Nationalitatenfrange und die sozial demokratie*, Vienna, Wiener Volksbuchhandlung, 1907, pp. 353-63. Et traduction française : BAUER Otto, *La question des nationalités et la social-démocratie*, Paris, FDI, 2 vol., 1987, 334 p. et 524 p. RENNER Karl, *Das Selbstbestimmungsrecht der Nationen in besonderer Anwendung and Osterreich*, Leipzig, Deuticke, 1918. Cité par Arend Lijphart : Democracy in plural societies. A comparative exploration, New Haven and London, Yale University Press, 1977, 248 p., p. 43 ; Democracies. Patterns of majoritarian and consensus government in twenty-one countries, New Haven and London, Yale University Press, 1984, 229 p., p. 183 ; et *Consociation and federation : Conceptual and empirical links*, in : Canadien Journal of Political Science, XII (3), September 1979, pp. 499-515. Cf également des textes de BAUER et RENNER ap.

du siècle, Otto Bauer, dans sa volonté de maintenir la cohésion de l'Empire austro-hongrois avait bien vu que l'aspiration première des nations était l'aspiration à préserver et développer leurs cultures propres, et d'abord leurs langues. Le programme national des années 20 insiste sur la promotion de *toutes* les cultures nationales à *égalité*.

D'autres auteurs, souvent considérés comme des déviants par les classiques du fédéralisme, se réfèrent explicitement à Bauer et Renner ou les rejoignent. Robert A. Dahl emploie l'expression de fédéralisme "sociologique" pour désigner le fédéralisme territorial[7]. William Livingston parle de "société fédérale" quand les segments sont géographiquement concentrés[8]. Carl J. Friedrich développe la notion de fédéralisme intégré (*corporate federalism*) en se référant à Otto Bauer et Karl Renner et au cas de la Constitution chypriote de 1960[9]. Kenneth D. MacRae distingue entre "principe de personnalité" et "principe de territorialité"[10]. Karl Aun analyse, suivant le principe de personnalité

Tom Bottomore and Patrick Goode (trans. and ed. by), Austro-marxism, Oxford, Clarendon Press, 1978, 308 p. Sur les idées de Bauer et Renner : KANN R.A., *The Multinational Empire. Nationality and National reform in the Habsburg Monarchy 1848-1918*, New York, Octagon Books, Third reprint, 1977, vol. II, pp. 157 sq. AGNELLI A., *Questione nazionale e socialismo. Contributo allo studio e al pensiero di K. Renner e O. Bauer*, Bologna, Il Mulin, 1969.

7 Cité par VERBA Sidney, *Some dilemmas in comparative research*, in : *Word Politics*, 20 (1), October 1967, p. 126.

8 LIVINSTON William S., *A note on the nature of federalism*, ap. Aaron Wildavsky (ed.), American federalism in perspective, Boston, Little-Brown, 1967, p. 37. Et STEIN Michael B., *Federal political systems and federal societies*, in : Word Politics, 1968 (20), pp. 727-747.

9 FRIEDRICH Carl J. : *Corporate federalism and linguistic politics*, paper presented at the 9th Word Congress of the International Political Science Association, Montreal, 1973 ; *Trends of federalism in theory and practice*, New York - London, Oxford University Press, 1968, trad. française par PHILIPPART André et Lucie, *Tendances du fédéralisme en théorie et en pratique*, Bruxelles, Institut belge de science politique, 1971, 205 p. Egalement : BOVIE Robert R. et FRIEDRICH Carl J., *Etudes sur le fédéralisme*, Paris, Librairie générale de droit et de jurisprudence, Bibliothèque de texte et études fédéralistes, 2 vol., 1960-1962.

10 MCRAE Kenneth D., *The principle of territoriality and the principle of personality in multilingual States*, in : *International Journal of the Sociology of Language*, 4 (1975), pp. 33-34.

d'après les propositions de Bauer et de Renner, le système de sauvegarde des minorités ethniques en Estonie en 1925[11].

D'après le grand penseur libanais Michel Chiha, on peut qualifier le fédéralisme personnel de fédéralisme de "législation". Il écrivait dans *Le Jour* du 30 juillet 1947 : "La Chambre des députés, au Liban représente au fond un aspect original du fédéralisme. Comme en Suisse, il y a des cantons, il y a ici des communautés confessionnelles. Les premiers ont pour base un *territoire*, les seconds seulement une *législation*, l'adhésion à un statut personnel"[12]. En effet, dans le "fédéralisme intégré" (*corporate*), personnel ou de législation, l'autonomie et le pouvoir de légifération et de décision ne se concrétisent pas sur des espaces régionaux, mais couvrent des unités culturelles quelle que soit la localisation géographique des personnes ou des institutions qui en relèvent. Ce sont les *personnes*, physiques ou *morales*, qui sont définies et des *lois* spéciales leur sont appliquées. Le fédéralisme géographique a pour base des territoires autonomes, alors que le fédéralisme personnel a pour base des unités culturelles autonomes. Dans le premier cas, les unités géographiques délèguent leurs représentants à une seconde Chambre fédérale autre que la Chambre des représentants, alors que dans le second cas, les unités culturelles délèguent leurs représentants, soit à une première chambre suivant des quotas affectés à chaque unité culturelle, ou à une seconde chambre sénatoriale, et les postes administratifs sont affectés suivant un quota pour chacune des unités culturelles.

Le fédéralisme territorial comporte certes de nombreux avantages. Il est plus aisé de déléguer des responsabilités gouvernementales et administratives à des unités territorialement concentrées qu'à des unités culturelles sans base régionale. Le fédéralisme territorial, parce que ses fron-

---

11 AUN Karl, *Cultural autonomy of ethnic minorities in Estonia : A model for multicultural society ?*, paper presented at the Third Conference of Baltic Studies in Scandinavia, Stockholm, 1 (1975), pp. 11-12.

12 CHIHA Michel, *Politique intérieure*, Beyrouth, Trident, 1964, 316 p., p. 135. Souligné par nous dans le texte. Des développements dans notre étude publiés ap. Thomas FLEINER-GERSTER et Silvan HUTTER (eds), Federalism and decentralisation, Fédéralisme et décentralisation, Suisse, Editions universitaires Fribourg, 1987, 488 p. et notre étude : *Principe de territorialité et principe de personnalité en fédéralisme comparé*, pp. 447-480.

tières sont mieux perçues, institue des relations moins quotidiennes entre les segments et, par suite, réduit les occasions de conflit. La territorialité jouit d'un autre avantage : En cas de conflit la sécession ou la partition est possible si son coût est faible et ses bénéfices supérieurs à ceux de l'union. Enfin le fédéralisme territorial consacre moins le cloisonnement et la classification des individus. Celui qui est gêné par les lois d'une province peut aller vivre dans une autre où la législation est différente, alors que dans le fédéralisme personnel la personne est soumise aux lois de son statut. Mais la catégorisation n'est pas fatale. Ce n'est pas en tout cas en *territorialisant* le fédéralisme qu'on le rend ouvert. Une territorialisation forcée, dans le but d'homogénéiser des régions historiquement non homogènes, signifie des mutations douloureuses de populations avec peut-être un coût disproportionné par rapport au profit de l'opération.

Le fédéralisme suivant le principe de personnalité comporte cependant, lui aussi, des avantages. Il peut être moins coûteux sur le plan administratif que le fédéralisme territorial qui contraint à la multiplication des unités locales. Le fédéralisme personnel favorise aussi le développement d'organisations communautaires dans chaque segment, organisations qui peuvent promouvoir un développement endogène des communautés. Ce fédéralisme permet surtout de limiter l'auto-segmentation exclusivement aux problèmes les plus conflictuels, alors que la fédéralisation territoriale contraint de segmenter outre mesure là où il est peut-être superflu de segmenter. Le fédéralisme personnel peut ainsi être facteur d'union parce que, justement, il ne provoque pas des ruptures dans les relations intercommunautaires quotidiennes dans un système où tous les segments peuvent, en termes de coût et profit, tirer profit de l'union à un coût acceptable. Mais le principe de personnalité implique, comme pour la copropriété immobilière, une perception psychologique claire des frontières du système et le respect de ces frontières, en vertu du principe de base d'un modèle consensuel : “Les bonnes frontières font le bon voisinage.”

2. LES DEUX CAIMACAMATS : PERSONNALITE OU TERRITORIALITE ?

L'histoire des sociétés pré-coloniales et celle des pays arabes, surtout sous l'Empire ottoman, offre des exemples de l'adoption du principe de personnalité pour la sauvegarde des identités culturelles. L'histoire constitutionnelle du Liban, plus que celle des autres pays sous l'Empire ottoman, permet de dégager la dialectique et le modèle du fédéralisme personnel.

Le choix entre principe de territorialité et principe de personnalité pour l'aménagement constitutionnel du Liban s'est posé en termes aigus à la suite de la décision, sur proposition de Metternich, approuvée le 15 septembre 1842, de diviser le Liban en deux caimacamats. Adel Ismail résume les différentes interprétations par les notions de "système de nationalité ou de l'extraterritorialité" et "système de territorialité"[13]. Jean Charaf analyse l'institution de la fonction de *wakîls* (procureurs) druzes et chrétiens dans chacun des deux caimacamats chargés des affaires de leurs coreligionnaires, à condition que ces wakîls relèvent directement de chacun des deux caimacamats[14].

Le mélange de populations autrefois comme aujourd'hui au Liban permet de poser le problème en termes clairs : S'agit-il d'une division territoriale en faisant abstraction de l'appartenance communautaire de la population ou d'une division communautaire de manière que chaque communauté soit régie par ses propres chefs ? Le problème s'est posé à propos des zones mixtes dans chacun des deux caimacamats, surtout dans le caimacamat druze où les zones mixtes sont nombreuses. Les solutions préconisées furent, soit le transfert de populations entre les zones mixtes en vue d'homogénéiser les deux caimacamats ou de désigner des *wakîls* druzes et chrétiens chargés des affaires de leurs communautés. Eugène Poujade, consul de France à Beyrouth, a proposé de

---

13 ISMAIL Adel, *Histoire du Liban du XVIIe siècle à nos jours*, Tome IV (1840-1861), Beyrouth, 1958, 418 p., pp. 216-217.

14 CHARAF Jean, *Sighat al-ta'âyush al-dustûrî fî Lubnân* (La formule de coexistence constitutionnelle au Liban), in : *Panorama de l'actualité*, 33, hiver 1984, pp. 29-47.

faire gouverner les chrétiens par les chrétiens et les druzes par les druzes par l'intermédiaire de *wakîls* relevant les uns du caimacam chrétien et les autres du caimacam druze. L'enclave de Deir el-Kamar serait gouvernée par deux *wakîls*, l'un chrétien et l'autre musulman[15]. L'Empire ottoman a réglé le dilemme en adoptant cette solution. Le 7 décembre 1842, la Montagne a été divisée en deux caimacamats, druze et chrétien, séparés par la route de Beyrouth-Damas, avec un statut spécial pour le village mixte de Deir el-Kamar.

LORD ABERDEEN, ministre anglais des Affaires étrangères, demanda à Bourée le 25 juin 1845 : "Mais vous qui avez vu les choses de près, en quel remède auriez-vous foi ?" "Je n'en connais qu'un, my Lord, répondis-je, dit Bourée, et non seulement je ne connais que celui-là, mais je ne crois pas qu'il en existe d'autres ; *on a échoué en voulant diviser ce qui était indivisible*, le remède serait de revenir à l'unité"[16]. Adel Ismail, qui expose les problèmes soulevés par la division de la Montagne et les différents projets, écrit que ce problème "fut incontestablement le plus délicat et le plus épineux de la Question du Liban au XIXe siècle"[17].

Le principe de personnalité couvrait non seulement la représentation, l'exercice de la décision et son assiette, le statut personnel et l'enseignement, mais aussi la juridiction même civile.

3. LE FEDERALISME SUIVANT LE PRINCIPE DE PERSONNALITE DANS LES SOCIETES MULTICOMMUNAUTAIRES CONTEMPORAINES

En Pologne, les juifs qui représentaient plus d'un million d'âmes constituent le dixième de la population. Groupés en quartiers populeux dans les villes (Cracovie, Posen) ou vivant dans des villages et hameaux perdus, ils appartiennent à un corps politique dont l'expression nationale,

---

15 POUJADE Eugène, *Le Liban et la Syrie (1845-1860)*, Paris, Librairie nouvelle, 1860, p. 30.

16 ISMAIL, *op. cit.*, p. 232.

17 ISMAIL, *op. cit.*, p. 263.

le *Wa'ad 'Arba Arasot* (Conseil des quatre pays : Grande-Pologne, Petite-Pologne, Ruthenie, Volhynie-Podolie) est reconnu par le roi. Le Wa'ad se réunit à Lublin et à Yaraslav lors des foires annuelles, répartit l'impôt, légifère et juge en appel les procès. Il délègue un représentant auprès du roi et de la diète polonaise. Sous l'impulsion du Wa'ad, les juifs adoptent un système d'enseignement généralisé. Ce grand âge du judaïsme polonais se clôt en 1648 avec la révolte des cosaques ukrainiens de Khmielnitsky[18]. Au Maroc, les juifs ont bénéficié d'un statut non moins favorable[19].

Ces traditions constitutionnelles séculaires ne sont-elles qu'un vestige historique d'un temps archaïque que les exigences de la modernité devraient effacer ? Le prétendre, c'est privilégier le principe de territorialité dans le fédéralisme, en vertu de critères contestables de la construction nationale, de l'Etat national et de l'intégration, et dénier par le fait même à nombre de sociétés plurales où les segments sont entremêlés toute chance de construction nationale sans mutations de populations. C'est aussi exclure de la notion de fédéralisme toute perspective autre que territoriale et condamner nombre de pays, dont la Belgique, le Liban, et des pays du tiers monde où les minorités sont peu consistantes ou non concentrées, à des solutions qui visent à l'extermination, à l'assimilation forcée ou au déplacement qui est une forme chirurgicale d'exclusion. Le fédéralisme, s'il se limite exclusivement au principe de territorialité, s'inspire finalement d'une culture majoritaire, même s'il vise à protéger les minorités. Le fédéralisme géographique ne prend en considération que les *minorités consistantes* et *concentrées*, donc majoritaires sur un *espace* bien à elles. Solution idéale peut-être, mais solution impossible dans beaucoup de pays, ou trop coûteuse, comme le montre l'exemple libanais où aucun segment ne réussit à "se tailler", sinon d'une manière trop artificielle et approximative, un espace à lui malgré des années de violence.

---

18 FILKENSTIEN L., *Jewish self-government in the Middle Ages*, New York, 2e ed., 1964. Cf. aussi *Encyclopedia Universalis*, vol. 9, pp. 535-536.

19 ZAFRANI Haim, *Mille ans de vie juive au Maroc*, Paris, Maisonneuve et Larose, Judaisme en terre d'islam, 1983, 320 p.

Pense-t-on aux mouvements autonomistes qui se multiplient dans le monde et au modèle normatif que propose la pensée politique comparative ? Yoichi Higuchi cite un best-seller japonais, *Kirikirijin* (peuple de Kirikiri), vendu à plus de 700.000 exemplaires en un an. Il s'agit d'un roman tragi-comique du fameux écrivain Inoue Hisashi sur un village qui ose faire sécession et se couper de l'Etat nippon. L'auteur a merveilleusement caricaturé la gloire et l'échec de l'indépendance éphémère[20]. Ce roman peut aussi être un best-seller au Moyen-Orient, et au Liban en particulier où chacun manipulait des cartes sur la configuration d'avenir des Etats confessionnels dans la région.

La recherche comparative permet de montrer que le fédéralisme suivant le principe de personnalité existe dans beaucoup de pays. Toutefois la culture dominante assimilant le fédéralisme à une provincialisation fait que dans ces pays le fédéralisme personnel, de législation ou intégré est interprété avec les schèmes culturels classiques de l'Etat unitaire et de l'Etat fédéral. Aristide R. Zolberg parle de "fédéralisation sans fédéralisme" à propos de la Belgique[21]. Ni Robert Senelle, ni F. Coppieters ne qualifient le système belge de fédéral. "Il s'agit en fait, écrit F. Coppieters, d'une évolution vers une structure fédérale[22]. Robert Senelle écrit : "Ce qui, en revanche, semble certain à la lecture des travaux préparatoires, c'est que le constituant a voulu exclure les minorités linguistiques du champ d'application du nouvel article 6 bis ("les droits et libertés des minorités idéologiques et philosophiques"), *afin de ne pas mettre en*

---

20 HIGUCHI Yoichi, *La décision de décentralisation*, ap. Thomas Fleiner-Gerster et Silvan Hutter (eds.), Federalism and decentralisation. Fédéralisme et décentralisation, Suisse, Editions universitaires Fribourg, 1987, 488 p., pp. 23-36.

21 ZOLBERG Aristide R., *Splitting the difference: Federalization without federalism in Belgium*, ap. Milton J. Esman (ed.), Ethnic conflict in the western world, Ithaca, Cornell University Press, 1977, pp. 103-142. HEISLER Martin O., *Managing ethnic conflict in Belgium*, in : Annals of the American Academy of Political and Social Science, 433 (1977), pp. 32-46.

22 COPPIETERS F., *Les structures politiques des communautés et des régions en Belgique*, in : Fiche documentaire (Institut belge d'information et de documentation, Montoyer 3, B 1040 Bruxelles), F.D. 324/1984/ 1, 39 p., p. 4. Souligné par nous dans le texte.

cause le principe de la territorialité de la législation linguistique"[23]. D'autres constitutionnalistes belges appellent la structure belge "semi-fédérale". Or le système belge règle essentiellement un transfert de pouvoirs par la nation à des entités sub-nationales qui sont les communautés et les régions.

La Constitution de la République de Chypre du 16 août 1960 adopte délibérément le principe de personnalité, avec une définition de ses communautés en termes non pas religieux, mais culturels. En 1960, lorsque les communautés grecque et turque étaient entremêlées (*interspersed*), il n'était pas possible de créer un fédéralisme territorial. Les deux communautés ont bénéficié d'une autonomie segmentaire au moyen de conseils locaux élus avec des attributions législatives dans les domaines religieux, éducatif et culturel et du statut personnel, et des conseils municipaux séparés dans les cinq grandes villes de l'île.

Si le système a échoué à Chypre, ce n'est pas parce qu'il porte en lui-même les germes de sa corruption, mais parce que les rapports de force à Chypre sont trop disproportionnés entre les deux communautés turque (18% de la population) et grecque, ce qui n'est pas le cas ni au Liban ni en Belgique. Il ne faut donc pas attribuer l'échec de la coexistence à Chypre à la nature même de son aménagement fédéral, mais aux rapports de force dans la société. Le principe de personnalité a en effet régi les rapports intercommunautaires dans les pays sous l'empire ottoman et sous-mandat français et anglais durant plus de quatre siècles, comme il régit aujourd'hui la Belgique[24].

---

23 SENELLE Robert, *La réforme de l'Etat belge*, Bruxelles, Ministère des Affaires étrangères, du Commerce extérieur et de la coopération au développement, 3 vol. vol. 3 (Les structures régionales prévues par les lois des 8 et 9 août 1980), 1980, pp. 177-178. Souligné par nous dans le texte. Cf. également in : *Acta Politica*, XIX, January 1984 : BILLIER J., *On Belgian pillarization : Changing perspectives*, pp. 117-128 ; HUYSE L., *A First meeting of Belgian and Dutch scholars of vanzuiling*, pp. 159-160 ; PIJNENBURG B., *Pillarized and consociational-democratic Belgium : The views of Luc Huyse*, pp. 57-71 ; DIERICKX G., *The management of subcultural conflict : The issue of education in Belgium (1850-1975)*, pp. 85-95. Pour une connaissance approfondie du système politique belge : DELPEREE Francis, Droit constitutionnel, Bruxelles, Maison F. Larcier s.a., 2 vol., 1987, 507 p. et 195 p.

24 Constitution de la République de Chypre, in : Notes et études documentaires, n° 2.761, 17 mars 1961, 44 p.

Les mouvements revendicatifs minoritaires d'aujourd'hui dans le monde ne visent pas toujours à l'obtention d'une autonomie du type régional. Parmi les 45 revendications des minoritaires sikhs de l'Inde figure "la mise à l'étude d'une législation sur les mariages, successions et autres affaires de famille sikhs"[25].

C'est en analysant la crise du fédéralisme territorial dans des pays pluraux, les controverses qu'il suscite et les impasses auxquelles il aboutit qu'on mesure l'intérêt de la distinction entre les deux principes de territorialité et de personnalité.

Le fédéralisme territorial adopté au Nigeria a-t-il réduit les conflits ? L'expérience nigériane montre qu'un fédéralisme territorial dont les frontières géographiques ne coïncident pas avec les frontières ethniques et idéologiques ne contribue pas à résorber les divergences entre les segments d'une société plurale. Au Nigeria en effet les frontières fédérales, qu'on a modifiées à plusieurs reprises, ne suivent pas les frontières ethniques et les plus petits segments n'ont pas obtenu leurs provinces. Ben O. Nwabueze écrit : "Le fédéralisme au Nigeria a échoué dans son objectif de bâtir des unités gouvernementales sur des groupes sociaux suffisamment homogènes pour qu'ils puissent gérer leurs affaires internes dans l'unité de l'ensemble"[26]. Gisèle Kayata Eid parle de "fédéralisme éclaté" à propos du Nigeria et préconise un "fédéralisme fonctionnel"[27].

Au Soudan, à l'occasion de l'application de la loi islamique, le président du Conseil du peuple soudanais, Izzeddine al-Sayyid, a déclaré le 13 juillet 1984 que les réformes constitutionnelles envisagées conformément à la *sharia* "ne porteront pas atteinte aux libertés et aux droits des non-musulmans".

---

25 In : *Le Monde*, 30 avril 1984.

26 NWABUEZE Ben O., *Constitutionalism in the emergent States*, London, Hurst, 1973, pp. 113, cité par Lijphart, Democracy..., p. 163.

27 KAYATA EID Gisèle, *Pluralisme au Liban et au Nigeria. Essai de sociologie politique comparative*, mémoire DEA en science politique, dir. A. Messarra,Université Saint-Joseph, Beyrouth, 1983, 88 p.

Depuis les années 50, les autorités de plusieurs pays du Proche-Orient ont supprimé le droit consenti aux communautés d'avoir leurs écoles, soit en nationalisant l'enseignement, soit en le contrôlant directement, sans que cela aboutisse à une plus grande intégration culturelle des groupes minoritaires. La représentation proportionnelle des communautés dans les assemblées politiques a également été progressivement supprimée. Quant au statut personnel, il n'est pas placé sur un pied d'égalité avec le droit musulman. Ce droit, qui s'incorpore au système juridique de l'Etat, "bénéficie d'une suprématie par rapport aux droits des communautés non musulmanes et s'applique d'emblée lorsqu'il se trouve en conflit avec ces derniers"[28].

Tel n'est pas le cas au Liban où aucun droit communautaire ne jouit d'une suprématie par rapport à l'autre, ce qui a d'ailleurs favorisé au Liban le recul de la fraude à la loi en matière de statut personnel. Pierre Gannagé écrit que "les divers statuts personnels en vigueur (au Liban) sont placés à pied d'égalité et chacun d'eux ne peut, en raison de sa nature, constituer un système de référence exclusif pour l'analyse des prétentions des plaideurs, dans les litiges de caractère international"[29].

La solution égalitaire tant en matière de statut personnel (art. 9 de la Constitution), d'enseignement (art. 10) et surtout de participation au pouvoir (art. 95) peut être qualifiée de *pleinement fédérale* suivant le principe de personnalité. Le système libanais a aussi trouvé en principe le moyen de pratiquer un fédéralisme personnel ouvert en prévoyant, par l'arrêté 60 LR du 13 mars 1936, la création d'une communauté de

---

28 Cf. GANNAGE Pierre, *Droit intercommunautaire et droit privé (A propos de l'évolution du droit libanais face aux droits proche-orientaux)*, in : *Journal du droit international*, 110 (1983), n° 3, juil.-sept. 1983, pp. 479-508. GANNAGE Pierre, *Le pluralisme des statuts personnels dans les Etats multicommunautaires* (Droit libanais et droits proche-orientaux), Bruxelles - Bruylant et Beyrouth - Presses de l'Université Saint-Joseph, 2001, 400 p. RONDOT Pierre, *Les communautés dans l'Etat libanais*, Paris, Cahiers de l'Association France nouveau Liban, n° 4, 1979, 72 p.

29 *Ibid*, p. 498. Et : *Anthimat al-Ahwâl al-shakhsiyya* (Les régimes du statut personnel), Beyrouth, Middle East Council of Churches, 1990, 396 p. ASSAF Georges, *Système communautariste et déconfessionnalisation: la problématique de la mutation de système politique libanais*, Travaux et Jours, n° 64, automne 1999, pp. 43-73.

droit commun, dont la législation ottomane ignorait l'existence. Ceux qui n'appartiennent à aucune communauté, ou qui désirent abandonner leur communauté de naissance, pourraient adhérer à la *communauté non communautaire* ou de droit commun. L'article 14 définit ainsi cette communauté : "Les communautés de droit commun organisent et administrent leurs affaires dans les limites de la législation civile." Aucun texte organique n'a cependant été publié pour l'organisation de cette communauté civile.

Le caractère fédéral personnel du système politique libanais aux niveaux tant culturel et politique permet de poser la question : le fédéralisme personne est-il compatible avec l'islam ? L'aliénation culturelle du monde arabe est telle que les traditions constitutionnelles les plus ancrées et les pratiques autochtones les plus confirmées sont considérées comme "étrangères". Le droit du Proche-Orient a comblé ses lacunes les plus apparentes par des lois empruntées à la législation occidentale, sans se soucier de la complète disparité créée par la réunion d'éléments aussi hétérogènes, ni des ruptures avec des traditions séculaires qui avaient favorisé l'intégration progressive de toutes les subcultures nationales[30].

Il n'y a pas de tradition de fédéralisme territorial au Proche-Orient, y compris à Chypre. Probablement la raison en est que la coexistence religieuse dans la région, berceau des trois grandes religions, le judaïsme, le christianisme et l'islam, a toujours connu des aménagements sur une base culturelle et que les minorités religieuses étaient en interaction étroite au point que les conflits communautaires et les ingérences extérieures n'ont jamais réussi à briser le tissu relationnel par delà les clivages religieux.

La création de l'Etat d'Israël, sur une base religieuse et en transformant le judaïsme religieux en nationalisme sioniste, introduit une division géographique et un *people engeneering* qui, par maints aspects, crée une impasse au sein même de l'Etat d'Israël et dans ses rapports avec son voisinage immédiat, en Palestine occupée, et son voisinage islamo-

---

30 TYAN Emile, *Histoire de l'organisation judiciaire en pays d'islam*, 2e éd., Leiden, E.J. Brill, 1960, 673 p., p. 93.

chrétien environnant. La guerre du Liban, de 1975 à 1990, a ressuscité des projets et velléités de territorialisation communautaire du Liban. La guerre contre l'Irak ressuscite aussi des appréhensions d'une balkanisation régionale.

4. RE-THEORISATION DU FEDERALISME

Il s'agit élargir le concept de fédéralisme, ou plutôt le ramener à son esprit, un peu à la manière de l'*Esprit des lois* de Montesquieu.

Nous vivons des phénomènes d'épuration ethnique, de génocide, de transfert de population et, dans la moins pire des situations, d'intégration forcée. Le but : se tailler un territoire et concrétiser une identité. Il ne s'agit pas du fédéralisme qui vise surtout à assurer l'efficience administrative, mais des fédéralismes qui cherchent à résoudre des problèmes aigus de diversité culturelle. Dans une approche comparative et pour re-théoriser, il faudrait étudier des situations de dysfonctionnement du fédéralisme territorial. Dans des situations multiples de fédéralisme territorial, en Afrique notamment, on trouve des adaptations, surtout dans des cas où les minorités, dont on entend régler l'autonomie, ne sont pas géographiquement concentrées.

Une *première* raison justifie la rethéorisation du fédéralisme : Beaucoup de fédéralismes territoriaux se font d'une façon chirurgicale. Il faut poser le problème de la genèse des fédéralismes. La genèse de beaucoup de fédéralismes a été chirurgicale, avec des déplacements de population. Que faire pour que le fédéralisme à l'échelle comparative soit humaniste ? Nous avons maints exemples, surtout au Proche-Orient. Au Liban en particulier, la géographie durant de longues années, a été brutalisée, violentée, avec des logiques identitaires impossibles. C'est logique d'après l'idéologie de l'Etat-nation, mais à une époque d'échange entre des espaces mouvants, des espaces autant physiques que virtuels et symboliques, il faudrait de plus en plus penser à des stratégies trans-identitaires, et non exclusivement spatiales.

Une *seconde* raison justifie la re-théorisation du fédéralisme : Il s'agit des nouveaux types de guerre qui se propagent dans le monde. Les guerres entre Etats sont en grande partie révolues. Nous assistons à des guerres internes, des guerres qu'on appelle civiles, où s'ingèrent des forces régionales et internationales, et qui exploitent les phénomènes ethniques et identitaires dans des stratégies qui dépassent ces pays.

Une *troisième* raison justifie la re-théorisation : la déliquescence des frontières. Les gens se déplacent, les frontières deviennent mouvantes, les minorités dont on entend sauvegarder l'autonomie vivent dans des zones de plus en plus mouvantes et de plus en plus va se poser le problème du respect de la minorité dans la minorité, du respect des droits culturels sur des bases qui ne sont pas nécessairement ou exclusivement géographiques. Le problème, fort actuel, incite à re-théoriser l'approche comparative internationale.

Le sionisme a introduit au Proche-Orient une logique identitaire territoriale dans une région qui n'a pas de traditions de territorialité fédérale. C'est une logique explosive dans une région qui a d'autres traditions. Nous vivons au quotidien aujourd'hui cette logique en Palestine. Une logique encore explosive pour Israël lui-même, avec des minorités arabes de plus en plus nombreuses à l'intérieur. Un grand penseur juif avait dit que l'idéologie de *nation-building* est un cadeau empoisonné de l'Occident à la pensée juive.

Une impasse sanglante perdure depuis plus d'un demi siècle, une impasse qui a propagé la victimisation. Victimisation des juifs, victimisation de la Palestine. Le Liban a été aussi victime durant quinze ans de ce contexte régional de territorialisation identitaire. Il a réagi.

Il y a une logique spatiale identitaire dans les correspondances de Moshe Sharett et Ben Gourion dans les années 1950. Tout un plan pour partager le Liban et créer des identités spatiales communautaires. Cela n'a pas abouti[31]. La question Kurde pose dans toute son ampleur le problème de la fédéralisation et des types d'autonomie.

---

31 Cf. les correspondances sionistes des années 50 sur les éventualités de partage du Liban, publiées dans *Davar (Israël)*, publiées dans *Beirût al-Masâ'* (Beyrouth), n° 97 et 98, 9 et 16 déc. 1975, publiées en hébreu dans les *Mémoires* de Moshe Scharet, 8 vol., Maariv, Tel Aviv, 1978, et ap. Yahya Ahmad al-Kaaki, *Lubnân wa-l-fidirâliyya* (Le Liban et le fédéralisme), Beyrouth, Dar al-Nahda al-arabiyya, 1989,

Il faudrait penser sérieusement au rapport territorialité / identité en tant que rapport explosif. On ne peut plus réfléchir innocemment sur les problèmes de territoire et de division des territoires. Nous étions peut-être autrefois plus tranquilles sur ce point, quand existait encore l'Union soviétique. Il y avait aussi sur le plan international un consensus sur le principe de l'intangibilité des frontières. Avec la chute de l'URSS le principe international de l'intangibilité des frontières s'est écroulé. Cela comporte des risques. Dans la charte de l'Union africaine, le principe de l'intangibilité des frontières est énoncé. Si vous changez les frontières au Proche-Orient, dans les Balkans, en Afrique…, vous avez des guerres internes ou civiles en cascades.

Certes, les systèmes de fédéralisme personnel, actuellement existants, ne sont pas idéaux. Il y a là d'énormes problèmes.

Il faudrait d'abord rendre le fédéralisme personnel *égalitaire*. Il était relativement égalitaire du temps des Ottomans. Il est *égalitaire* au Liban, c'est-à-dire en cas de conflit entre deux statuts personnels, aucun statut ne domine l'autre. Dans d'autres pays arabes, en cas de conflit de lois de statut personnel, c'est la loi musulmane qui s'applique. On relève des prostestations en Egypte et ailleurs pour que les statuts personnels soient réellement égalitaires.

Il faudrait aussi moderniser le fédéralisme personnel en le rendant *ouvert*. En fait le régime libanais, par un arrêté de 1936, du temps du Mandat français, prévoyait la création d'une communauté de droit commun. Cela existait aussi en ex-Yougoslavie et à Chypre, ce qui implique la possibilité de ne pas être membre d'une communauté. Il y a un grand débat au Liban pour la création d'un statut civil facultatif. C'est un grand problème que de *démocratiser* et *moderniser* les régimes de statut personnel[32]. C'est aussi un grand problème que de rendre plus opérationnel et moderne le fédéralisme territorial.

---

184 p. SHAMIR Moshé, *Yûjad hal : taqsîm Lubnan* (Il y a une solution : Le partage du Liban), in : *Maariv* (Jérusalem), trad. en arabe in : *al-Safir*, 24 oct. 1983.

32 TRABOULSI Ibrahim, *al-kânûn al-urtodoksî al-jadîd li-l-ahwâl al-shakhsiyya* (Le nouveau code de statut personnel de la communauté grecque-orthodoxe), *an-Nahar*, 11/1/2004.

Fédéralisme personnel et territorial en Belgique

André ALEN / Jan CLEMENT

§ 1er INTRODUCTION

On attend beaucoup de l'expérience belge comme l'exemple le plus remarquable d'un fédéralisme combinant les aspects territoriaux avec des aspects personnels. A cet égard, Thomas Fleiner et Lidija Basta écrivaient en 1991 :

> *"[...], it still remains to be seen if this system of personal federalism – adopted in Belgium by the end of seventies and the beginning of eighties by vesting the competences not only with determined territories but also with linguistic communities – can bring to a positive solution of the existing minority problems"*[1].

Dans le même sens Ronald Watts écrivait en 1994 :

> *"[...], within federal political systems it has in practice been possible to provide protection for both territorial and non-territorial minorities through the constitutional protection of basic rights. [...] This raises the question whether non-territorial federal arrangements for power-sharing might be possible. In this respect the Belgian combination of territorial and community organization appears to break new ground, although it is still too early to judge its efficacy"*[2].

Nous démontrerons ci-après que, bien qu'il y ait eu en Belgique une réception de la théorie du fédéralisme personnel de Renner et Bauer, le

---

1 FLEINER Th. et BASTA L.R., *Federalism, Federal States and Decentralization*, in : The Territorial Distribution of Power in Europe (III), European Summer University, Fribourg, 1991, 11.

2 WATTS R.L., *Contemporary Views on Federalism*, in : B. de Villiers (éd.), Evaluating Federal Systems, Kenwyn, Juta & Co Ltd, 1994, 11.

fédéralisme belge est essentiellement territorial. Afin de pouvoir comprendre ce paradoxe, il est nécessaire de donner une brève explication du système institutionnel belge.

§ 2. LES LOIS LINGUISTIQUES ET LE FEDERALISME EN BELGIQUE[3]

L'Etat belge de 1831 était un Etat unitaire décentralisé et une "nation francophone", dans laquelle la bourgeoisie francophone gardait le pouvoir, notamment grâce au suffrage censitaire. La prépondérance démographique des Flamands ne pouvait être traduite en pouvoir politique qu'après l'introduction du suffrage universel lors des révisions constitutionnelles de 1893 et de 1921.

Par des lois linguistiques successives, les Flamands militaient pour la reconnaissance de leur langue en matières législative, administrative, judiciaire et scolaire. Les Wallons souhaitant préserver l'homogénéité linguistique de la Wallonie refusaient d'attribuer des droits linguistiques aux Flamands en Wallonie et s'opposaient à un bilinguisme généralisé de l'administration. Ceci a mené à l'inscription du *principe de territorialité* dans les lois de 1932 et de 1935 : désormais, la langue de la région unilingue est la langue de l'administration, de l'enseignement et de la justice. D'après le modèle du *multilinguisme par juxtaposition*[4], chaque langue est reconnue à l'intérieur d'une partie déterminée du territoire. Les lois linguistiques de 1962 et de 1963 ont divisé le pays en quatre régions linguistiques: trois régions linguistiques unilingues – à savoir: la région de langue néerlandaise, au Nord; la région de langue française, au Sud; la région de langue allemande, au Sud-Est – et une

---

3 ALEN A. et ERGEC R., *Le principe de territorialité dans la jurisprudence belge et européenne. Un essai de synthèse*, Journal des Tribunaux, 1998, 785-790; ALEN A. et ERGEC R., *La Belgique fédérale après la quatrième réforme de l'Etat de 1993*, Textes et Documents, Ministère des Affaires Etrangères, du Commerce Extérieur et de la Coopération au Développement, Bruxelles, 1998.

4 HÉRAUD G., *Pour un droit linguistique comparé*, Revue internationale de droit comparé, 1971, 309-330.

région bilingue, à savoir la région bilingue de Bruxelles-Capitale, au centre.

Le principe d'unilinguisme dans les régions linguistiques unilingues souffre de tempéraments dans les communes à statut linguistique spécial (les "communes à facilités"). La législation linguistique a prévu des "*facilités linguistiques*" pour les habitants de vingt-sept communes (municipalités) contiguës à une autre région linguistique qui ont le droit de demander, dans leurs rapports avec les autorités locales, qu'une langue différente de celle de la région dans laquelle ces communes sont situées soit employée. En ce qui concerne ces "*facilités linguistiques*", une resolution adoptée le 26 septembre 2002 par l'Assemblée parlementaire du Conseil de l'Europe a donné lieu à beaucoup de controverses en Belgique. La difficulté posée par la Résolution 1301 (2002) réside dans le fait que les francophones, les néerlandophones et les germanophones dans les autres régions unilingues et *en dehors des communes à statut linguistique spécial* sont considérés comme des "minorités nationales". Les francophones sont évidemment favorables à cette thèse leur conférant le statut de "minorité nationale" dans l'ensemble de la Flandre. Mais, en dehors des communes à statut linguistique spécial, aucune disposition constitutionnelle ou législative ne leur reconnaît un statut de groupe minoritaire dans la région de langue néerlandaise. Il en est de même pour les néerlandophones et les germanophones dans les communes de la région de langue française autres que les communes à statut linguistique spécial. La thèse adoptée par l'Assemblée parlementaire, suite au rapport de Mme Nabholz-Haidegger, va donc à l'encontre de l'ordre constitutionnel belge basé sur le principe de territorialité[5].

L'Etat unitaire décentralisé belge s'est lentement mais sûrement transformé en un État fédéral à la suite de la constitution de communautés et de régions en 1970. La Belgique est maintenant un Etat fédéral qui se compose des communautés et des régions (article 1er de la Constitution). La Belgique comprend trois communautés : la Communauté fla-

---

5 ALEN A., *Deux rapporteurs suisses sur les minorités nationales belges*, in : P. Hänni (éd.), Mensch und Staat. Festgabe der Rechtswissenschaftlichen Fakultät der Universität Freiburg für Thomas Fleiner zum 65. Geburtstag, Universitätsverlag Freiburg (Schweiz), 2003, 241 et 253.

mande, la Communauté française et la Communauté germanophone (article 2 de la Constitution). La Belgique comprend trois régions : la Région flamande, la Région wallonne et la Région bruxelloise (article 3 de la Constitution). La compétence territoriale des trois régions et des trois communautés se définit en fonction des quatre régions linguistiques dont les limites ont été arrêtées en 1963. Ainsi, la Région flamande voit son territoire circonscrit aux limites de la région de langue néerlandaise, la Région wallonne à celles des régions de langue française et de langue allemande, et la Région bruxelloise à celles de la région bilingue de Bruxelles-Capitale. Les décrets de la Communauté germanophone n'ont force de loi qu'en région de langue allemande.

La sphère de compétence territoriale des deux grandes communautés est plus compliquée car, si leurs décrets s'appliquent aux institutions *et aux personnes* respectivement en région de langue néerlandaise et en région de langue française, la Communauté flamande et la Communauté française voient également leur compétence territoriale s'étendre à la région bilingue de Bruxelles-Capitale *mais uniquement aux institutions*. Ces deux communautés agissent donc concomitamment dans cette région mais de manière indépendante l'une vis-à-vis de l'autre. En pratique, les Bruxellois se voient appliquer les décrets de l'une ou de l'autre communauté, en fonction de l'appartenance communautaire de l'institution à laquelle ils ont recours. Hormis la réglementation de l'emploi des langues, ces deux communautés ont une vocation légitime à déborder de leur région linguistique respective, celle de langue néerlandaise et celle de langue française, pour exercer des compétences à Bruxelles-Capitale, où habitent tant des néerlandophones que des francophones. Mais comme le droit public belge ne connaît pas de sous-nationalité pour déterminer juridiquement qui, des personnes physiques, est neérlandophone ou francophone, l'exercice des compétences communautaires dans la région bilingue de Bruxelles-Capitale ne s'exerce qu'à l'égard des institutions. Dans les matières culturelles et l'enseignement ainsi que dans les matières "personnalisables" (la politique de santé et l'aide aux personnes), le champ d'application des décrets des communautés s'étend aux institutions établies dans la région bilingue de Bruxelles-Capitale qui, en raison de leurs activités ou de leur organisation, doivent être considérées comme appartenant exclusivement à l'une ou à l'autre communauté. En matière d'enseignement, par exemple, les parents seront tenus par les décrets de la Communauté flamande s'ils ont décidé d'inscrire leur enfant dans une école flamande; si un autre de leurs enfants suit les cours dans l'enseignement francophone, ils seront tenus, pour ce qui concerne cet enfant, par les décrets de la Communauté française. Par le choix qu'ils font librement de leurs institutions (écoles, associations sportives, etc.), les habitants de Bruxelles-Capitale se soumettent indirectement aux normes communautaires[6]. L'appartenance communautaire des Bruxellois n'est dès lors, ni directe, ni exclusive, ni définitive.

La nature quelque peu particulière de la "communauté" typique du fédéralisme belge, a engendré des divergences conceptuelles sur la notion même de communauté et, par là, sur le cadre spatial des normes communautaires. Dans la conception de la Communauté française, la communauté s'adresse à un ensemble d'individus unis par la langue et la culture. Dès lors, c'est le principe de la personnalité qui détermine l'exercice des compétences communautaires. La Communauté française pourrait, le cas échéant, s'adresser à tous les francophones du pays, quand bien même ils se trouveraient dans la région de langue néerlandaise. On songe en particulier aux francophones des "communes à facilités" (n° 5) situées dans la région de langue néerlandaise. Cette conception doit être rejetée. En suivant Yves Lejeune, il est parfaitement possible de considérer les trois communautés comme des collectivités territoriales, les Communautés flamande et française étant en outre dotées, à l'égard des *institutions* bruxelloises, d'une compétence extraterritoriale fondée sur la "sous-nationalité de ces institutions"[7]. Le principe de territorialité est la pierre de touche de la répartition des compétences et exclut toute immixtion de la Communauté française dans la région de langue néerlandaise, en ce compris dans les "communes à facilités", c.à.d. les communes avec une minorité francophone. En effet,

---

6 DELPÉRÉE F., *Le peuple, la nation, l'Etat et la communauté dans la Constitution belge*, in : F. Rigaux (éd.), Le concept de peuple, Bruxelles, Story-Scientia, 1988, 70.

7 LEJEUNE Y., *La notion de collectivité en droit public belge*, in : Liber Amicorum E. Krings, Bruxelles, Story-Scientia, 1991, 217-218; ALEN A., *Le fédéralisme belge*, in : Centre d'Etude du Fédéralisme, Le fédéralisme. Approches politique, économique et juridique, Bruxelles, De Boeck, 1994, 151-152.

le modèle institutionnel belge repose entièrement sur le compromis historique qui était le *principe de territorialité*. Comme on expliquera plus loin (n°s 20-24), ce principe a été consacré tant par la Cour européenne des droits de l'homme que par la Cour constitutionnelle belge.

Enfin, il faut remarquer que le système institutionnel belge est "un ensemble complexe de freins et de contrepoids" (voir n° 23). Le fédéralisme belge est un fédéralisme "bipolaire"[8], parce que les institutions *fédérales* sont tellement organisées qu'il y a "une gestion paritaire des compétences fédérales"[9]. En 1970, la majorité flamande (± 60 %) fut neutralisée grâce à des garanties constitutionnelles pour la minorité francophone (± 40 %). Les membres élus de chaque Chambre législative sont répartis en un groupe linguistique néerlandais et un groupe linguistique français. Les lois en matière de réforme de l'Etat doivent être adoptées par chaque Chambre législative à une majorité spéciale : d'une part, une majorité simple des suffrages dans chaque groupe linguistique, et, d'autre part, une majorité des deux tiers des suffrages émis dans les deux groupes linguistiques. Pour les autres lois, "une procédure de sonnette d'alarme" est prévue : une motion motivée et signée par les trois quarts au moins des membres d'un des groupes linguistiques peut déclarer que les dispositions d'un projet ou d'une proposition de loi qu'elle désigne sont de nature "à porter gravement atteinte aux relations entre les communautés"; dans ce cas, la procédure parlementaire est suspendue et la motion est déférée au Conseil des ministres (composé paritairement) qui invite la Chambre législative saisie à se prononcer soit sur son avis motivé, soit sur le projet ou la proposition éventuellement amendés. Le Conseil des ministres compte, le Premier Ministre éventuellement excepté, autant de ministres d'expression néerlandaise que d'expression française. Cette parité existe, en vertu de

---

8 ALEN A., *La Belgique: un fédéralisme bipolaire et centrifuge*, Textes et Documents, Ministère des Affaires Etrangères, du Commerce Extérieur et de la Coopération au Développement, Bruxelles, 1990; ALEN A., *Deux rapporteurs suisses sur les minorités nationales belges*, *l.c.*, 243-244.

9 RIMANQUE K., *Réflexions concernant la question oratoire: Y a-t-il un Etat belge?*, in : H. Dumont et al., Belgitude et crise de l'Etat belge, Bruxelles, Fac.univ. Saint-Louis, 1989, 67.

la loi, également au sein des juridictions supérieures, et, à partir d'un certain grade, dans les services centraux de l'administration de l'Etat.

§ 3. LA RECEPTION DE LA THEORIE DE RENNER ET BAUER EN BELGIQUE[10]

Bauer et son grand inspirateur Renner sont encore considérés aujourd'hui comme étant les principaux théoriciens d'un fédéralisme personnel, en tant qu'alternative au fédéralisme territorial.

En 1995, Pierré-Caps écrivait au sujet de la théorie austro-hongroise des nationalités, telle qu'elle avait été portée à son paroxysme par Renner et Bauer :

> *"C'est cette pensée brillante, originale et audacieusement actuelle qu'il est indispensable d'évoquer aujourd'hui, dans la mesure où elle est porteuse de solutions adéquates aux conflits nationalitaires européens"*[11].

Otto Bauer[12] s'était fondé sur les idées de Karl Renner, et plus particulièrement sur le système que ce dernier avait développé en 1902 dans *Der Kampf der Österreichischen Nationen um den Staat*[13]. Ces deux théoriciens et politiciens autrichiens ont essayé d'élaborer une solution pour l'Autriche multinationale du début du vingtième siècle, où habitaient, outre des germanophones, de nombreux autres groupes de population, au premier rang desquels des Tchèques.

Ce qui est caractéristique, dans les idées de Bauer et de Renner, c'est qu'ils dissocient très nettement les concepts de nation et d'Etat. Le territoire est simplement un élément constitutif de l'Etat, mais pas de la nation. Pour Bauer, tenir exclusivement compte de la frontière linguis-

---

10 Le texte de ce paragraphe est basé sur CLEMENT J., *Taalvrijheid, bestuurstaal en minderheidsrechten. Het Belgisch model*, Anvers, Intersentia, 2003.

11 PIERRÉ-CAPS S., *La multination. L'avenir des minorités en Europe centrale et orientale*, Paris, Odile Jacob, 1995, 257.

12 BAUER O., *La question des nationalités et la social-démocratie*, 2 vol., Montréal-Paris, Guérin Littérature-Arcantère Éditions, 1987.

13 Renner a mieux exposé son système en détail dans : RENNER K., *Das Selbstbestimmungsrecht der Nationen in besonderer Anwendung auf Österreich. Erster Teil: Nation und Staat*, Leipzig-Vienne, Franz Deuticke, 1918.

tique pour procéder à la division administrative d'un pays était, dans une économie moderne, un anachronisme. D'une part, le principe de territorialité accorde une importance excessive à la diversité nationale de la population en voulant à tout prix diviser l'Etat en des circonscriptions administratives basées sur la frontière linguistique. D'autre part, le principe de territorialité oblige les nations à céder à d'autres nations d'importantes parties de leur population, à savoir celles qui n'habitent pas dans leur propre région linguistique. Bauer affirmait que le principe de territorialité absolue avait pour conséquence de livrer partout les minorités à la majorité. Renner ne considérait pas que le principe de territorialité était erroné en soi, mais qu'il n'était pas une solution pour l'Autriche de l'époque, dans laquelle, par suite de circonstances historiques, sociales et économiques, les groupes de population s'étaient fortement mélangés. Selon Renner, la territorialité et la personnalité pouvaient être considérées comme une thèse et une antithèse, devant conduire à une synthèse supérieure. On ne peut donc pas affirmer que Renner aurait répudié le principe de territorialité au profit du principe de personnalité :

> *"Natürlich existiert kein Volk ohne Gebiet, kann der innere Aufbau nicht von der örtlichen Schichtung der Bevölkerung unabhängig sein. Ist das Prinzip der Personalität das konstitutive, welches die Scheidung der Nationen und die Zusammenfassung der einzelnen zum Ganzen herbeiführt, so wird das territoriale seine bedeutende Rolle als organisatorisches Prinzip zu spielen haben"*[14].

Dans le système de Renner, qui est repris par Bauer, on établit un registre indiquant la nationalité choisie librement par chaque citoyen. Ceux qui sont inscrits dans le registre paient des impôts à leur nation. Les nations acquièrent la personnalité juridique. De la sorte, elles peuvent créer elles-mêmes, et partout où elles le désirent, leurs propres écoles, théâtres, musées, académies, etc. Par ailleurs, les nations se voient attribuer des institutions autonomes, dotées de compétences propres.

---

14 *Ibid.*, 108.

Alors que les nations sont constituées sur une base personnaliste, Renner et, à sa suite, Bauer[15], délimitent des zones territoriales, appelées "districts", pour l'organisation concrète du système. Il faut opérer une distinction entre les districts mixtes (sur le plan linguistique) et les districts homogènes (ou unilingues), en remarquant toutefois qu'il n'est pas exclu que, même dans ces derniers, puissent vivre également des minorités ou des individus "dispersés" ayant opté pour une nationalité (ou une langue) autre que celle du district. Cette répartition entre deux types de districts définit l'intensité avec laquelle les nations peuvent exercer leur droit national. Dans ses districts homogènes propres, la nation peut faire jouer pleinement son droit national. Dans les districts mixtes, l'enjeu est le droit de la majorité ou de la minorité. A cet égard, il est essentiel qu'en ce qui concerne les matières spécifiquement nationales, au premier rang desquelles les écoles, l'art et la littérature, les décisions soient prises par des organes composés de personnes ayant la même nationalité. Pour les individus qui vivent de manière dispersée dans les districts homogènes dont la nationalité n'est pas la leur, le système prévoit un simple droit de protection. Ces individus peuvent faire appel à leur nation pour l'enseignement public dispensé à leurs enfants ainsi que pour une assistance juridique dans leurs rapports avec l'administration et les tribunaux du district homogène dans lequel ils vivent. Renner veut transposer dans le droit interne le principe de personnalité du droit international selon lequel les Etats défendent aussi leurs ressortissants en dehors de leur territoire. En dehors des districts mixtes, les nations peuvent, en quelque sorte, offrir une protection diplomatique dans les districts des autres nations. *En résumé, le système proposé présente trois facettes* : la première est celle de l'autonomie pour les matières nationales dans les districts homogènes propres, la seconde est celle de cette même autonomie dans les districts mixtes et

---

15 Bauer explique à ce sujet que le système de Renner n'est pas une application pure et simple du principe de personnalité, étant donné que s'il est vrai que ce principe peut être immédiatement appliqué aux religions, il ne peut l'être à la diversité nationale-culturelle, qui est bien plus importante pour l'homme moderne (BAUER O., *o.c.*, II, 368). Dans la doctrine belge, Dumont n'a pas vu cette nuance quand il écrit que Bauer fait de la nationalité un attribut individuel comparable à l'appartenance religieuse (DUMONT H., *Le pluralisme idéologique et l'autonomie culturelle en droit public belge*, Vol. 1, Bruxelles, Bruylant, 1996, 140, note 42).

la troisième est celle d'un droit de protection dans les districts homogènes des autres nations.

L'octroi aux parlements nationaux propres de la pleine souveraineté sur les matières "nationales" était un élément qui convenait bien au plaidoyer de Renner, pour qui l'Etat fédéral était la forme d'Etat la plus parfaite. Pour Renner, le fédéralisme était la concrétisation idéale de ce que l'on désigne aujourd'hui par le terme de "principe de subsidiarité" :

> *"Wer das, was von Natur aus gesondert ist, sondert und den Sonderteil, der der Selbstregierung bedarf, auch mit Selbstregierung ausstattet, zugleich aber für die organische Verbindung der Teile, für ihre harmonische Eingleiderung in das Ganze sorgt, der ist Föderalist, jeder andere nicht"*[16].

A la différence de Bauer, Renner ne voulait pas seulement dissocier les intérêts nationaux spécifiques des compétences générales existantes de l'Etat et confier ceux-ci à des organes autonomes spécifiques; il voulait également faire de même pour les matières territoriales spécifiques qui devaient être confiées à des organes constitués sur une base purement territoriale. Renner citait l'agriculture comme l'élément principal des compétences "liées au territoire", mais il soulignait qu'il ne s'agissait là que d'un simple exemple de compétences plus larges. Renner proposait donc un fédéralisme à deux niveaux, tel qu'il existe aujourd'hui en Belgique. Le parlement fédéral et le gouvernement fédéral restent seulement responsables des matières qui ne sont pas spécifiquement nationales ou territoriales[17].

En 1913, le Parlement belge examinait le projet de loi linguistique sur l'armée[18] introduite par de Broqueville, Ministre de la Guerre. Le parlementaire Camille Huysmans s'est exprimé à cette occasion :

---

16 Renner K., *o.c.*, 234.

17 C'est la juridiction fédérale qui doit trancher les conflits de compétences (*ibid.*, 273 et 292).

18 Le Constituant belge du 7 février 1831 conçut la Belgique comme un Etat unitaire décentralisé. Bien que la population flamande ait toujours été majoritaire, la langue française était en pratique la seule langue officielle au 19ème siècle. Le Mouvement flamand remporta une victoire importante en imposant "la loi de l'égalité" du 18 avril 1898, en vertu de laquelle les lois sont votées, sanctionnées, promulguées et publiées en langue française et en langue néerlandaise.

"[...] si la Belgique constitue une nation, elle est composée de deux nationalités distinctes. Cette nation doit être basée sur l'unité politique, tandis que les nationalités flamande et wallonne ont besoin de l'autonomie de culture. Cette autonomie de culture, nous la réclamons pour la Wallonie, mais nous la voulons également entière et complète pour la Flandre.

Ces idées, messieurs, ont été développées au point de vue théorique par des hommes qui ont eu l'occasion d'examiner cette question dans des pays plurilingues beaucoup plus étendus, et notre camarade Otto Bauer, certainement un de nos meilleurs théoriciens, est arrivé, pour l'Autriche, exactement aux mêmes conclusions"[19].

Huysmans avait fait la connaissance de Bauer en 1907 lors du congrès de l'Internationale à Stuttgart. Durant la même année, Bauer publiait *Die Nationalitätenfrage und die Sozialdemokratie*, dans lequel il prolongeait les raisonnements de Karl Renner.

En ce qui concerne l'autonomie culturelle en Belgique, Huysmans songeait en premier lieu à ce que nous avons appelé ci-dessus la première facette du système proposé par Renner et Bauer, à savoir l'autonomie pour les matières culturelles dans les régions homogènes. En 1919, il lançait un plaidoyer visant à conférer au groupe linguistique flamand une autonomie pour toutes les institutions culturelles en Flandre :

"[...] en Flandre, groupez l'académie flamande, les théâtres flamands, les écoles techniques flamandes, les écoles de musique flamandes, les nombreuses sociétés flamandes, tâchez d'arriver à une communauté d'idées non seulement entre les fonctionnaires, mais aussi entre toutes les forces vives de la Flandre, les littérateurs, les artistes, tous ceux qui pensent et réflètent les idées, la vie, le milieu et la nationalité. Faites la même chose pour la Wallonie, et alors vous aurez une Belgique unie".

Il soulignait qu'il n'y avait donc aucun risque pour l'unité du pays :

"Je n'ai jamais été partisan de la disjonction que dans un seul département: celui des sciences et arts. Je veux non pas une séparation administrative, puisque je ne veux qu'un seul ministre des sciences et des arts, mais je veux à côté de ce seul ministre deux sous-secrétaires d'état, l'un s'occupant de la Wallonie, l'autre de la Flandre"[20].

L'application aux deux groupes linguistiques de Belgique de la première facette du système proposé par Renner et Bauer a eu pour consé-

19 *Ann.* Chambre, 23 mai 1913, 1320.

20 *Ann.* Chambre, 5 juin 1919, 1046.

quence évidente l'application de la deuxième facette dans le district mixte de Bruxelles. Les deux groupes linguistiques pourraient ainsi exercer leur autonomie à Bruxelles pour les matières culturelles. S'agissant des autres matières, il ne serait procédé à aucune scission en groupes linguistiques.

Huysmans a donné une portée limitée à l'autonomie culturelle proposée par Renner et Bauer. Il n'a parlé nulle part de l'enregistrement individuel volontaire des "nationalités" flamande et wallonne. Huysmans a implicitement donné une base territoriale à l'autonomie culturelle introduite par lui en Belgique en reprenant seulement les deux premières facettes du système de Renner et Bauer. La troisième facette de ce système, qui suppose l'instauration de sous-nationalités, n'a jamais été réalisée en Belgique.

§ 4. LA CONSECRATION DU PRINCIPE DE TERRITORIALITE PAR LA COUR CONSTITUTIONNELLE BELGE ET LA COUR EUROPEENNE DES DROITS DE L'HOMME[21]

A. La jurisprudence de la Cour constitutionnelle belge

La Cour d'arbitrage (la Cour constitutionnelle belge) a décidé que les dispositions constitutionnelles "ont déterminé une répartition exclusive de compétence territoriale. Un tel système suppose que l'objet de toute norme adoptée par un législateur communautaire puisse être localisé dans le territoire de sa compétence de sorte que toute relation et toute situation concrètes soient réglées par un seul législateur". C'est là un rejet clair de la conception personnaliste[22]. La Cour consacre clairement le principe de territorialité, mais la motivation de l'arrêt dit "*Car-*

---

21 Le texte de ce paragraphe est basé sur ALEN A. et ERGEC R., *Le principe de territorialité dans la jurisprudence belge et européenne. Un essai de synthèse*, *l.c.*

22 La jurisprudence de la Cour confirme aussi que le droit public belge ne connaît pas de sous-nationalités (par ex. Cour d'arbitrage, n° 33/2001, 13 mars 2001, *M.B.* 27 mars 2001, *J.T.*, 2002, 3, note D. DE BRUYN et *R.B.D.C.*, 2001, 209, note DELGRANGE X.).

refour I" du 3 octobre 1996 n'est pas sans équivoque[23]. A l'origine de cet arrêt se trouve la politique de la Communauté française consistant à aider financièrement les multiples associations francophones œuvrant dans les communes à statut linguistique spécial de la Région flamande. La Cour a égard à "la nature même de la promotion de la culture" pour reconnaître que, dans une certaine mesure, la compétence communautaire dans ce domaine puisse produire des effets sur le territoire d'une autre région unilingue. "Toutefois", ajoute la Cour, "ces effets extraterritoriaux potentiels des mesures de promotion de la culture ne peuvent contrarier la politique culturelle de l'autre communauté". En somme, dans cet arrêt la Cour reconnaît en matière culturelle la possibilité pour les normes communautaires de déployer des effets sur le territoire d'une autre communauté. A cela il y a deux limites : le principe général de proportionnalité et l'interdiction d'édicter des normes qui s'appliqueraient uniquement dans les communes à statut linguistique spécial situées sur le territoire de l'autre communauté.

Dans les arrêts *Carrefour* suivants[24], la Cour d'arbitrage a systématiquement répété, sans la moindre ambiguïté, que la Communauté française est incompétente pour assurer la protection des francophones dans la région de langue néerlandaise. Selon le professeur Scholsem, la possibilité de l'existence d'effets extraterritoriaux est étroitement liée à la nature budgétaire de la mesure :

> *"à moins d'enterrer l'argent dans son jardin (dans quel cas, il est à strictement parler localisé) une dépense, entrant dans un circuit économique ouvert, a toujours certains effets 'extraterritoriaux'. Qu'on pense, à cet égard, aux subsides aux entreprises"*[25].

---

[23] Cour d'arbit rage *Carrefour I,* n° 54/96, 3 octobre 1996, *M.B.* 10 octobre 1996, *J.T.*, 1997, 477, note UYTTENDAELE M. et WITMEUR R., *T.B.P.*, 1997, 782, note HENRARD K., *Journ. proc.*, 1996, n° 312, 29, note SCHOLSEM J.-C..

[24] Cour d'arbitrage *Carrefour II,* n° 22/98, 10 mars 1998, *M.B.* 10 avril 1998; Cour d'arbitrage *Carrefour III*, n° 50/99, 29 avril 1999, *M.B.* 19 juin 1999; Cour d'arbitrage *Carrefour IV*, n° 56/2000, 17 mai 2000, *M.B.* 1er juillet 2000; Cour d'arbitrage *Carrefour V*, n° 145/2001, 20 novembre 2001, *M.B.* 4 décembre 2001.

[25] SCHOLSEM J.-C., *Observations sous l'arrêt n° 54/96 du 3 octobre 1996 de la Cour d'arbitrage*, Journ. Proc., 1996, n° 312, 31.

Dans l'arrêt *Carrefour I*, la Cour d'arbitrage semble donc avoir plutôt souligné un fait qui est de notoriété publique, sans que l'on puisse affirmer pour autant que la frontière linguistique serait devenue plus perméable à la suite de cet arrêt. Le considérant de la Cour d'arbitrage relatif aux possibles effets extraterritoriaux des mesures visant à la promotion de la culture signifie que lorsque les communautés n'agissent pas en vue de la protection de la minorité linguistique dans l'autre région linguistique, mais prennent une mesure de promotion de la culture, tout en restant dans les limites de leur compétence territoriale, leur compétence matérielle peut malgré tout, le cas échéant, devoir subir une limitation en raison des effets disproportionnés des conséquences extraterritoriales de la mesure sur la compétence de l'autre communauté[26].

B. La jurisprudence de la Cour européenne des droits de l'homme

On trouve une première consécration jurisprudentielle du principe de territorialité dans l'arrêt du 23 juillet 1968 "relative à certains aspects du régime linguistique de l'enseignement en Belgique"[27]. La loi du 30 juillet 1963 prescrit comme langue de l'enseignement celle de la région linguistique. La méconnaissance de ce principe est notamment sanctionnée par le retrait des subsides ou le refus d'homologation des diplômes. Le principe souffre de tempéraments dans les communes à statut linguistique spécial (les "communes à facilités": voir n° 5), notamment dans les six communes de la périphérie bruxelloise, où des écoles primaires dispensant l'enseignement en langue française peuvent être instituées. La même loi s'abstint cependant de préciser exactement la région linguistique dont ces six communes devaient faire partie: elles étaient considérées comme à régime spécial ou, pour reprendre une expression de l'époque, elles étaient "en l'air". La Cour européenne des

26 ALEN A. et PEETERS P., *The Competences of the Communities in the Belgian Federal State: The Principle of Exclusivity Revisited*, European Public Law, 1997, vol. 3, 172.

27 Cour eur. D.H., arrêt *Affaire linguistique belge* du 23 juillet 1968, *Publ. Cour eur. D.H.*, Série A, n° 6.

droits de l'homme a rejeté les griefs de discrimination fondée sur la langue et de violation du droit à l'instruction que les requérants adressaient contre l'unilinguisme de l'enseignement dans la région de langue néerlandaise. La Cour a vu dans la "défense de l'homogénéité linguistique de la région" une pratique dénuée d'arbitraire: "Elle repose, tout d'abord, sur cet élément objectif que constitue la région. Elle s'inspire en outre d'un intérêt public, celui d'assurer que tous les établissements scolaires dépendant de l'Etat et existant dans une région unilingue, dispensent leur enseignement dans la langue qui est, au premier chef, celle de la région". Sans doute le même arrêt a-t-elle valu à la Belgique une condamnation pour violation de l'article 14 de la Convention européenne des droits de l'homme (interdiction de discrimination) en combinaison avec l'article 2 du Premier protocole additionnel à la Convention (droit à l'instruction). La condamnation reposait sur le fait que, selon le système de la loi précitée, l'enseignement en langue française dans les six communes périphériques n'était pas accessible aux enfants dont les parents résidaient en dehors des communes considérées, alors que le même enseignement, dispensé en langue néerlandaise, l'était à tout enfant, quels que soient sa langue maternelle ou le lieu de résidence de ses parents. Dans un mémorandum du 12 avril 1972 adressé au Comité des ministres du Conseil de l'Europe, le Gouvernement belge a expliqué comment la Belgique a executé l'arrêt du 23 juillet 1968 lors de la révision constitutionnelle de 1970. En rangeant les six communes périphériques dans la région de langue néerlandaise, les écoles francophones dans ces communes furent traitées sur un pied d'égalité avec les autres écoles de la minorité situées dans une région unilingue, à propos desquelles la Cour européenne des droits de l'homme n'avait constaté aucune violation[28].

---

28 On s'est étonné du fait que deux résolutions récentes de l'Assemblée parlementaire du Conseil de l'Europe, à savoir la Résolution 1172 du 25 septembre 1998 et la Résolution 1301 du 26 septembre 2002 (n° 5), appellent encore la Belgique à exécuter l'arrêt du 23 juillet 1968 (ALEN A., *Deux rapporteurs suisses sur les minorités nationales belges*, *l.c,* 242 ; CLEMENT J., *L'emploi des langues en matière administrative, les facilités et la résolution Nabholz du Conseil de l'Europe. Pas de langue, pas de liberté?*, *A.P.T.*, 2003, 198).

Le mode de composition des ("grands") Conseils (Parlements) de communauté et de région avant les réformes institutionnelles de 1993 a donné lieu à l'important arrêt du 2 mars 1987 de la Cour européenne des droits de l'homme[29]. Après avoir relevé que "la loi spéciale du 8 août 1980 s'insère dans un système institutionnel général de l'Etat belge, *inspiré par le principe de territorialité*", la Cour de Strasbourg observe :

> *"Encore inachevée, la réforme en cours cherche à réaliser un équilibre entre les diverses communautés culturelles et régions du Royaume moyennant un ensemble complexe de freins et de contrepoids; elle a pour but d'apaiser, par la création de structures plus stables et décentralisées, les différends linguistiques au sein du pays".*

Et la Cour de poursuivre à propos du système électoral incriminé :

> *"Il entraîne, pour les minorités linguistiques, la nécessité d'accorder leurs suffrages à des personnes aptes et prêtes à user de la langue de leur région. Une obligation analogue se rencontre dans nombre d'Etats pour l'organisation de leurs élections.*
>
> *Pareille situation, l'expérience le montre, ne menace pas forcément les intérêts de ces minorités. Il en va surtout ainsi, en présence d'un système qui dans son ensemble, s'inspire de la loi du sol, quand l'ordre politique et juridique fournit des garanties, sous la forme par exemple de l'exigence de majorités qualifiées, contre des modifications intempestives ou arbitraires".*

La Cour conclut qu'elle ne discerne dans les griefs des requérants aucune violation de la Convention. Il faut voir dans cet arrêt une nouvelle consécration européenne du principe de territorialité, après celle de l'arrêt de 1968.

La jurisprudence européenne d'après laquelle les minorités linguistiques peuvent êtres astreintes à n'accorder leurs suffrages qu'à des personnes aptes et prêtes à user de la langue officielle est bien établie. A propos de l'obligation imposée en Lettonie aux candidats au Parlement – en ce compris ceux issus de la minorité russe – de connaître la langue officielle (le Letton), la Cour de Strasbourg estima dans un arrêt du 9 avril 2002 : "eu égard à la marge d'appréciation de l'Etat défendeur, la Cour conclut que le fait d'exiger qu'un candidat au parlement ait une

---

29 Cour eur. D.H., arrêt *Mathieu-Mohin et Clerfayt c. Belgique* du 2 mars 1987, *Publ. Cour. eur. D.H.*, Série A, n° 113 (souligné par nous).

connaissance suffisante de la langue officielle poursuit un but légitime"[30].

La Cour constitutionnelle belge[31], suivie par la Commission européenne des droits de l'homme[32], a confirmé que le droit de vote ou d'être élu ne peut s'exercer qu'à l'égard des assemblées législatives compétentes pour le territoire où résident les personnes qui invoquent ce droit.

§ 5. CONCLUSIONS ET EVALUATION

Le système institutionnel belge est essentiellement territorial atténué par trois éléments dits personnels :

- les "facilités linguistiques" prévues par la législation linguistique pour les habitants de vingt-sept communes à statut linguistique spécial (n° 5);
- la compétence des deux grandes communautés s'étendant à la région bilingue de Bruxelles-Capitale (n° 7);
- la jurisprudence de la Cour constitutionnelle belge d'après laquelle la compétence communautaire dans le domaine de la culture peut produire des effets sur le territoire d'une autre région unilingue (n° 20).

Toutefois, il serait incorrect d'en déduire que la Belgique aurait adopté le fédéralisme personnel. Reprenons les trois éléments précités. En premier lieu, les "facilités linguistiques" ne peuvent pas porter atteinte à l'homogénéité linguistique d'une région[33]. En second lieu, la compé-

30 Cour eur. D.H., arrêt *Podkolzina c. Lettonie* du 9 avril 2002, http://www.echr.coe.int ; voir DESMECHT C., *L'emploi des langues dans les assemblées parlementaires*, *C.D.P.K.*, 2003, 311-317.

31 Cour d'arbitrage, n° 90/94, 22 décembre 1994, *M.B.* 12 janvier 1995, *Jaarboek Mensenrechten 1994*, 295, note THEUNIS J..

32 Comm.eur.D.H., 8 septembre 1997, *Clerfayt et autres c. Belgique*, requête n° 27.120/95.

33 Voir notamment Cour d'arbitrage, n° 17, 26 mars 1986, *M.B.* 17 avril 1986, *J.T.*, 1986, 562, note UYTTENDAELE M., *T.B.P.*, 1986, 343, commentaire VELAERS J. : "L'article [4] de la Constitution [...] constitue [...] la garantie constitutionnelle de la primauté de la langue de la région unilingue ou du caractère bilingue de la région [bilingue de Bruxelles-Capitale]".

tence extraterritoriale des Communautés flamande et française ne s'étend qu'à des *institutions* unilingues établies dans la région bilingue de Bruxelles-Capitale (n°s 7-8). En troisième lieu, la possibilité pour les normes communautaires de déployer, en matière culturelle, des effets sur le territoire d'une autre communauté est limitée par le principe général de proportionnalité et par l'interdiction d'édicter des normes qui s'appliqueraient uniquement dans les communes à statut linguistique spécial situées sur le territoire de l'autre communauté (n°s 20-21). Enfin, il ne faut pas perdre de vue que tous ces éléments dits personnels ne sont que des "pseudo-exceptions" au principe de territorialité étant le vrai fondement du "système institutionnel général de l'Etat belge" (n° 23). En Belgique, la législation linguistique a jeté les bases du principe de territorialité qui aujourd'hui a pour effet de confiner l'activité législative, gouvernementale et administrative de chaque entité fédérée principalement à son territoire défini, en substance, à l'aide des régions linguistiques et d'assurer, à l'intérieur de chaque région linguistique unilingue, la primauté de principe de la langue de cette région[34].

Dans le cadre du fédéralisme belge, les deux premières facettes du système de Renner et Bauer se retrouvent dans la scission qui existe entre les matières régionales et les matières communautaires et dans le fait que, s'agissant de la région bilingue de Bruxelles-Capitale, les Communautés flamande et française sont simultanément compétentes pour les matières communautaires. La Belgique est donc l'un des rares pays au monde qui fasse application du modèle de Renner et Bauer[35].

Le fédéralisme personnel au sens de ce que nous avons appelé la troisième facette du système de Renner et Bauer (n° 13) n'est pas une so-

---

34 ALEN A. et ERGEC R., *Le principe de territorialité dans la jurisprudence belge et européenne. Un essai de synthèse*, *l.c.*, 785.

35 Durant l'entre-deux-guerres, les conceptions de Renner en matière d'autonomie culturelle ont été appliquées en Estonie et en Lettonie, mais leur annexion par l'Union soviétique y a mis fin (KANN A., *Renners Beitrag zur Lösung nationaler Konflikte im Lichte nationaler Probleme der Gegenwart*, Sitzungsberichte Österreichische Akademie der Wissenschaften. Philosophisch-Historische Klasse, 279, Band 4, Vienne, 1973, 9). En Hongrie, il existe aujourd'hui un régime des minorités qui s'inspire des idées de Renner, mais il ne s'agit pas là d'un fédéralisme (PIERRÉ-CAPS S., *Le principe de l'autonomie personnelle et l'aménagement constitutionnel du pluralisme national. L'exemple hongrois*, Rev. dr. Publ., 1994, 401-428).

lution pour la Belgique, parce qu'il suppose l'instauration de (sous-)nationalités séparées. Outre les objections de principe à cette séparation des citoyens sur la base de leur "appartenance linguistique", l'on peut craindre avec raison que cette troisième facette ne profite à la langue dominante[36]. Comme le démontre l'exemple belge, le principe de territorialité est une technique institutionnelle de protection d'un groupe linguistique. L'introduction du principe de territorialité équivaut à la création d'une *security area* linguistique, à l'intérieur de laquelle le groupe peut faire prospérer sa langue et sa culture[37]. Affirmer que la problématique des groupes linguistiques trouve une solution dans la concession de droits individuels aux membres de ces groupes implique de présupposer que toutes les langues sont par nature intrinsèquement égales. Un tel raisonnement ne tient nullement compte d'une situation, telle la situation belge, où une langue dominante (la langue française) entre en contact avec une langue non-dominante (la langue néerlandaise). Il est généralement admis que dans une telle situation, les locuteurs de la langue dominante sont moins enclins à s'adapter à l'environnement où la langue non-dominante est parlée – que du contraire –, de telle manière que les processus de glissement linguistique auront toujours lieu au détriment de la langue non-dominante. Dans ces circonstances, le principe

---

36 Le principal reproche que l'on peut faire au système de Renner et Bauer est qu'il est au service d'une langue dominante. Les écrits de ces deux théoriciens ne laissent planer aucun doute à ce sujet. Bauer écrivait que les germanophones voulaient pouvoir trouver partout en Autriche des écoles de langue allemande pour leurs enfants, et il y voyait un facteur non négligeable de puissance pour la nation allemande. Renner s'attendait à ce que d'autres citoyens optent pour la nationalité allemande. C'est ainsi qu'il pensait que les parents appartenant aux minorités tchèque, polonaise, slovène et italienne de Vienne souhaiteraient que leurs enfants fréquentent des écoles allemandes, ne fût-ce que pour permettre à ces minorités de se comprendre entre elles en allemand.

37 LAPONCE J.A., *Relating Linguistics to Political Conflicts : the Problem of Language Shift in Multilingual Societies*, in : Etats multilingues, problèmes et solutions. Multilingual Political Systems, Problems and Solutions, Travaux du Centre International de Recherche sur le bilinguisme, Québec, Presse de l'Université de Laval, 1975, 200. Voir. aussi CLEMENT J., *Taalvrijheid, bestuurstaal en minderheidsrechten, o.c.*, n° 1440; DONEUR A., *La solution territoriale au problème du multilinguisme, ibidem*, 211 ; WOEHRLING J., *La Constitution du Canada, la législation linguistique du Québec et les droits de la minorité anglo-québécoise*, in : N. Levrat (éd.), Minorités et organisation de l'Etat, Bruxelles, Bruylant, 1998, 615 ; VANDERNOOT P., *Les aspects linguistiques du droit des minorités*, *R.T.D.H.*, 1997, 352.

de territorialité, compris comme la création d'une *security area* linguistique, est une technique particulièrement importante de protection du groupe linguistique qui parle la langue non-dominante. Il existe certes une tension entre le principe de territorialité et les droits des minorités, mais le fait que cette tension existe ne doit pas faire perdre de vue que les deux pôles qu'elle oppose ont une seule et même finalité, à savoir la protection des groupes linguistiques[38]. Enfin et surtout, il faut souligner que le principe de territorialité ne peut en aucun cas porter atteinte aux droits fondamentaux individuels, en particulier le principe d'égalité et de non-discrimination.

Le concept de l'Etat moderne est à l'origine du principe de territorialité[39]. L'Etat de droit moderne où les droits de l'homme universels sont respectés se traduit en un système juridique territorial où les règles, sans distinction de personnes, valent pour tous les habitants dans un territoire déterminé, et non en un système juridique personnel, où les droits et les obligations de l'individu diffèrent en fonction du groupe auquel il appartient. Dans l'arrêt de la Cour européenne des droits de l'homme du 31 juillet 2001 relatif au Parti de la prospérité turc, il fut affirmé qu'un système juridique personnel où le statut de chacun dépend de sa religion est contraire à la Convention européenne des droits de l'homme[40]. A propos de l'interdiction d'une mention, même facultative, de la religion sur les cartes d'identité en Grèce, la Cour estima que "lorsqu'un Etat opte pour l'introduction d'un système d'identification par des cartes d'identité, il convient d'admettre que celles-ci constituent simplement des documents officiels permettant d'identifier et d'individualiser les personnes en leur qualité de citoyens et dans leurs rapports avec l'ordre juridique de l'Etat. Les convictions religieuses, [...] ne constituent pas une donnée servant à individualiser un citoyen dans ses rapports avec l'Etat ; non seulement elles relèvent du for intérieur de

38 CLEMENT J., *Taalvrijheid, bestuurstaal en minderheidsrechten, o.c.*, n° 1465.

39 DUMONT H., *Au-delà du principe de territorialité : fédéralisme, intégration et subsidiarité*, *A.P.T.*, 1999, 64.

40 Cour eur. D.H., arrêt *Refah Partisi, Erbakan, Kazan et Tekdal c. Turquie* du 31 juillet 2001, http://www.echr.coe.int; voir notamment CLEMENT J., *Taalvrijheid, bestuurstaal en minderheidsrechten, o.c.*, n° 1449.

chacun, mais elles peuvent aussi, comme d'autres données, changer au cours de la vie d'un individu ; leur mention dans un document risque aussi d'ouvrir la porte à des situations discriminatoires dans les relations avec l'administration ou même dans les rapports professionnels"[41].

Le fédéralisme belge est essentiellement un fédéralisme territorial. Il n'est nullement certain qu'un fédéralisme purement personnel – à supposer qu'il soit réalisable[42] – poserait moins de problèmes du point de vue de la protection des groupes minoritaires, et même du point de vue de la protection des droits de l'homme en général.

41 Cour eur. D.H., arrêt *Sofianopoulos c. la Grèce* du 12 décembre 2002, http://www.echr.coe.int .

42 Un "fédéralisme personnel" intégral existait ou existe seulement à Chypre et au Liban, qui ne sont certainement pas les exemples de fédéralisme les plus réussis (ALEN A., *Nationalism – Federalism – Democracy. The Example of Belgium*, European Review of Public Law, 1993, Vol. 5-N° 1, 1993, 69).

"Multicultural Switzerland : How to Accommodate (Religious) Diversity?"

Matthias SCHNYDER

A century ago the cultural uniformity of France was seen as a normal phenomenon, the cultural diversity of Switzerland, however, as an exception. Nowadays the multicultural composition of Switzerland is nothing atypical anymore – the way how Switzerland accommodates cultural diversity, however, still is.[1]

Today around 95% of the people in the world live in multicultural states, fragmented into different cultural communities.[2] That makes multiculturalism a major social phenomenon, a source of enrichment and/or conflict, particularly in a globalising world with very high mobility, including migration (legal or not).

Multicultural societies are, of course, nothing new, but the phenomenon of multiculturalism is growing and changing, especially through the aforementioned population movements of various kinds.[3] Particularly

---

1 DEUTSCH Karl W., *Die Schweiz als friedenspolitisches Lehrstück. Integration als Friedensgemeinschaft*, in: Matthies Volker (Hrsg.), Der gelungene Frieden. Beispiele und Bedingungen erfolgreicher Konfliktbearbeitung, Bonn 1997.

2 FLEINER (I) Thomas / KÄLIN Walter / LINDER Wolf / SAUNDERS Cheryl, *Federalism, Decentralization and Conflict Management in Multicultural Societies*, in: Federalism in a Changing World. Learning from Each Other. Scientific Background, Proceedings and Plenary Speeches of the International Conference on Federalism, Montreal/Kingston/London/Ithaca 2002, 197.

3 GALTUNG (I) Johan, *Multicultural Society. From a Multicultural World to Multicultural Persons*, 22nd of August 2002, www.transcend.org.

after the fall of the Berlin Wall multicultural societies have to cope with problems that were formerly overshadowed by the potential for conflict between capitalism and communism[4]. Another factor explaining the new prominence of multiculturalism is the greater consciousness of racism, not at the least associated with the rights revolution. The reaction against globalism is a further important factor.[5] As globalisation increases, localisation is likely to increase accordingly. The fragmentation of multicultural states thus will continue. If they do not develop the capacity to meet these new challenges, they will be unable to meet increasing demands for localisation, and will be confronted with major conflicts.[6]

With regard to the peaceful management of conflict(s) in multicultural societies the famous Norwegian Peace Researcher Johan Galtung writes, "of these (…) [multicultural societies] only one single society has managed a symmetric co-habitation of nations: Switzerland. In all the others there is one dominant nation « more equal than the others »".[7]

In Switzerland federalism enabled the peaceful coexistence of different regional/cantonal, linguistic, and religious identities and even promoted diversity.[8] Switzerland is often presented as an example of success in nation-building as the presence of diverse communities on the same national territory did not prevent their harmonious coexistence, unlike in other culturally heterogeneous or multicultural countries, even prosperous and democratic ones like Belgium or Canada. Today the Swiss consensual and participatory model of federalism/good governance is

---

4 FLEINER (I), 197.

5 SAUNDERS Cheryl, *Federalism, Decentralisation and Conflict Management in Multicultural Societies*, in: Federalism in a Changing World. Learning from Each Other. Scientific Background, Proceedings and Plenary Speeches of the International Conference on Federalism, Montreal/Kingston/London/Ithaca 2002, 33.

6 FLEINER (I), 197.

7 GALTUNG (I), www.transcend.org.

8 REILLY Harris / REILLY Peter / REILLY Ben (Eds.), *Democracy and Deep-Rooted Conflict. Options for Negotiators, Deep-rooted Conflicts. The Structure of the State: Federalism and Autonomy*, www.idea.int/publications/democracy_and_deep_rooted_conflict/home.htm.

on the agenda of institutional engineering, not at the least as a device for peaceful transition to democracy in deeply divided societies.[9]

With regard to the role of Swiss federalism as a tool for conflict management in multicultural societies it has, however, to be stated, that Swiss multicultural federalism would, of course, most certainly not work in another environment simply by transplanting the system. In cases of minority conflicts, where the basic conditions for introducing federalism or decentralisation are lacking, to turn to such models might even be contraproductive. The purpose of studying the political systems of other countries is, however, not to find models to copy, but to find inspiration from existing models and to seek ways of adapting some of their elements to the particular circumstances of one's own country. This requires a lot of un-dogmatic new thinking, creativity and good will by all (cultural) communities. I hope that this presentation of the specific particularities of Swiss multicultural federalism may be one of several sources of inspiration that can enrich the discussion with regard to a peaceful transformation of the violent conflict(s) in the Near East. The Swiss system *itself* is a result of influence and inspirations from different systems abroad.[10]

The following presentation will illustrate how Swiss federalism enabled the peaceful coexistence and integration of different regional/cantonal, linguistic, and religious identities and even promoted diversity. The present paper will, however, also illustrate that this accommodation of linguistic and religious diversity was and is mainly focused on indigenous minorities. The European integration, globalisation, and, in this context, increased migration led to a, at least partial, questioning of the Swiss federal arrangement, though not of federalism as such. Often the actual Swiss federal arrangement does not provide "new" minorities

---

9 PAPADOPOULOS Yannis, *Connecting minorities to the Swiss Federal System. A frozen conception of representation and the problem of the "requisite variety"*, Paper presented at the Common Congress of the German, Austrian, and Swiss Political Science Associations "Der Wandel föderativer Strukturen", Humboldt-Universität zu Berlin, 8-9 June 2001.

10 FLEINER (II) Thomas (ed.), *Multiculturalism and Federalism, The Swiss Case*, www.federalism.ch.

with the necessary instruments to enforce their interests.[11] But also with regard to indigenous minorities a certain questioning of the Swiss federal system can be remarked. In this context the new phenomenon of language corporativism (see Belgium) between German and French speaking Switzerland needs to be named.[12]

Taking into account the topic of the present Colloquium "Federalism: A tool for conflict management in multicultural societies with regard to the conflicts in the Near East" I would furthermore like to put a strong accent on the role the Swiss system played and plays with regard to the accommodation of religious diversity. The accommodation of religious diversity was one of the most difficult tasks in the history of Switzerland. In the Near East, which is divided by religious diversity not only between Jews, Muslims and Christians but as well between different subgroups of these religions, the accommodation of religious diversity plays a very important role with regard to the peaceful transformation of violent conflicts. And with a growing number of immigrants with a non-Christian, mainly Muslim, background, the question of how to accommodate, integrate and legally recognise religious minorities is again very relevant in Switzerland too.[13]

---

11 SUTTER Alex, *Welche kulturellen Rechte für marginale Minderheiten?*, erschienen in: Schnyder A. (Hrsg.), Sozialrechte und Chancengleichheit in der Schweiz. Sozialalmanach 2000. Caritas-Verlag. Luzern 2000, S. 179-192; see also: BADE Klaus J. (Ed.), *Europa in Bewegung. Migration vom späten 18. Jahrhundert bis zur Gegenwart*, 378-454.

12 ALTERMATT (I), *Das Fanal von Sarajevo. Ethnonationalismus*, Zürich 1996, 145-155.

13 CATTACIN Sandro / FAMOS Cla Reto / DUTTWILER Michael / MAHNIG Hans, *Staat und Religion in der Schweiz. Annerkennungskämpfe, Anerkennungsformen.* Eine Studie des Schweizerischen Forums für Migrations- und Bevölkerungsstudien im Auftrag der Eidgenössischen Kommission gegen Rassismus, Bern, September 2003; see also: MINKENBERG Michael / WILLEMS Ulrich, *Neuere Entwicklungen im Verhältnis von Politik und Religion im Spiegel politikwissenschaftlicher Debatten*, in: Aus Politik und Zeitgeschichte, Beilage zur Wochenzeitung "Das Parlament", B 42-43/2002, Bonn, 21. Oktober 2002; see also: FRANRAHE Monika / SCMICKER Melanie / HÖRIG Christian, *Grenzen der Modernisierung im Hinblick auf die europäische und die arabische Kultur*, Alber-Ludwigs-Universität Freiburg i. Br, 2002; TAYLOR Charles, *Drei Formen des Säkularismus*, in: Otto Kallscheuer (Hrsg.), Das Europa der Religionen, Frankfurt/M. 1996.

Switzerland is a multi-lingual and multi-confessional state with important historical, cultural and economic differences between these groups. It is composed of 20 cantons and 6 half-cantons, each with their own identity and history. These territorial divisions are not purely administrative units but self-governing entities with original (residual) powers. The creation of the Swiss State was based on the attempt to safeguard the existing sovereignty of the cantons while enabling a limited degree of common decision making.[14] The cantons themselves are the aggregate of in total 2842 communes (2003).[15] All cantons accorded autonomy to their communes. Cantonal and communal self-rule enabled the development and preservation of independent traditions and ideas and even of an independent identity and culture.[16]

It is this reality of the fragmented Swiss society, which has induced the drafters of the updated Swiss Constitution of 1999 to provide already in the preamble a clear mandate of the confederation to be "determined to live our diversity in unity respecting one another". And article 2 paragraph 2 of the Constitution does oblige the confederation to foster the cultural diversity of the federation. Such provision of a promotion of cultural diversity is certainly unique compared with most other constitutions of the world.

The formula of "diversity in unity" describes the federal principle according to the Swiss understanding of its multiculturality.[17] It does not only emphasise, that different cultural communities can be united by their firm will to be a political union, but it expresses also the dialectic tension between self-rule, shared rule and solidarity.[18]

There are different reasons why this unique constitutional promotion of diversity and the peaceful cohabitation of different cultural communi-

---

14 FLEINER (II).

15 STEINER Reto, *Gemeindezusammenschlüsse sind in der Schweiz kein Tabu mehr, In 155 Jahren 361 Gemeinden weniger*, Unipress, Heft 117, Juni 2003, Bern 2003.

16 FLEINER (II).

17 See GREBER Anton, *Die vorpositiven Grundlagen des Bundesstaates*, Diss. Fribourg 1999.

18 ELAZAR D. J, *Exploring Federalism*, Tuscaloosa/London 1987, 5.

ties developed in Switzerland. First of all cleavages between linguistic, religious, and cantonal groups do not overlap but there is a crosscutting of cleavages. Crosscutting of cleavages normally mitigates tensions, overlapping cleavages enhances them, not at the least with regard to inter-religious issues.[19] In Switzerland this is well illustrated, where in the past long disputes between urban Protestants and rural Catholics often (since the 16th century) reached the level of violent conflict that lead to civil war in 1847/48.[20] The Swiss success of overcoming these violent hostilities began with the overlapping of conflict lines, when the French- and Italian-speaking cantons joined the Swiss Confederation. Since the 19th century the boundaries between religions, that is Catholics and Protestants, the languages, that is German, French, Italian and the socio-economic conditions are no longer identical.[21] They only rarely coincide with cantonal borders. Because the aforementioned factors overlap, every Swiss is in some regards in a majority and in other regards in a minority.[22] This crosscutting of cleavages not only prevents the creation of violent conflicts, but they make co-operation between the various cultural subgroups necessary.[23] Nevertheless a latent ethnisation can be remarked in Switzerland since the mid 1980s. The mass media plays a key role in his development. Language corporativism mainly between French- and German-speaking Switzerland is winning ground in everyday life. Linguistic cleavages, which unfortunately overlap with ideological and partly social cleavages are increasingly questioning the Swiss unity and consensus. One of the basics of

---

19 HOLMES Stephen, *Gag Rules or the Politics of Omission*, in: Elster Jon / Slagstad Rune, Constitutionalism and Democracy, Cambridge 1997, 47.

20 LINDER (I) Wolf, *Swiss Democracy. Possible Solutions to Conflict in Multicultural Societies*, Second Edition, New York 1998, 18f.; see also: STEINBERG Jonathan, *Why Switzerland*, Second Edition, New York 1996, 206-233.

21 KÄLIN Walter, *Federalism and the Resolution of Minority Conflicts*, in: Bächler Günther (ed.), Federalism against Ethnicity. Institutional, Legal and Democratic Instruments to Prevent Violent Minority Conflicts, 179f.

22 ALTERMATT (I), 243ff.

23 KÄLIN, 179f.

Swiss conflict management is being eroded in the beginning of the 21st century.[24]

Even though the crosscutting of cleavages mitigates tensions, this factor is not the only reason why peaceful cohabitation succeeded in Switzerland. The aforementioned development of a balanced combination of self-rule and shared rule and the specificity of a consensus driven direct democracy on all three, the municipal, the cantonal and the federal levels, is part of the success of the peaceful accommodation of diversity in Switzerland. Furthermore the makeup of the unique Swiss (multi[25]) nation-concept and with regard to that the concept of multiple loyalties as a positive factor of peaceful cohabitation of cultural communities need to be mentioned.[26]

The three-level federalism in Switzerland is the pragmatic outcome of the balancing between the highest possible degree of self-rule and a necessary centralisation for common decision-making (shared rule). Until the end of the 18th century the organisation of the Swiss political system as a confederation was sufficient for achieving the common aim. The loose union maintained the sovereignty of the cantons but organised common defence and introduced arbitration among the cantons. Common defence could protect the cantons from its neighbours. Arbitration provided peaceful conflict management among the cantons.

Despite various conflicts (violent and non-violent) between the cantons and between the confederation and neighbouring powers the loose union served Switzerland well for more than 500 years. Modernisation and with it nation building processes in neighbouring countries (esp. Italy and Germany) however necessitated the restructuring of the union. The armies of the cantons could no longer compete with the national armies of its neighbours. With the creation of a German and an Italian nation, which was not only based on language but included language as major identifying criteria, the meaning of being Swiss gained impor-

---

24 ALTERMATT (I), 145ff.

25 See KYMLICKA Will, *Multicultural Citizenship*, New York 1995, 13f.

26 FLEINER (II).

tance. Last but not least industrialisation called for bigger markets and closer integration.

While Switzerland opted for a stronger centralisation in order to survive and to compete with the neighbouring nation-states, it nevertheless cherished the given diversity. The aim of the adoption of a federal system was not so much to modernise but to allow as much centralisation as necessary for the maintenance of existing diversity.[27] The maintenance and promotion of preconstitutional diversity was accepted as common value and therewith became a unifying element. As the Swiss Political Scientist Wolf Linder argues, Switzerland is a multicultural antithesis to nation-building and national unification in the neighbouring countries.[28]

Self-rule gave and gives the cantons the possibility to decide on their own over certain issues. They have a final say for some subject matters, e.g. for education. Shared rule guaranteed and guarantees their participation in the decision making process on the federal level, e.g. the subunits are represented in a second chamber of parliament and have therefore a special input in the decision-making at the federal level. In this sense shared rule includes always an institutional set-up through which sub-national entities (in this case the cantons) are accorded special participation and input in the decision-making on the federal level.[29]

Although the history of Switzerland is a history of centralisation, the highly decentralised structure of its political institutions, that is a high level of decentralisation of power (a power that is rather institutional and not personal and that is well-founded in an active civic society) was and is central for the prevention of possible conflicts in Switzerland. Through self-rule many conflicts could be prevented or delegated to and transformed on a low and less conflictual level. Through shared rule, that is compromise and togetherness founded on political values, a balance could be found between local diversity and common identity that lead to a mostly peaceful transformation of conflicts.

---

27 LINDER (II) Wolf, *Politische Kultur*, Zürich 1999, 15.

28 Ibid. 15.

29 FLEINER (II).

Over the centuries a Swiss nation (or "multination"[30]) developed based on the voluntary association of the peoples of the cantons. Switzerland was able to establish its own, very singular, concept of a nation that differs decisively from the major western (esp. German and French) nation concepts.

In Germany the nation as preconstitutional ethnic homogeneous people legitimises the German state.[31] The unity derives from ethnicity. The French nation is a creation of the state and encompasses all French citizens who accept certain universal values. In the French case the unity of a democratic "citizen-state" is created against ethnicity.[32]

Neither the French and the German, nor most other major nation concepts take cultural diversity seriously. Culture is either ignored, or is so central to the nation that all other cultures are excluded. The multicultural nature of the state is not a significant factor in constituting the political order. None of them readily accommodates different cultures within their concept of political unity.[33]

Also in immigration countries like the United States, where the unity of a polity is focused on the territory, culture or history are considered as irrelevant as nation-building factors. Here too, culture may be considered a threat to the state, but in this case, it is likely to be ignored. The basis on which immigration nations are typically established assumes the need to separate political unities from cultural unities, including the culture of any indigenous peoples. An immigration state can accommodate the different cultures of its immigrant citizens on the basis of private pluralism, but not as political instruments that fragment the unity of the state.[34]

---

30 See KYMLICKA, 13f.

31 See Preamble German Constitution 1948: "(...) the German people [not the people of Germany] have adopted, by virtue of their constituent power, this Constitution."

32 FLEINER (II).

33 FLEINER (I), 199.

34 Ibid. 199.

The Swiss system takes cultural diversity seriously. It relies partly on the idea of citizenship like in France and on preconstitutional criteria such as an internalised very particular corporate direct democracy like in Germany. The cantons as preconstitutional entities form as equal partners the federation while the citizenry of the cantons form the nation.[35] The Swiss nation concept does neither rely on culture blindness nor on one unifying culture but accepts the equal value of different cultures.

When Ernest Renan delivered his famous lecture at the Sorbonne University in Paris in 1882, his aims were to challenge traditional conceptions of nationhood based on race, language, religion, geography and dynastic rule as an appropriate basis for nationhood in a modern democratic state. For Renan Switzerland represented the ideal example of a nation that was not held together by the aforementioned nation concepts, but by political values only. He called Switzerland "la nation la plus légitimement composée".[36]

If a nation is held together by political values only, it can incorporate other cultures as long as no political recognition is claimed for them. The multicultural nature of the state is ignored as a structural factor that might serve to unite or decentralise the political society. For this reason a political nation denies culture as a nation-building factor. The nation can exist only on the basis of the equality of individuals. This implies that individuals are conceived as rational human beings, who ignore their cultural roots. Nations that deny culture thus assume rational citizens, who may not pursue their cultural identity as part of the political identity of the state. All rational citizens are equal with regard to each other. Their cultural identity is of no political value.[37]

---

35 FLEINER (II).

36 TANNER Albert, *Willensnation versus Kulturnation*, in: Bosshart-Pfluger Catherine / Jung Joseph / Metzger Franziska, Nation und Nationalismus in Europa. Kulturelle Konstruktion von Identitäten. Festschrift für Urs Altermatt, Frauenfeld 2002, 179.

37 FLEINER (I), 200.

The Swiss type of federal state takes into account the reality of its diversity and recognises the political value of its different cultural communities. It is the basis for a concept of multiple loyalties, a concept that the Swiss historian Urs Altermatt calls the model of the "hyphen citizen" ("Bindestrich-Bürger"), as is provided in Switzerland with regard to local and national citizenship (the federation and the canton are both considered states).[38] Double and triple identities/loyalties, of course, can always create tensions. But as long as political loyalty in a multicultural society does not depend on colour, language or race, but on civic identity, conflicts will be transformed institutionally and not with violence.

In addition to that, multiple identities help people to imagine identities outside the set of their own identities. To imagine other identities does not necessarily mean that one is willing to consider the interests of the people with these other identities, but the chances are better that one would do so. Considering the interests of other groups can lead to a learning process, whereby it becomes a habit to imagine other identities and to consider the interests of the people holding these other identities. Such a process will not necessarily happen, but if it does, we are on the path to an ethics of discourse – a discourse that the classical nation state is not or at least less open for.[39]

There are, however, also severe risks if a country takes the described path. Fluid boundaries can weaken domestic political structures, which, in turn, may lead to feelings of insecurity among many citizens. They feel at a loss and long for the well-established order of the classical nation state with its firmly set boundaries.[40]

There is, however, a model that goes even a step further than the described model of tolerance and discourse. It is the transition from a multi-cultural society to multi-cultural persons, which means the active

---

38 ALTERMATT (I), 243ff.

39 STEINER (I) Jürg, *Switzerland and the European Union – A Puzzle. Switzerland today: models, issues and lessons for Canada*. Presented at the conference at the UBC Institute for European Studies.

40 STEINER (I).

coexistence of more than one culture inside one person, not only inside a society.[41] This model gives us another perspective on multiculturalism, namely as an infinite resource for enrichment if other cultures are really taken on, not only tolerated. Conflicts must be handled not only non-violently to avoid violence, but also creatively for joint enrichment. This concept, however, at least for the moment, still seems to be quite utopian.[42]

As I have mentioned in the introduction of my presentation, with regard to the topic of the colloquium the question of the accommodation of religious diversity is probably one of the most crucial issues. To accommodate religious diversity was and with regard to new minorities still is for Switzerland and, of course, was and still is for the Near East a very decisive question. Compromises in the area of religion are extremely painful to the different parties involved. However, as the history of Switzerland shows, compromises are the only way to deal with religious differences.

Religious strife in Switzerland culminated in a civil war in 1847, which was primarily a conflict between Catholic dominated cantons (conservatives) and Protestant dominated cantons (progressives/radicals), both of them representing the two traditional religions in Switzerland.[43] Although the cause of the war was religious and it can thus be labelled as a confessional conflict, it opposed more fundamentally two social coalitions with competing interests. The emerging industrial and progressive protestant bourgeoisie on the one side and the Catholic traditionalist landlords, who lived in backward, agricultural areas of the countryside on the other side. As Switzerland fought its wars between Catholics and Protestants in times of relative religious peace in the surrounding countries, there never really existed the danger of a complete disintegration of the country.[44]

---

41 GALTUNG (I), www.transcend.org.

42 GALTUNG (II), *Rethinking Conflict : the Cultural Approach*, www.transcend.ch.

43 FLEINER (II).

44 PAPADOPOULOS.

The Federal Constitution, which was drafted and voted in 1848 after the short civil war (won by the protestant side), clearly was a compromise. The passage from the former confederation to a federal state did not go as far in terms of centralisation as the radicals would have wished. Institutions were established that allowed for some degree of protection of the defeated Catholic-conservative cantons. In particular, broad competencies of self-government were clearly intended as a mechanism of external protection in order to avoid that the minority be negatively affected by decisions of the wider society. This typically "consociationalist" solution can be explained by two different theoretical paradigms: a) the federalist compromise should be primarily interpreted as an equilibrium resulting from political choice: as the winners were not thoroughly homogeneous they needed the support of the losers for their federation, and the latter could also find some good reasons to accept the institutional arrangement and b) another perspective, more in line with a historical and sociological institutionalist way of thinking would stress the influence of the past on actors' perceptions, and more accurately the inheritance of norms of peaceful coexistence that originated in previous consociational solutions intended to overcome confessional conflicts. This is not to say that the protestant winners did not concede any governmental power to the Catholic-conservative forces at the federal level, and this is also a signal of the power relations at the time. They retained a thorough monopoly at the level of the central executive, and occupied all seats in the Federal Government for almost 50 years.[45]

Despite the fact that Catholic conservatives eventually achieved a quite good constitutional compromise, the first decades after the Constitution of the Swiss federation led to segregation of the Catholic minority. The Catholic regions were mainly rural and cut off from the industrialisation. The First Vatican Council of the Catholic Church was hostile to the modernisation of society and scientific progress, as well as to the separation of religion and state. The declaration of papal infallibility, which was viewed by the radicals as a threat to Swiss liberty and de-

---

45 Ibid.

mocracy further led to segregation. A tight web of social and para-political organisations kept Catholics together. It was in these years that a Catholic university was founded in Fribourg. No wonder that this kind of segmentation lead to conflict over religious issues, especially in the religiously mixed cantons. In Swiss history we speak of the "culture struggle" (Kulturkampf) because the issue went beyond religion to different views of society.[46]

The revision of the Federal Constitution in 1873/74 was influenced by this cultural struggle. It aimed at a fully secularised state and led to the elimination of public functions of the church. The Constitution of 1874 also granted legal freedom to all religious communities.[47] While the Constitution of 1848 denied legal freedom to the Jewish community, it was granted to them in 1874. Free establishment was, however, already granted in 1866, but only under (economic) pressure of France, the Netherlands and the USA.[48]

During the period of the cultural struggle, it was the aforementioned instruments of peaceful cohabitation, the combination of shared and self rule, that is the highly decentralised power structure of Switzerland and the instruments of direct democracy that gave the Catholics a certain space of manoeuvring and influence on decision making. Institutional compromises made the inclusion of the Catholic minority possible.

Self-government allowed the Catholics to preserve or develop to a great extent autonomously specific regulations (e.g. in the provision of religious education). Because of federalism the Catholic cantons could still decide on the role of the Catholic religion in their canton.[49] The conservative party became thus able to exert in some cantons a governmental monopoly comparable to the monopoly of the radicals at the federal

46 Ibid.

47 ALTERMATT (II) Urs, *Katholizismus und Moderne*, Zurich 1991, 147.

48 See "Antisemitismus", www.dhs.ch.

49 KRIESI Hanspeter, *Federalism and Pillarization: the Netherlands and Switzerland compared*, Acta Politica 25, 433-450.

level.[50] The Christian-democrats were able to convert their local dominance into national influence too, although such a process took several decades.[51]

The introduction of proportional representation of the population in one chamber of the Federal Assembly strengthened predominantly Catholic parties and increased their negotiating power. This mitigated the feeling of oppression by the Catholics and contributed to their gradual reintegration within the national community and facilitated the bargaining for more Catholic seats in the Federal Council (Bundesrat).[52]

The Catholics acquired yet another instrument that proved useful to them. With the constitutional revision of 1874 it became possible to oppose federal legislation (of mostly Radical inspiration) by resorting to referendums by petition. Within two decades twenty federal bills were challenged by way of referendum mainly by the Catholic opposition, and the Federal Government of radical obedience was defeated fifteen times.[53] In order to avoid further perturbations by the Catholics, who increasingly became thereby dangerous veto players, the radicals coopted in 1891 one of their representatives into the seven members' federal executive. It was of course not the end of radical dominance, but it was the beginning of powersharing at the executive central level.[54]

In the 20th century inter-religious issues could only lead to political mobilisation when there was an overlapping of cleavages. In the case of the secession of the canton of Jura from the canton of Bern, the popula-

---

50 KLÖTI Ulrich, *Kantonale Parteiensysteme. Bedeutung des kantonalen Kontexts für die Positionierung der Parteien*, in: H. Kriesi et al. (eds.), Schweizer Wahlen 1995, Bern 1998, 45-72.

51 ALTERMATT (III) Urs, *Der Weg der Schweizer Katholiken ins Ghetto*. Freiburg 1995, 433.

52 ALTERMATT (IV) Urs, *Le Catholicisme au défi de la modernité. L'histoire sociale des catholiques suisses aux XIXe et XXe siècles*, Lausanne, 49.

53 TRECHSEL Alexander, *Feuerwerk Volksrechte. Die Volksabstimmungen in den schweizerischen Kantonen 1970-1996*, Basel 2000, 142.

54 PAPADOPOULOS.

tion of the Jura did not only have a different religion but spoke a different language and were economically disadvantaged.[55]

One of the main reasons, why religious issues lost increasingly importance in the 20th century was not at the least because the neutrality of the federal state in religious matters dismissed religious disputes to the cantonal level except for issues of representation. Religious disputes could not directly threaten the national unity. Only when religious disputes had gone so far as to destroy the solidarity among the cantons and imbalance the power structure in the federation could it threaten the national unity.[56] Only because the Swiss federal state was removed from religious conflicts could it create an overarching national identity, which is not questioned by diversity but on the contrary incorporates diversity.

The neutrality of the Swiss federal state towards religion is however not complete. The freedom of religion clause in the Federal Constitution, in which the relationship between state and church is founded, does not demand a complete separation of state and church, although this decision is delegated to the cantonal level. The church model in Switzerland can be called a "partial separation of church and state".[57] But in addition to that the Constitution shows, although not explicitly, a clear attachment to the Christian tradition. The preamble of the updated Federal Constitution of 1999 starts with the evocation of the Almighty God and the responsibility with regard to the creation ("Schöpfung").[58]

Although the Federal Government explicitly guarantees the religious neutrality of schools, freedom of creed and the free exercise of religion[59], these rights are not absolute. They can be limited in the interest

---

55 STEINBERG, 90-93.

56 Ibid., 206-233.

57 KOCH Kurt, *Das Verhältnis von Staat und Kirche im Entwurf der neuen Bundesverfassung*, SKZ 12/1999; see also: NZZ, 28.10.1999, 5.

58 See Schweizerische Bundesverfassung vom 18. April 1999 (Stand 15. Oktober 2002).

59 Ibid.

of religious peace.[60] The state can find himself in a conflict between the collective right of religious communities and individual human rights (Rechtsgüterkonflikt). In the frame of a growing religious plurality in den Western societies, this phenomenon will gain importance and lead to serious conflicts.[61] And it is the question of how to manage this religious plurality that the sociologist Roland Campiche from Lausanne calls the major defiance for the accommodation of religious diversity in Europe, but very much also in Switzerland, in the coming years.[62]

The breakdown between the different religious denominations has shifted noticeably over the past several years in Switzerland. Traditionally, over 95 percent of the population has been evenly split between the Protestant and the Catholic Church, but since the 1970s, there has been a steady increase of persons formally renouncing their church membership. In the Catholic Church, immigration from Southern Europe has countervailed this trend. The arrival of immigrants from other parts has contributed to the noticeable growth of religious communities, which in the past had no or no strong presence in the country. According to the Federal Government's Statistics Office, membership in religious denominations in the year 2000 was as follows: 41.8 percent Roman Catholic, 33.0 percent Protestant, 1.8 percent Orthodox, 0.2 percent Old Catholic, and 0.2 percent other Christian groups; 4.3

---

60 Decision of the Swiss Federal Court: BGE 49 I, 138-159. See aslo: KALLSCHEUER Otto, *Die Trennung von Politik und Religion und ihre "Globalisierung" in der Moderne*, in: Aus Politik und Zeitgeschichte, Beilage zur Wochenzeitung "Das Parlament", B 42-43/2002, Bonn, 21. Oktober 2002.

61 PRITTWITZ Volker von, *Fundamentalismus, Religionsfreiheit und die Verantwortung des zivilen Staates*, in: Aus Politik und Zeitgeschichte, Beilage zur Wochenzeitung "Das Parlament", B18/2002, Bonn 2002.

62 CAMPICHE Roland J., *Religion: Herausforderung für die Kirchen.* Studien und Berichte aus dem Institut für Sozialethik des SEK, 43-46. See also: MINKENBERG Michael / WILLEMS Ulrich, *Neuere Entwicklungen im Verhältnis von Politik und Religion im Spiegel politikwissenschaftlicher Debatten*, in: Aus Politik und Zeitgeschichte, Beilage zur Wochenzeitung "Das Parlament", B 42-43/2002, Bonn, 21. Oktober 2002; see also: FRANRAHE Monika / SCMICKER Melanie / HÖRIG Christian, *Grenzen der Modernisierung im Hinblick auf die europäische und die arabische Kultur*, Alber-Ludwigs-Universität Freiburg i. Br, 2002; see also: TAYLOR Charles, *Drei Formen des Säkularismus*, in: Otto Kallscheuer (Hrsg.), Das Europa der Religionen, Frankfurt/M. 1996.

percent Muslim, 0.2 percent Jewish, and 0.8 percent other religions (Buddhist, Hindi, and other); 11.1 percent no formal creed.[63]

Most striking: the Muslim population has doubled to more than 310,000 in the 1990s, due to the influx of refugees from the former Yugoslavia. Although only two mosques exist – in Zurich and Geneva – there are approximately 120 Islamic centres throughout the country, making Muslims the country's largest non-Christian minority.[64]

As aforementioned, Article 72 of the Swiss Constitution stipulates that "the regulation of the relations between the Church and the State falls within the jurisdiction of the Cantons" ("Church" stays religious communities in general).[65] In others words, each canton has the responsibility to regulate its own relations with the different religious communities, although all have to comply with certain fundamental rights, in particular the freedom of conscience and belief. It is therefore mainly the cantons, who have to deal with the new phenomenon of the accommodation of religious diversity.

The precarious peace that was achieved between the Catholics and the Protestants in Switzerland in the 19th century was of such urgent concern to the Swiss history that the rights of other religious communities lay unattended for a long time; freedom of religion for Jews and other non-Christians was, as aforementioned, first provided for only in 1874 under economic pressure from other countries. The recognition of non-Christian religious communities ("öffentlich-rechtliche Anerkennung") came only much later. The cantons in Switzerland differ greatly with regard to this recognition. Some, such as Bern, Basle City, St. Gallen and Fribourg, have already recognised the Jewish religion that now has the state of a legal person and can e.g. levy taxes. Others only recognise Christian churches. Only in the cantons Geneva and Neuchâtel are all religions treated the same. Other cantons have so far rejected such a move. But some are looking into the issue, which could have conse-

63 Swiss Federal Statistical Office, http://www.statistik.admin.ch.

64 Ibid.

65 See Schweizerische Bundesverfassung vom 18. April 1999 (Stand 15. Oktober 2002).

quences for both recognised and non-recognised religious communities.[66]

Latest example with regard to the recognition of new religious communities: In November 2003 a cantonal referendum on an amendment to the cantonal constitution that provides for the recognition of non-traditional religious communities and allows them to levy a tax on their members and to receive public funds was carried out in Zurich. The referendum was, however, rejected.[67]

This case exemplifies the increasing conflicts in Western European societies in general and in Switzerland in particular with non-Christian forms of life and the importance to find solutions on how to accommodate religious diversity.

As has been illustrated, in Swiss history religious differences were for a long time the major source of tensions. Switzerland was torn by religious strife and threatened by internal violence. A readiness to peaceful coexistence of confessions was only achieved step by step. The process of growing insight into the possibility of political co-operation despite religious plurality and an accompanying development of the required institutions took decades. In this, Switzerland's federal structure was of primary importance, not at the least because of the balanced combination between self-rule (e.g. self-government: possibility to live local culture/religion) and shared rule (e.g. compromise through representation in one chamber of the parliament).

In its history Switzerland has shown that pragmatic institutional or quasi-institutional compromises are the most important instruments to ensure the inclusion of all groups and to preserve the national unity, also with regard to religious diversity. Solutions that work in one country or in this case in Switzerland, will not necessarily be viable solutions for another country. A theory of the proper resolution of a conflict between different cultural communities in a country must take the spe-

66 CATTACIN, 5.

67 See "Switzerland", in: International Religious Freedom Report 2003. Released by the Bureau of Democracy, Human Rights and Labor, http://www.state.gov/g/drl/rls/irf/2003.

cial background in the concerned country into account. In Switzerland it is especially the nature of its nation concept that needs to be considered.

With regard to the future of the accommodation of diversity in Switzerland, the Swiss people have to ask themselves, if their instruments that led to a peaceful accommodation of indigenous minorities need to be reformed, not at the least because of the influx of new minorities? Do the Swiss still see themselves as an open country with fluid borders and multiple identities or not? Nowadays, this may be the key question with which not only Switzerland but every country has to deal with.

Nation, Religion and Identities in the Near East : Challenge or Opportunity for Federal Solutions ?

Multicultural Qualifications : A Legal Analysis in Respect of the Palestinian-Arab Minority of Israel

Michael Mousa KARAYANNI*

I. INTRODUCTION

Multiculturalism has become a central theme in many academic disciplines from philosophy to education, social work and psychology, ultimately reaching political science and law. However, it should be added at once that the study of diverse societies existed all throughout history, for there is really nothing new in the phenomenon of having different sets of people live in one sovereign unit. Nevertheless, what seems to be unique in current studies on multiculturalism is not merely the observance and display of societies that happen to be diverse in terms of the religious, cultural, national and ethnic affiliation of their members. Rather, it is the central argument that such divergence is legitimate and should be accommodated. So instead of diversity being the cause of animosity and hate, as was the case in many countries in the past, it is seen today as a cause for tolerance and acceptance. Indeed, some have also come to realize that diversity could also be in itself a value that should be cherished – given the inter-group dialogue and the exchange of ideas it manages to create. In addition, multiculturalism has also had an influence that far exceeds the confinements of this or that academic

* Vice-Dean and holder of the Edward S. Silver Chair in Civil Procedure, Faculty of Law, The Hebrew University of Jerusalem. LL.B., Bar Ilan University, LL.M., George Washington University; LL.D., Hebrew University of Jerusalem; S.J.D., University of Pennsylvania.

discipline. The high moral ground now belongs to those who accept and support multiculturalism as an ethical standard. Accepting other groups in society and the legitimacy of accommodating them has become a virtue of tolerance.

Despite the sweeping influence of multiculturalism, the movement has not been as successful in composing a comprehensive scheme of rules and standards that are attuned to the needs and concerns of different countries. Though many governments would like to accommodate different members of society based on their group membership (group differentiated rights), there is still much discussion as to the form of such accommodations: should they be molded into exemptions from laws that penalize or burden cultural practices, should they guarantee certain quotas of representation of minority groups in different government bodies or maybe even reach the level of granting groups some powers of self-government.[1] Some forceful arguments claim that accommodating particular groups might resolve one set of problems, but at the same time create another set no less acute. One worrisome reality is that the accommodation granted to one group is seen to be at the expense of other groups, promoting inter-group tensions rather than tolerance. In due course this tension could lead to demand of secession from the original sovereign unit. Another dilemma is concerned with relativism of values: what if the group accommodation leads the group to apply norms that go against universal notions of liberal thought, e.g. when a religious group is accommodated making it possible for its institutions to apply norms that overtly discriminate against women.

Worries and dilemmas of this sort have lead some to question the desirability of having group accommodations in the first place. Whatever multiculturalism seeks to promote in terms of accommodating different groups can be sought through the regular guarantees of a democratic society that build on safeguarding individual rights.[2] Individuals who

---

1 LEVY Jacob T., *Classifying Cultural Rights*, in : Nomos XXXIX: Ethnicity and Group Rights 22 (New York and London: New York University Press, Ian Shapiro & Will Kymlicka eds., 1997).

2 *See* BARRY Brian, *Culture and Equality, An Egalitarian Critique of Multiculturalism* (Cambridge Mass.: Harvard University Press, 2001).

want to nourish their group identity can do so by associating, as they are free to do under the basic guarantee of the freedom of association. Multicultural theorists have argued in return that such associations, especially when initiated by minority groups, will not get far if not assisted by additional guarantees. As a result, serious efforts were made to find answers to the worries and dilemmas by modifying the theory of multicultural accommodations.

This paper does not take issue with those who support group accommodations in multicultural societies or with those who oppose them, at least not directly. Rather, the article argues that we must first look into multicultural theory itself to discover what can be called “multicultural qualifications”. These are in essence pre-conditions without the presence of which group accommodations, even if granted based on group membership, should not be considered as multicultural in nature. In other words, for a multicultural accommodation to be considered as such it is not enough that it is accorded on a group basis, but it itself together with the legal and political environment that embodies it must be able to meet such multicultural qualifications.

With multicultural theory as a backdrop, the first part of this article intends to identify such multicultural qualifications. In an effort to facilitate the discussion further I have chosen the Palestinian-Arab minority in Israel in its constellation as both a national minority group and as a religiously diverse group as an object for testing the application of the identified multicultural qualifications. This move is motivated by two principle reasons. The first is personal. This is the community I happen to belong to, and so I am naturally closely acquainted with its characteristics, aspirations, problems and dilemmas. Second, this community is situated in a state that has traditionally ascribed a number of accommodations based on group membership, although usually to the Jewish majority, primarily in its immigration laws, national symbols and its de facto policies in terms of settlement and land development.[3] The Pales-

---

3 *See e.g.*, ROSENFELD Henry, *The Class Situation of the Arab National Minority in Israel*, 20 Comparative Studies in Society and History. 374 (1978); ZURIEK Elia, *The Palestinians in Israel: A Study in Internal Colonialism* (London: Routledge and Kegan Paul, 1979).

tinian-Arab minority has been largely excluded from equivalent accommodations. Instead this minority has been granted certain group accommodations, such as the recognition of Arabic as an official language, having a separate public school system and an exemption from army conscription. However, it is questionable whether these so-called accommodations can be regarded as multicultural. The status of Arabic is diminished, far overshadowed by English, which has no official standing; the schools are under-funded, with minimal infrastructure and mostly a low academic level; and the exemption from army service is at times a liability in gaining employment, housing and education benefits. Obviously, such group accommodations can hardly be considered multicultural, especially given the kind and substance of the group accommodations given to the Jewish majority.

In terms of religion, large portions of the Ottoman *millet* system are still part of the local legal corpus. Today, there exist 12 different Palestinian-Arab religious communities: ten Christian communities, the Moslem community, and the Druze. Such communities are granted exclusive jurisdiction to adjudicate in their own religious courts and under their own religious norms matters of marriage and divorce of their members. Moreover, the religious courts of these communities are competent to adjudicate other matters of personal status, such as custody of children, maintenance and inheritance, as long as certain pre-conditions are met, the principal condition being that of consent of all concerned parties. As a result, such religious accommodations have also been regarded as a sort of an autonomy granted by the State of Israel to the different Palestinian-Arab religious communities as groups.[4] But yet again can such group accommodations qualify as multicultural accommodations given the fact that certain religious norms applied by the different

---

4 LANDAU Jacob M., *The Arab Minority in Israel, 1967-1991: Political Aspects* 24 (Oxford: Clarendon Press, 1993); KRETZMER David, *The Legal Status of Arabs in Israel* 163–168 (Boulder; Westview Press, 1990); SABAN Ilan, *Minority Rights in Deeply Divided Societies: A Framework for Analysis and the Case of the Arab-Palestinian Minority in Israel*, 36 *N.Y.U. J. Int'l L & Pol.* 885, 942-946, 954-960 (2004); ZAMIR Itzhak, *Equality of Rights for Arabs in Israel*, 9 *Mishpat Umimshal* 11, 26, 30 (2005) [in Hebrew]; RUBINSTEIN Amnon and MEDINA Barak, *The Constitutional Law of the State of Israel: Basic Principles* 429-435 (6th ed. Jerusalem and Tel Aviv: Schoken, 2005)[in Hebrew].

religious communities overtly discriminate against women; given the fact that Israel has noot adopted a civil institute of marriage and divorce that one can opt out to, and given the fact that individual members of the different relgious communities were not asked whether they are interested in the form and structure of the granted religious jurisdiction?

These relations between the state of Israel and the Palestinian-Arab minority are of particular relevance also to the current debate in Israel that has also specifically implicated multiculturalism as a framework for conflict management.[5] However, multiculturalism in Israel is really a misnomer; Israel has many cultures, but to my mind is not truly multicultural. Therefore my discussion will also consider the normative side of multiculturalism, i.e. the standards for determining what is right and what is wrong in terms of group accommodations, rather than referring to the factual reality of diverse forms of group accommodations as necessarily multicultural.

II. MULTICULTURALISM : THEORY AND DILEMMAS

A. On Multicultural Qualifications

In the second half of the twentieth century, particularly after the end of the Cold War, a number of countries witnessed clashes among minorities and majorities over such issues as ethnic and cultural autonomy, religious freedom, national symbols (*e.g.*, national anthem, public holidays) and more.[6] This phenomenon is widespread and ubiquitous.[7] It

---

5 MAUTNER Menachem, SAGI Avi and SHAMIR Ronen (eds.), *Multiculturalism in a Democratic and Jewish State, The Ariel Rosen-Zvi Memorial Book* (Tel-Aviv, Ramot – Tel-Aviv University, 1998) [in Hebrew]; DANÉL Adam D., *A Jewish and Democratic State, A Multiculturalist View* (Jerusalem: Israel Democracy Institute, 2003) [in Hebrew]; NACHTOMY Ohad (ed.), *Multiculturalism in the Israeli Context* (Jerusalem: The Hebrew University Magnes Press, 2005) [in Hebrew]; YONNAH Yossi, *In Virtue of Difference: The Multicultural Project in Israel* (Tel-Aviv: The Van Leer Jerusalem Institute – Hakibutz Hameuchad, 2005) [in Hebrew].

6 KYMLICKA Will, *Introduction*, in : The Rights of Minority Cultures 1 (Oxford: Oxford University Press, Will Kymlicka ed., 1995).

7 *See* KELLY Paul, *Introduction: Between Culture and Equality*, in : Multiculturalism Reconsidered 1 (London: Routledge, Paul Kelly ed., 2002) ("All modern states

has been noted that in the almost 200 states that exist today there are more than 5,000 different ethnic groups.[8] It also seems that the era of globalization, with its advanced means of transportation and communications, has not promoted the envisioned understanding among the different groups, but has worked to aggravate ethnic conflicts even more.[9] One substantial effort aimed at easing ethnic, religious and cultural conflicts among different groups was the intellectual interest of political scientists, sociologists, philosophers and legal scholars, the intention of which was to create a theoretical framework capable of accommodating both the needs of one sovereign entity to stay as such on the one hand and needs of the different ethnic and religious groups that want to retain and foster their group identity on the other hand.[10] One theoretical course in this effort was the neo-liberal argument stressing the need of a state to keep a neutral preference when it comes to the ethnic and religious identity of its citizenry (an approach commonly termed "blindness to difference"). According to this approach, no ethnic or religious group deserves any preferential treatment by state authorities. Critics of minority rights have argued that to ascribe rights or benefits on the basis of membership in a particular group is an arbitrary and inherently discriminatory act that will eventually lead to a ranking of first and second class citizens.[11] The sole entity that is entitled to rights and protections from this point of view is the individual, and from the point of view of liberalism all individuals are to be treated equally, especially on the normative level, i.e. when state institutions come to prescribe norms of conduct. Under this conception, individuals of course have a right to join in different societies as they see fit, but have no right to ask the

---

face the *problems* of multiculturalism even if they are far from endorsing multiculturalism as a policy agenda or official ideology.").

8 KYMLICKA Will, *Multicultural Citizenship, A Liberal Theory of Minority Rights* 1 (Oxford: Clarendon Press, 1995).

9 *See* CHUA Amy, *World on Fire: How Exporting Free Market Democracy Breeds Ethnic Violence and Global Instability* (New York: Anchor Books, 2004).

10 LEVY Jacob T., *The Multiculturalism of Fear* (Oxford: Oxford University Press, 2000).

11 KYMLICKA Will and NORMAN Wayne, *Citizenship in Culturally Diverse Societies: Issues, Contexts, Concepts*, in : Citizenship in Diverse Societies 1, 3 (Oxford: Oxford University Press, Will Kymlicka and Wayne Norman eds., 2000).

state for preferable treatment from state authorities. Among the notable adherents of this line of argument is Brian Barry. In his view, "there should be only one status of citizens… so that everybody enjoys the same legal and political rights. These rights should be assigned to individual citizens, with no special rights (or disabilities) accorded to some and not others on the basis of group membership."[12]

The first to challenge such strict notions of liberalism as a basis for political theory were those adhering to communitarian thought. Communitarians first took issue with the liberal paradigm that citizens, as rational autonomous agents, are imagined to make choices on the basis of values and commitments they have judged to be valid, independent of any external factor, such as their society, history or culture. Communitarians have argued that individuals' ties to society, history and culture are contingent aspects of their identity and part of their being. Moreover, it has been argued that people, in an ontological sense, must be understood as 'constituted' by relations with others without which they will cease to be who they are.[13] So according to "the communitarian view, individuals engage even in thinking and acting not in a detached reflective mode but as fully embedded personalities defined and shaped by a social milieu."[14]

The above notions of strict liberalism have also been refuted by what came to be called the multicultural movement. Societies composed of a majority group and minorities cannot be neutral among all of their members even if they adopt the most liberal framework of administration.[15] Government in all of its branches will be more closely connected to the interests of the majority group than to the interests of the minor-

---

12 BARRY, *supra* note 2 at 7.

13 SANDEL Michael J., *Liberalism and the Limits of Justice* 62 (Cambridge: Cambridge University Press, 1982).

14 CHRISTMAN John, *Social and Political Philosophy. A Contemporary Introduction* 131 (London: Routledge, 2002).

15 SHACHAR Ayelet, *Multicultural Jurisdictions, Cultural Differences and Women's Rights* 22-23 (Cambridge: Cambridge University Press 2001) (indicating that "[a]t the heart of many contemporary justifications for multicultural citizenship lies a deep concern about power, particularly about the power of the state and dominant social groups to erode minority cultures").

ities. This is an inevitable reality in democratic societies as well, since the majoritarian mode of government guarantees the majority group the greater share in government administration.[16] This point has long been acknowledged by research in the social sciences. In what came to be known as May's theorem, it was proven that if all persons are permitted to participate in all decisions under conditions that ensure that one person's identity or preferred outcomes have special status but that each person has an equal chance to cast the decisive vote, then the decision will inevitably give preference to majority interests.[17] Therefore, one way of protecting minority groups is by empowering them in relation to the majority through a number of multicultural accommodations intended to reinforce their group identity and political strength. Without such protection the minority group could be assimilated, thereby endangering its very *nomos*[18] – aside from the dangers of excluding the minority group from the political process. Therefore, it was argued that states should work to grant minority groups preferable treatment both for the sake of empowering the minority group in its relations with the majority group and for the sake of enabling the minority group to preserve its distinctive features, which may be national, ethnic, religious or cultural.[19]

Other multiculturalists advocated the need for group rights from a purely liberal point of view.[20] Individuals need to belong to a group as a matter of self-fulfillment. It has been argued that a person's autonomy

---

16 KYMLICKA Will and NORMAN Wayne, *supra* note 11 at 3-4.

17 MASHAW Jerry L., *Administrative Due Process: The Quest for a Dignity Theory*, 61 *Boston University Law Review* 885, 899-900 (1981).

18 Referring to the culture distinctions of groups in terms of *nomos* was introduced in COVER Robert M., *The Supreme Court 1982 Term, Forward: Nomos and Narrative*, 97 *Harvard Law Review* 4 (1981). The use of the term dates back to ancient Greek philosophy whereby a distinction was made between a universal and divine law (*logos*) and the law expressed in relation to human life as created in the polis, the city-state, which was referred to as the *nomos*.

19 *See* YOUNG Iris Marion, *Justice and the Politics of Difference* (Princeton: Princeton University Press 1990); YOUNG Iris Marion, *Polity and Group Difference: A Critique of the Ideal of Universal Citizenship*, 99 *Ethics* 250 (1989).

20 RAZ Joseph, *Multiculturalism*, 11 *Ratio Juris* 193 (1998); RAZ Joseph, *Multiculturalism: A Liberal Perspective*, 41 *Dissent* 67 (1994).

of choice and judgment, cornerstones of liberal thought, are intrinsically tied to the community from which that person comes. People grow up in households and communities that tend to shape their virtues and qualities as individuals, and therefore have a personal need to continue to belong to their group as a form of individual realization. Liberalism as such demands that groups, particularly minority groups, be accommodated, for in preserving the group identity individuals in the group can operate in their full capacity.[21]

But as soon as this multicultural argument crystallized, those advocating the need for group rights were faced with two major issues. The first was the possible conflict between norms of minority communities and the individual rights of members of such communities.[22] For instance, how should the multiculturalism movement deal with minority ethnic or religious groups that have a strong patriarchal structure or even outright norms that discriminate against women?[23] Can liberal thought possibly advocate at the same time two opposing measures, on the one hand promoting group rights for the sake of certain individuals, and on the other hand making it possible for groups to mistreat other individuals belonging to it? Scholars who side with multiculturalism offer a number of devices that have the potential of lessening the tension between the right of a group and the right of an individual. Will Kymlicka, a prominent political philosopher who has worked extensively on multiculturalism, offers a basic distinction between group rights in the form of "external protections" and group rights in the form of "internal restrictions". In his view the legitimate claim of group rights is present only when it includes schemes intended to offer groups external protections, that are group accommodations intended to guard

---

21 KYMLICKA, *Multicultural Citizenship*, *supra* note 8; KYMLICKA Will, *Liberalism, Community and Culture* (Oxford: Oxford University Press 1989).

22 *See* EISENBERG Avigail and SPINNER-HALEV Jeff (eds.), *Minorities within Minorities: Equality, Rights and Diversity* (Cambridge: Cambridge University Press, 2005); GREEN Leslie, *Internal Minorities and Their Rights*, in : The Rights of Minority Cultures 257, 258 (Oxford: Oxford University Press, Will Kymlicka ed., 1995).

23 MOLLER OKIN Susan, *Is Multiculturalism Bad for Women?* 9-24 (Cambridge: Cambridge University Press 1999).

the minority group from majority domination. In this category one can include the protection of minority language, adequate representation in public institutions by guaranteeing a certain quota of representatives from members of minority groups, restricting geographically certain areas for the housing of certain minority groups, and so forth. However, liberal multiculturalism does not justify granting group rights in the form of internal restrictions under which, for example, a minority group is granted the right to apply norms that discriminate against or hinder the well-being of certain members of the group, such as woman and children.

Although the distinction offered by Kymlicka has a sound theoretical basis, in the opinion of other multiculturalists its practical utility is questionable. In many cases of group rights, especially with respect to traditional patriarchal societies or religious communities, the mere existence of the community itself, if supported exclusively by external protections alone will mean the undermining of certain individual liberties. This is mainly so since the external protections will inevitably re-enforce the power hierarchies within the group which in turn will work to the detriment of vulnerable individuals within groups with a patriarchal structure, e.g. women.[24] On way of dealing with this is to accept that any sort of multicultural accommodation will necessarily sacrifice certain individual liberties in the group's interest. Liberal justification for such a sacrifice is found by the possibility "opting out" or "exit" by individual members of such groups – an option that will make it possible for such members to receive the neutral parcel of rights and liberties provided to all citizens.[25]

Of course, the right of exit from a community may not be possible for a number of reasons.[26] First, the very decision to leave a group may prove impractical for children and women in a traditional society.[27] Ad-

---

24 SHACHAR, *Multicultural Jurisdictions*, *supra* note 15 at 17.

25 KUKATHAS Chandran, *Are There Any Cultural Rights?*, 20 *Political Theory* 105 (1992).

26 KYMLICKA Will, *The Rights of Minority Cultures, Reply to Kukathas*, 20 *Political Theory* 140 (1992).

27 *Cf.* Wisconsin v. Yoder, 406 U.S. 205 (1972).

ditionally, group identity may mean that a person is unable to function or be in a severe disadvantage – culturally, religiously, economically – alone, outside the group.[28] This would empty all meaning out of multiculturalism, which essentially builds on the well-being of individuals.

The preceding discussion underlines the importance of finding a way to ease the tension between group norms and individual liberties, since the multiculturalism that advocates the need for group rights has not abandoned the rights of individuals.

This leads me to the second major problem multiculturalism faces. If a state is willing to grant minority groups the ability to organize separately and to grant territorial autonomy, this may lead to growing demands on behalf of that group for secession and independence. Underlying this forecast is the assumption that groups, like individuals, work to maximize their interests, which entails the desire on the part of minority groups of becoming a majority in a territory of their own. But even if this does not happen, whether because the type of group right granted is not in the form of territorial autonomy, or because the group is tied by other means to the majority, still, granting groups the ability to advance their group identity could lead, at the very least, to tensions among the different groups.

To ease this inter-group tension a series of techniques have been proposed. One such technique advocates inter-group dialogue. Ways and modes of tolerance and respect among the different groups should be advanced with the encouragement and backing of state authorities in order that groups, through their members, come to realize that sharing cultures can also be a self-fulfilling experience. The objectives of such dialogue facilitating institutions is by no means intended to assimilate the different groups into one, but builds on the intention of those members of society that want to take part in dialogue activities to be able to do so without abandoning their own culture. Activities that can materially benefit such inter-group dialogue can range from the creation of joint townships, joint schools, joint educational activities, the promotion of tolerance and respect towards the other in school curricula and

---

28 GREEN, *supra* note 22 at 266.

the public media, joint cultural centers, etc. In order for such results to emerge, the government must be actively involved by giving such activities preference in terms of budgets and other forms of state support.

Bhikhu Parekh, a spokesperson for dialogue among the different groups captures precisely the value of diversity.[29]

> *[C]ultural diversity enriches and vitalizes collective life, and is desirable not only for minority communities but also for the society as a whole. It adds a valuable aesthetic dimension to society, widens the range of moral sympathy and imagination, and encourages critical self-reflection. Since no culture realizes all that is valuable in human life, each needs others to correct its inescapable biases, to appreciate its specificity, to help it arrest its tendency to absolutize itself, and to deepen its appreciation of the nature and possibilities of human existence. Furthermore, every culture fosters specific traits of temperament, psychological and moral dispositions, a particular kind of imagination, and needs constructive interactions with others to revitalize, regenerate and enrich itself. In short cultural diversity, being a both a vital component of human freedom and well-being and a necessary condition of human progress, is a valuable social asset.*[30]

The experience of dialogue in a multicultural society is thus not only a device for easing the tension among the different groups but a positive ideal for all members of society, who in turn might even strive for pluralistic society.[31]

Recent writings on multiculturalism have also come to appreciate more than before the need for what might be called a shared concept of citizenship in a multicultural society.[32] This concept comes to compensate for the fractious implications of the multicultural discourse in an effort to lessen the prospect of inter-group conflicts. Functionally, the shared concept of citizenship stresses the fact that a modern democracy depends not only on the justice of its institutions towards minority groups but also on the qualities and attitudes of its citizens – e.g. their sense of identity, their view with respect to conflicts, their ability to tolerate and

---

29 PAREKH Bhikhu, *Rethinking Multiculturalism – Cultural Diversity and Political Theory* (New York: Palgrave, 2000).

30 PAREKH Bhikhu, *A Commitment to Cultural Pluralism*, http://www.krachtvancultuur.nl/uk/archive/commentary/parekh.html.

31 SHACHER Ayelet, *Two Critiques of Multiculturalism*, 23 *Cardozo Law Review* 253, 261 (2001).

32 *See* KYMLICKA Will and NORMAN Wayne, *supra* note 11 at 1.

work together with members of other groups, their readiness to participate in the political process in order to promote the public good, their willingness to show self-restraint, and their sense of justice and commitment to a fair distribution of resources. The articulation of a sphere of shared citizenship in a multicultural society will serve as a ground for promoting inter-group cooperation and serve the object of a feel of solidarity among the different members.[33] Without a sense of common citizenship "there is little hope for the sort of mutual understanding, deliberation, trust and solidarity required by a flourishing democracy."[34] This is why governments with a multicultural body of citizenry have worked lately to promote citizenship as a civil institution.[35] If the debate will concentrate on minority rights only, what might emerge is a politicization of ethnicity which might create a spirit of competition, mistrust and antagonism between ethnic groups.[36]

This concept of a shared citizenship is necessarily of a limited and relative meaning. Surely it cannot demand that all citizens should share the same virtues and identify equally with the same values. The differential treatment of citizens is after all a basic impetus of multiculturalism. This is why when speaking about the concept of "multicultural citizenship" authorities make it clear that it is essentially synonymous with "differentiated citizenship rights" or "differentiated citizenship".[37] On the other hand, this shared concept of citizenship cannot be restricted in a multicultural society only to the most basic attributes of citizenship, such as the carrying of one's passport and having the right to vote. It should include a civic base which all citizens can identify with, feel a sense of belonging to, care for and be equally sensitive to its diminish-

---

33 *Id.* at 10.

34 *Id.* at 35.

35 *Id.* at 6.

36 *Id.* at 10.

37 *See* KYMLICKA, *Multicultural Citizenship*, *supra* note 8 at 26; YOUNG Iris Marion, *Polity and Group Difference*, *supra* note 19 at 258 (1989); SHACHAR Ayelet, *The Puzzle of Interlocking Power Hierarchies: Sharing the Pieces of Jurisdictional Authority*, 35 *Harvard Civil Rights and Civil Liberties Review* 385, 387 (2000).

ment. This sphere is the "common culture" that Joseph Raz has emphasized in his writings.[38]

This sphere of common citizenship has an important utility in a multicultural society other than saving the general framework from dismantlement. It serves as a basis for legitimizing the intervention of state institutions in the internal affairs of the different groups when the individual liberty of a group member has been severely infringed upon. Moreover, even when such an intervention is deemed inappropriate one can build on this basic bond with the different group members to create a parallel course of regulation that competes with regulation offered by the group. Stressing the basic bond with its citizens, the state can justifiably work in areas regulated by the group, but in a direction that will maximize the interests of the individual citizens. Eventually, such a course of parallel regulation will offer a path of "exit" for group members, and maybe even a "race to the top" mode of regulation on the part of the group and the state, if each genuinely strives to draw the individual to its side on the specific issue of regulation.[39] This sphere of a common citizenship could also serve as a basis for the insertion of inter-group mechanisms that can work to promote mutual activities among group members with the intention of producing a tolerant atmosphere. Be the case as it may, I think that a multicultural regime to qualify as such must offer all citizens a sphere of common citizenship, in lieu of the bond each member has with his or her group.

To conclude this section, it appears that multiculturalism as it has now developed has not only worked to justify why certain groups are entitled to specific rights in light and for the sake of their group identity, but has also identified the basic tensions such accommodating rights might produce. In an effort to deal with such tensions, the multicultural movement has proposed a number of ideas aimed at easing the level of conflict generated by multicultural accommodations. On the intra-group level the multicultural movement has stressed the fact that in order to lessen the conflict between group practiced norms and individual rights,

---

38 RAZ, *Multiculturalism*, *supra* note 20 at 202.

39 SHACHAR, *Multicultural Jurisdictions*, *supra* note 15.

individuals should be offered an exiting route which would enable them to do away with groups and their imposed restrictions. Moreover, it has also been suggested that when affording minority groups certain accommodations, one should try to limit such accommodations to what could be defined as those of the external protections type that are supposed to be different than those affording authority to impose internal restrictions. On the inter-group level the fear is from inter-group tensions that might turn into inter-group violence. In this respect it becomes extremely important to provide certain channels of dialogue between the different groups, whether by guaranteeing that the composition of different official institutions, such as courts, have members representing the different communities, or by setting up schools, townships and other frameworks where all groups members can have the opportunity to meet and become more tolerant. And finally, on the group-state level there should be established some form of a "common bond" or a "common sphere of citizenship" in order to prevent the state from falling apart. The sense of a mutual interest and the individually felt obligation towards shared ideals could work to strengthen the general civic identity of all citizens, thereby creating a balancing effect between group identity and civic identity. Moreover, this concept of a common bond could also work to justify government initiatives designed to promote inter-group dialogue, giving additional legitimacy for the state to interfere and advocate the dialogue channels. Similarly, the concept would also give legitimacy for the state to intervene on behalf of individual group members and offer them alternative normative schemes that respect their individual liberal rights in lieu of the schemes offered by their groups. So this concept of a common bond can serve as a basis for lessening not only the tension on the group-state level, but tension on the other two levels as well.

B. Two Multicultural Caveats

The preceding discussion on multiculturalism has set the background for justifying why group accommodations are essential to a society with a majority-minority situation. However, the discussion has been based on assumptions implicit in the legal cultures from which the multicultural movement has evolved, namely western democracies such as Australia, Canada, Great Britain and the United States. For instance, the discussion with respect to the right of exit has been preoccupied with the difficulty of practicing the right itself in light of individual constraints. The assumption was that societies in the mentioned countries do provide a sphere to which one could exit to if one chooses to exercise his or her right to exit. But in many other countries it is doubtful whether there is at all a sphere to which one could exit. In other words, exiting can fail not only because of a lack of capacity of certain individuals to exit but also because of the lack of a sphere that can host the individual if and when he or she eventually decides to exit.[40]

One other observation concerns the "voice" of community members. In the discussion of multicultural accommodations of minority groups it seems taken for granted that a group accommodation comports with the will of the group, or at least with the will of the majority of the group. But there is no real discussion in the literature dealing with multiculturalism of the question of how to guarantee that a group accommodation will actually suit the interests of the minority group. It seems essential in my view that for a multicultural accommodation to be regarded as such that it also accords with the basic notion of justice, that everyone who is required to follow the accommodation "must in principle have an effective voice in its consideration and to be able to agree to it without coercion."[41] I will relate to this point in more detail below, when discussing the nature and practice of religious jurisdiction of the Palestinian-Arab religious communities in matters of personal status. As I will argue there, this practice cannot be regarded as a derivative of multiculturalism, inter alia because of the fact that the nature of the jurisdiction accorded to a number of Palestinian-Arab religious communities does not comport with the will of those communities.

---

40 REITMAN Oanagh, *On Exit*, in : Minorities within Minorities, Equality, Rights and Diversity 189, 191 (Cambridge: Cambridge University Press, Avigail Eisenberg and Jeff Spinner-Halevi eds., 2005).

41 YOUNG, *Justice and the Politics of Difference*, *supra* note 19 at 34.

III. APPLICATIONS : THE CASE OF THE PALESTINIAN-ARAB MINORITY OF ISRAEL

Almost one-fifth of the about seven million citizens of the State of Israel are non-Jewish. The non-Jewish population is overwhelmingly Palestinian-Arab, who are also an indigenous minority. In the lexicon of the Arab world this minority is known as the "1948 Arabs", to reflect the fact that the population is that portion of the Palestinian-Arabs who stayed in what came to be Israel after the 1948 war. In terms of its religious composition, the Palestinian-Arab community is formed mainly of Moslems, with communities of Christians and Druze. The Christian community is further divided into ten recognized religious communities.

The existence of different national and religious groups in Israel has been a constant cause of tension. Underlying this Jewish-Arab tension is of course the Israeli-Palestinian conflict, with the Palestinian narrative stressing the tragic outcome by which the majority of the Palestinian people were deprived of a homeland, and the Jewish (Zionist) national movement stressing the emancipation of the Jewish people by becoming sovereigns in a state of their own. But the reality of relations between Arabs and Jews in Israel goes well beyond the question of competing narratives. Israel as a state has assumed a Jewish character. This is evident first and foremost in the commitment of Israel to Jewish immigration, Jewish heritage and Jewish settlement. Moreover, state symbols such as the flag, the national anthem, and the state emblem are all Jewish in character. This has taken its toll on the Palestinian-Arab minority of Israel. Given the background of the conflict, this community has been traditionally seen as a security threat, thus bringing it under different policies of control.[42] The most notable schemes of control were military government, which administered the affairs of the Palestinian-Arab minority for 18 long years (1948-1966), massive expropriation of land and property, and the application of different policies of fragmentation. Topping all of this was widespread discrimination, prin-

---

42 LUSTICK Ian, *Arabs in the Jewish State – Israel's Control of a National Minority* (University of Texas Press, 1980).

cipally in budget allocations, planning and zoning, and job opportunities.

The Israeli legal system, it is true, has worked relentlessly and forcefully to adopt basic guarantees of human rights characteristic to many democracies.[43] A principle player in this move was the Israel Supreme Court. Sitting in its capacity as High Court of Justice the court oversees the legality and reasonableness of the acts of government which impact on citizens, and can overrule such acts if it finds them in conflict with basic notions of justice. In addition, as a result of the enactment of two major Basic Laws in 1992, Basic Law: Human Dignity and Liberty and Basic Law: Freedom of Occupation, courts in Israel have been accorded some measure of judicial review over legislation of the Knesset, the Israeli parliament. Utilizing such capacities, the Israeli judiciary worked to adopt a whole list of civil liberties concerned with individual civil rights, such as the freedom of expression, freedom of association, the freedom of worship, freedom of movement, equal treatment and due process when faced by actions of state authorities. Such guarantees proved to be instrumental for the Palestinian-Arab minority in the sense that they offered its members a cause of action before the courts in their endeavors to bring remedy and change. Indeed, over the years, major decisions were handed down by Israeli courts bringing some relief in respect of the petitions filled before them.

The synthesis of the Jewish character of the State of Israel and the basic commitment to civil liberties had two major consequences in respect of the collective rights of its national and religious groups. As a Jewish state, Israel's primary commitment is to maintain its Jewish majority in terms of accommodations fostering this group's ideals, heritage, culture

---

43 ZYSBLAT Allen, *Protecting Fundamental Rights in Israel without a Written Constitution*, in : Public Law in Israel 47, (Oxford: Oxford University Press, Izhak Zamir and Allen Zysblat eds.,1996); SHAPIRA Amos, *The Status of Fundamental Individual Rights in the Absence of a Written Constitution*, 9 *Israel Law Review* 497 (1974). This statement is made with respect to guarantees of human rights in respect of Israel within the 1967 borders without the West Bank and Gaza Strip. On this latter issue *see* KRETZMER David, *The Occupation of Justice, The Supreme Court of Israel and the Occupied Territories* (Albany: State University of New York Press, 2002).

and collective memory. As indicated before, Israel's immigration policy and the nature of its public sphere stand witness to this. The Palestinian-Arab community as a national group has largely remained "outside of the collectivity's boundaries as nonmembers of 'Israel'."[44] This minority's national character, traditions, cultures and heritage have not received a fair share of what the State of Israel proclaims in terms of its common good and national ideals. This Israeli dilemma is quite clear:

> *If Arabs are to be truly integrated, if they are to be truly equal, then how will Israel remain a Jewish state? But if Israel is not to be a Jewish state, then what have the Jews been fighting for, what has all their effort been about, what have they died for? And if the Arabs are not integrated, do they not pose a continuing threat to Israel's security?*[45]

The Palestinian-Arab minority has been given a variety of designations that refer to this exclusion, such as the "the most remote, excluded community from the state's meta-narratives",[46] as "the invisible man",[47] or as the "odd man out,"[48] whose status is that of "second",[49] or even "third"[50] class citizenship. Palestinian-Arab citizens of Israel do enjoy civil rights, as recognized for all Israelis, Jewish and non-Jewish alike. But still the principle beneficiary of these rights is considered to be the individual citizen instead of the group as such. The outcome of this reality was a schism in the notion and contents of Israeli citizen-

---

44 KIMMERLING Baruch, *Sociology, Ideology, and Nation-Building: The Palestinians and their Meaning in Israeli Sociology*, 57 *American Sociology Review* 446, 450 (1992).

45 LIEBMAN Charles S. & DON-YEHIYA Eliezer, *Civil Religion in Israel, Traditional Judaism and Political Culture in the Jewish State* 162 (Berkeley: University of California Press, 1983).

46 BARZILAI Gad, *Communities and the Law, Politics and Cultures of Legal Identities* 7, 42 (Ann Arbor: University of Michigan Press, 2003).

47 SMOOHA Sammy and PERETZ Don, *The Arabs in Israel*, 26 *Journal of Conflict Resolution* 451 (1982).

48 MIGDAL Joel S. and KIMMERLING Baruch, *The Odd Man Out, Arabs in Israel*, in : Through the Lens of Israel: Explorations in State and Society 173 (Albaney: State University of New York Press, Joel S. Migdal ed., 2001).

49 SAIDI Ahmad H., *Israel as Ethnic Democracy: What are the Implications for the Palestinian Minority?*, 22 *Arab Studies Quarterly* 25 (2000).

50 SHAFIR Gershon and PELED Yoav, *Being Israeli: The Dynamics of Multiple Citizenship* 110 (Cambridge: Cambridge University Press, 2002).

ship.[51] In respect of the Jewish majority, citizenship has strong republican underpinnings embodying a shared national purpose and a shared common good. On the other hand, the contents of citizenship in respect of the Palestinian-Arab citizen is confined to individual liberties as guaranteed by the Israeli legal system.[52]

Such characteristics reveal at least two major impediments in having Israel qualify as a multicultural state. First, in light of the fact that what determines the collective common good are the collective ideals and the national aspirations of the Jewish majority, little basis is left for legitimizing the grant of group rights to the Palestinian-Arab community to begin with. Interestingly, a number of Israeli scholars have argued that because of Israel's Jewish nature and the definition of its common good, the case of group rights for its Palestinian-Arab minority becomes especially strong.[53] For this minority happens to be not only a minority that is subject to the dominance of a Jewish majority but is also subject to the dominance of the whole Israeli establishment, which is overtly dedicated to the common good and national aspirations of its Jewish majority. Thus in terms of multicultural theory itself, the empowerment justification for having group rights for the Palestinian-Arab minority becomes particularly strong. Theory and legitimacy aside, in practice there has been only very little acceptance of the claim of according the Palestinian-Arab minority national group rights. In fact the more pervasive view in Israel today is that the grant of group-differentiated rights to the Palestinian-Arab minority might carry with it a security risk. Another popular argument in this respect is that collective accommodations of the Palestinian-Arabs is to be realized in the Palestinian state that is yet to be established beside the state of Israel. It is no

---

51 ROUHANA Nadim N., *Palestinian Citizens in an Ethnic Jewish State: Identities in Conflict* (New Haven: Yale University Press, 1997).

52 PELED Yoav, *Ethnic Democracy and the Legal Construction of Citizenship: Arab Citizens of the Jewish State*, 86 *American Political Science Review* 432 (1992).

53 KLEIN Claude, *Israel as a Nation-State and the Problem of the Arab Minority: In Search of a Status* (Tel Aviv: International Center for Peace in the Middle East, 1987); MARGALIT Avishai and HALBERTAL Moshe, *Liberalism and the Right to Culture*, 61 *Social Research* 491 (1994); SMOOHA Sammy, *Autonomy for Arabs in Israel?* (Raananah: The Institute for Israeli Arab Studies, 1996).

wonder that what can be identified as group rights at present and the kind of group rights proposed in existing constitutional drafts are few and far between when compared to the kind of group rights accorded to the Jewish majority. To get a sense of these arguments, I would like to refer to what are generally regarded as a number of group accommodation made by the State of Israel to the Palestinian-Arab minority and demonstrate how slim such accommodations are both in substance and in volume.

In referring to the group differentiated rights actually granted to the Palestinian-Arab minority in Israel, four accommodations stand out. One is the recognition of Arabic as an official language, the second is the existence of a separate education system for the Palestinian-Arab community, the third is the jurisdiction granted to the Palestinian-Arab religious communities in matters of personal status and the fourth is the exemption granted to a large portion of Palestinian-Arab members from military service.[54] But looking into the actual realization of such accommodations reveals their flimsiness and marginality. In respect of language, the Israel Supreme Court was prepared to recognize the official status of the Arabic language only insofar as such recognition does not threaten the status of Hebrew, notwithstanding the fact that under black-letter law Arabic is as official as Hebrew is.[55] In practice all that this means is the addition of Arabic inscription to road signs posted on Israeli Highways and in some mixed Jewish-Arab cities but not much more. Laws, court decisions and other public records are usually not published in Arabic, nor is the language widely spoken or understood by Jewish citizens of Israel. As to the education system, there are a number of studies showing how in fact this system was controlled by different government agencies in an effort to better control the minority at large. Appointments of teachers and other executives in the Palestinian-Arab school system often involve the approval of the internal security authorities. In addition, at different periods throughout Israel's history the school curriculum relevant for the Palestinian-Arab schools

---

54 *See* SABAN, *supra* note 4 ; RUBINSTEIN and MEDINA, *supra* note 4.

55 H.C.J. 4112/99.*Adalah, The Legal Center for Arab Minority Rights in Israel v. The Municipality of Tel-Aviv-Jaffa*, 56 (v) P.D. 393 (2002).

was suited more to satisfy the interests of the government than the needs of the minority group itself.[56] In terms of the exemption from military service, insofar as this exemption was made in an effort to save the Palestinian-Arab citizens of Israel from bearing arms against members of their own people, this accommodation seems to be considerate of the group identity of this minority. But still, such an accommodation only slightly manages to sustain the kind of virtue multicultural accommodations seek to actualize, whether in terms of guarding the personal autonomy of the individual members and the empowering the minority in its dealings with the majority. And the exemption from military service, instead of strengthening inter-group understanding, has the opposite effect, for it tends to support the stereotype of the minority's untrustworthiness in the eyes of the majority. As to the nature of the accommodations made in respect to the Palestinian-Arab religious communities, I will seek to demonstrate in the next section that though such accommodations may be group based, they are still far from being regarded or justified on multicultural grounds.

The second impediment that arises from the fact that the Israeli public sphere is largely committed to the common good of its Jewish majority, while the Palestinian-Arab community is supposed to enjoy individual guarantees to basic human rights, is the reality this schism has brought about in terms of a sense of common bond and a shared sense of Israeli citizenship. Probably the most telling piece of evidence to this is the fact that there exists no one single official holiday that is celebrated jointly by Arabs and Jews in Israel – all official holidays and days of rest are Jewish centered. Moreover, there is an inherent impediment for the Palestinian-Arab citizens of Israel to even relate to the state flag, official emblem and national anthem – for once again such symbols are all centered around Jewish national symbols.

---

56 *See* KHALIL MARI Sami, *Arab Education in Israel* (Syracuse: Syracuse University Press, 1978); AL HAJ Majid, *Education, Empowerment and Control: The Case of Arabs in Israel* (Albany: State University of New York Press, 1995); JABAREEN Yousef T., *Law and Education, Critical Perspective on Arab Palestinan Education in Israel*, 49 *American Behavioral Scientist* 1052 (2006).

A third impediment which in a sense is external to the schism in citizenship, but still very much connected to it, concerns the current state of Jewish-Arab dialogue and co-existence. Indeed, as far as both the Jewish and the Arab communities are concerned assimilation has never been a common goal. Each side would prefer to keep its identity instead of being assimilated into a joint identity. As a result, both communities live in a willing state of segregation from one another in almost every sphere of social life. Villages and towns in Israel are almost entirely either Arab or Jewish, except for a number of cities that were historically mixed. The school system is also divided into Arab and Jewish "sectors". Mixed marriages are rare.

Over the years, Arab and Jewish individuals have worked against such barriers to create a number of Jewish-Arab schools. At the moment there are four such schools, in Jerusalem, in the Galilee (Misgav), in the northern Tirangle (Kuffer Karea') and in Neveh-Shalom-Wahat El Salam. In addition, Neveh-Shalom-Wahat El Salam was established as a joint Jewish-Arab township from the start. What characterizes these initiatives is that they all began as private initiatives of a group of Jewish-Arab individuals who sought a joint framework – none were initiated by the government. For example, the Ministry of Education has not yet developed a proper curriculum for the joint Jewish-Arab schools, despite the fact that it eventually certified and accredited them.

The domination of the public sphere by the Jewish character of the State of Israel has also been substantial in terms of religion and religious accommodations. Though some studies indicate that Israel is not considered to have an established religion and do not consider Judaism to be its official religion, Jewish religious institutions have received wide statutory recognition and substantial state budgets unparalleled by any other religious community.[57] This state of affairs has also been attributed to the Jewish nature of the State of Israel, for Judaism entails

57 EDELMAN Martin, *Courts, Politics, and Culture in Israel* 48-99 (Charlottesville: University Press of Virginia, 1994); RUBINSTEIN Amnon, *Law and Religion in Israel*, 3 *Israel Law Review* 380, 400 (1967); RUBINSTEIN Amnon, *State and Religion in Israel*, 4 *Journal of Contemporary History* 107, 116 (1967).

not only a nationality but a religion as well.[58] The conflict inherent in the mixture of state and religion is seen in the recognition of Jewish religious institutions and the type of norms such institutions are supposed to apply. These have been major political issues within Israel, and have often been the central issue in government coalition agreements. The arguments over reform always stress the risk such change might bring about in terms of Jewish unity. In addition, the preservation of Jewish traditions is taken to be a central role of the State of Israel also given the tragic past of the Jewish people, especially the Holocaust, that destroyed many centers of Jewish learning.[59] But religion and state within the Jewish community in Israel has had one additional component; ever since the establishment of the State of Israel there was a struggle on behalf of a large section within the Jewish community against what was deemed to be religious coercion. The fact that the secular Jewish community in Israel has had to put up with the governing authority of religious norms in matters of marriage and divorce, with restriction on public transportation and the opening of shops on Jewish religious holidays, brought to surface much resentment among secular Jews against Jewish religious norms and institutions. Other intra-group tensions abound, as between the orthodox religious camp and the Reform and Conservative streams. As a result, a strong move for liberal and secular norms has been felt within the Jewish community. Jewish political parties have argued for more secular norms and the Israel Supreme Court, using concepts of human rights, has also taken an active role in promoting secularism. This reality of religious coercion within the Jewish community has brought legal scholars to admit that whatever the justification for having religious accommodations for the Jewish community may be, it is hard to consider them a

---

58 MAOZ Asher, *Religious Human Rights in the State of Israel*, in : Religious Human Rights in Global Perspective, Legal Perspectives 349 (The Hague: Kluwer, John D. van der Vyver & John Witt, Jr., ed. 1996).

59 *Id.* at 369.

form of multicultural accommodations. Rather they have been characterized as anti-multicultural[60] and a blot on Israel's democracy.[61]

The kind of justifications and political forces that stand behind the religious accommodations granted to the Palestinian-Arab religious communities are different.[62] In general, the Palestinian-Arab religious communities were accommodated more as a matter of preserving the religious autonomy granted to these communities under the Ottoman *millet* system.[63] The religious affairs of such communities are not the subject of government coalitions, nor are worries about their disunity on the Israeli political agenda. Another important ingredient that has helped form the view on the Palestinian-Arab religious communities is the fact that the political and religious leadership of the community itself has accepted this basic perception about the religious accommodation to the different religious communities being a form of an autonomy that accommodates the group as such.[64] Moreover, there is no real secular reform movement within the Palestinian-Arab community, at least not in the form of having political organs actively solicit change in religious law and religious jurisdiction. Thus unlike the schism that took place on the national level in terms of groups and individuals, where the Palestinian-Arab citizens are seen only in the individual capacity, in matters

---

60 HALPERIN-KADDARI Ruth, *Women, Religion and Multiculturalism in Israel*, 5 *UCLA Journal of International Law and Foreign Affiars* 339, 343 (2000); COHN Margit, *Women, Religious Law and Religious Courts in Israel*, 27 *Retfaerd: Scandinavian Journal of Social Science*. 57, 58 (2004) (characterizing the problem of institutionalizing religion in respect of the Jewish community as an infringement on the rights of a liberal majority instead of the right of a religious majority to express their beliefs); EDELMAN, *supra* note 57 at 60-61 (noting the troublesome fact that Rabbinical courts in Israel decide matters of personal status of on the basis of *halachic* norms to which the majority of the Jewish community does not subscribe).

61 COHN Haim, *Personal Introduction – Autobiography* 242 (Jerusalem: Zmora Bitan-Dvir, 2005.

62 ENGLARD Izhak, *Law and Religion in Israel*, 35 *American Journal of Comparative Law* 185, 189-190 (1987).

63 *See* supra note 4.

64 KARAYANNI Michael Mousa, *Separate and Different: Religious Accommodations for the Palestinian-Arab Minority in Israel* (forthcoming).

of religion it is the Palestinian-Arab religious community that takes center stage.[65]

But can the religious accommodations granted to the Palestinian-Arab religious communities be regarded as multicultural? I think not. In this respect I would like to point to three different reason why the existing accommodation cannot qualify as multicultural. First, the religious jurisdiction accorded to the different Palestinian-Arab religious communities embodies a number of rather extreme forms of internal restrictions, especially in respect of gender inequality. Take for example the divorce norms applied by some of these communities. Under Islam and Druze family law the husband can unilaterally dissolve the marriage without the need to state any cause for his action while the wife cannot.[66] Another example can be found in the Code of Family Law of the Greek Orthodox community, which is essentially a code compiled in the fourteenth century in the Byzantine Empire.[67] The Code allows for only a limited number of causes for divorce that are asymmetric in nature in terms of gender. Thus, for example, under the Code the husband can petition the Greek Orthodox court for divorce if his wife slept outside of their house without his permission. However, such a cause does not apply when the husband chooses to do the same without his wife's consent. Most revealing are two causes for which divorce is not to be granted: a wife cannot petition for divorce in cases where she was whipped by her husband with a lash or hit by him with a stick.

Second, there exists in Israel no right to exit mainly because there is no civil regulatory-scheme of marriage and divorce that can offer a sphere for one to exit to. So even if we are able to assume that Arab couples,

---

65 TESSLER Mark A., *The Identity of Religious Minorities in Non-Secular States: Jews in Tunisia and Morocco and Arabs in Israel*, 20 *Comparative Studies in Society and History* 359, 360 (1978) (noting the fact that the Arabs in Israel are viewed as a religious minority). *See also* BARZILAI, *supra* note 46 at 107 ("State law has mainly defined Arabs residing in Israel in terms of religious groups").

66 It should be noted that a unilateral act of divorce is considered to be a criminal offence in Israel, its religious validity notwithstanding. Moreover, such an act can serve the divorced wife as a civil cause of action against the husband.

67 *See* GOADBY F.M., *International and Inter-Religious Private Law in Palestine* 134-135 (Jerusalem: Hamadpis Press, 1926).

especially women, can exit their group jurisdiction,[68] given the exclusive jurisdiction still accorded to their community religious courts in matters of marriage and divorce they really have no where to exit to.

Third, if we were to look into the history of the internal organization of the Palestinian-Arab religious communities it is not at all clear whether such an organization accords with the will and voice of community members. Take for example the Greek Orthodox community. This community is controlled by a group of foreign clergy from Greece, who can barely speak the mother tongue of the local Palestinian-Arab Greek Orthodox community – Arabic. The judges appointed to the Greek Orthodox ecclesiastical courts are appointed at the sole discretion of the Church's administration without any input or supervision from either State authorities or community members. This reality existed in the past in a number of other Middle Eastern countries, such as Egypt, but was changed through reform that abolished foreign control of local churches. However, calls from the local Palestinian-Arab community for change have not been successful, neither before nor after the establishment of the State of Israel.[69] Thus, serious questions arise as to whether the existing accommodation granted to this community is really an autonomy or multicultural given the fact that its form and practice runs against the wishes of the constituency. Take also the Moslem community, though their community affairs have been handled over the years by *qadis* and *imams* coming from the ranks of the community itself, state authorities have applied different control policies over the handling of community affairs. This policy was evident in the

---

68 *See* MACKINNON Catherine A., *Sex Equality under the Constitution of India: Problems, Prospects, and 'Personal Laws'*, 4 *I.Con* 181, 198-202 (2006) (arguing that women in India are capable of opting out from their group in family disputes, despite all difficulties).

69 *See* TSIMHONI Daphne, *The Greek Orthodox Community in Jerusalem and the West bank, 1948-1978: A Profile of a Religious Minority in a National State*, 23 *Orient* 281 (1982). Indeed it is because of this distance between the local Greek Orthodox community and the Greek clergy that associations and clubs, governed by community members, developed among the Greek Orthodox community. *See* TSIMHONI Daphne, *Continuity and Change in Communal Autonomy: The Christian Communal Organizations in Jerusalem 1948-80*, 22 *Middle Eastern Studies* 398 (1986).

appointment process of such religious figures to their posts, always conducted under the close supervision of government authorities. A request made by Moslem leaders to have a Moslem as head of Moslem affairs in what was the Ministry of Religious Affairs was denied."[70] But more importantly, the community's control over its own affairs was curtailed by the handling of the Moslem religious endowments (*waqf* property) by state authorities. Through legal constructs, such property was characterized as absentee property, given the fact that various members of the Supreme Moslem Council, the body that administered such property in Mandatory Palestine, had left the country.[71] In turn this made it possible for the State of Israel, through the authority granted to a governmental organ, Custodian of Absentee Property, to take over such property. Thus, it is once again questionable whether the jurisdiction and authority granted to the Moslem community in Israel is autonomy or multicultural in nature, even leaving aside the question of internal restrictions and the option to exit.

IV. CONCLUSION

In its normative form, multiculturalism is intended to make it possible for different groups of people to live together in one sovereign unit but yet apart within their own groups. In addition, the movement seeks to fulfill theses objectives while also trying to satisfy universal notions of human rights. It is no wonder that much effort has been made to find a state of equilibrium between all of these considerations. This paper, however, sought to achieve something different. Essentially, I tried to extract from the already held discussion the kind and type of qualifications that make it possible for us to regard group accommodations as multicultural. This task was carried out from a legal point of view in respect of the Palestinian-Arab community in Israel. It is my hope that

70 TESSLER Mark A., *The Middle East: The Jews in Tunisia and Morocco and Arabs in Israel*, in : Protection of Ethnic Minorities, 245, 265 (New York: Pergamon Press, Robert G. Wirsing ed., 1981).

71 *See* KRETZMER, *The Legal Status*, supra note 4 at 167-168. *See also* Alisa RUBIN-PELED, *Debating Islam in the Jewish State, The Development of Policy Toward Islamic Institutions in Israel* (Albany: State University of New York Press, 2001).

such a discussion can also trigger similar discussions in other countries, where groups are accommodated because of their identity, but where questions still arise whether such accommodations are truly multicultural. This is offered also as a caveat to countries that do not accommodate groups because of their group identity: if they seek to do so, they need to do so while also making guarantees in the legal culture that surrounds the group; for as I have also tried to emphasize throughout this paper, multiculturalism is not just about living apart but also about living together.

Le "statu quo" entre religieux et non-religieux en Israël : un arrangement d'esprit fédéraliste

Ilan GREILSAMMER

On emploie souvent l'expression – paradoxale – "Israël en danger de paix". Paradoxale, cette expression signifie bien que l'état de paix entre Arabes et Israéliens, le jour où il surviendra, risque d'être aussi explosif pour la société israélienne que la situation de guerre. Car si la guerre que le monde arabe a menée contre le sionisme et Israël menace la survie physique de l'Etat juif, la paix, elle, menace de façon mortelle le tissu social israélien et risque de provoquer sa dissolution brutale ou son implosion. Parfois, certains conseillent même cyniquement aux pays hostiles à Israël : faites donc la paix... et l'Etat juif cessera d'exister par voie interne, par auto-destruction !

C'est un fait que la société israélienne, mosaïque d'immigrants venus des quatre coins du monde, est traversée par de très profonds clivages, des fractures essentielles, des désaccords existentiels : Juifs et Arabes, sepharades et achkenazes, anciens et nouveaux arrivés, grandes villes et villes de développement, riches et pauvres, sociaux-démocrates défendant l'Etat-providence et capitalistes sauvages à la Milton Friedman, faucons ultra-nationalistes et colombes pacifistes, etc... Seul le "couvercle" de la guerre, qui a tout fermé, tout bloqué, la nécessité de se défendre contre l'ennemi, a fait "tenir ensemble" ces éléments disparates et antagonistes. Mais dès que le processus de paix a débuté avec l'Egypte en 1977, puis s'est renforcé avec les Palestiniens (accords d'Oslo) et les Jordaniens (accord de paix de 1994), ce couvercle a commencé à se soulever, et cet ensemble fragile pourrait très bien éclater...

Parmi les multiples fractures de la société israélienne, mon sentiment est que le clivage le plus grave est celui qui sépare le monde *religieux* (toutes tendances confondues, sionistes-religieux et ultra-orthodoxes non sionistes) du monde *laïque* (toutes tendances confondues, colombes ou faucons politiques). Y a-t-il encore une chance que ces deux mondes hostiles puissent coexister ?

Pendant très longtemps, depuis les débuts du sionisme politique et l'établissement juif en Palestine à l'époque contemporaine, cette coexistence était basée sur *un arrangement entre religieux modérés et laïques modérés*. L'entente se trouvait concrétisée sur le plan politique par l'alliance entre le Parti travailliste Mapai, qui était le principal parti laïque) et le Parti National Religieux (Mizrahi). De leur côté les ultra-religieux, les orthodoxes extrémistes, ne participaient pas à la vie publique, ils s'étaient en quelque sorte "retirés" dans leurs ghettos volontaires. L'alliance consensuelle entre laïques et religieux modérés était fondée sur une expression-miracle : le "statu quo". Le sens de ce statu quo était très simple : il tenait précisément en un mot, cher à John Locke et à Montesquieu: *modération.*

Les laïques travaillistes de Ben-Gourion, souvent doués d'une forte culture juive, acceptaient que le "contenu" de la société israélienne soit un contenu juif, et que soient respectés les principaux acquis du Judaisme, les principales ordonnances de la tradition juive. En se fondant sur les arrangements mis en pratique et acceptés à l'époque du mandat britannique, la société israélienne serait fondée sur un "minimum commun", qui comprendrait surtout le respect public du chabbat comme jour chômé dans l'ensemble du pays, le respect des fêtes juives, l'observance des lois alimentaires dans les institutions publiques, et le statut spécial du rabbinat. Ce dernier point est fondamental: dans la lettre dite du "statu quo" adressée par David Ben-Gourion à la population orthodoxe à la veille de la création de l'Etat, le premier ministre acceptait en fait qu'il n'y ait pas de séparation de la religion et de l'Etat, puisque toutes les questions d'état-civil (qui est juif?, mariages, divorces, etc...) étaient remises à la compétence exclusive des tribunaux rabbiniques.

De leur côté, les religieux et les ultra-religieux, du moment que ces acquis étaient respectés et que leur système d'éducation autonome et soutenu par l'Etat était garanti, acceptaient de *modérer leurs exigences* vis-à-vis de l'Etat. Ils reconnaissaient en fait le caractère libéral, moderne et démocratique de l'Etat juif, renonçaient officieusement à le transformer en un Etat théocratique, réduisaient leurs exigences de législation religieuse, bref acceptaient de ne pas pousser les laïques dans leurs retranchements, de ne pas "les rendre fous" et de ne pas rendre leur vie impossible.

Cette époque de modération mutuelle, fondée sur ledit statu quo, a duré très longtemps. L'alliance politique entre le parti travailliste et le parti national religieux, déjà en place avant la création de l'Etat dans les institutions d'auto-gouvernement juif sous mandat britannique, s'est maintenue jusque dans les années 1970. Ils s'agit de longues années d'entente et de collaboration mutuelle, des années où sionistes laïques et religieux communiaient largement dans les mêmes "valeurs" non explicites : recherche de la paix avec le monde arabe, défense et sécurité de l'Etat, promotion d'une société démocratique, pluraliste et tolérante, accueil des immigrants juifs venus du monde entier, service militaire des jeunes gens, etc... On pourrait presque dire que les Israéliens laïques de l'époque étaient, d'une certaine façon, "religieux" : le sionisme – socialiste avait pour eux le caractère d'une véritable "religion civile", avec ses mythes et ses symboles. Ces deux religions, la religion civile du sionisme laïque, et la religion traditionnelle des Juifs pratiquants, rapprochaient fortement les deux communautés. On retrouve ici l'idée classique selon laquelle un système de type consensualiste ou d'esprit fédéraliste fonctionne d'autant mieux que les différents groupes communient dans un même esprit religieux.

Certes, il ne faut pas exagérer cette entente, cette "communion" dans les mêmes valeurs ! Il y a eu beaucoup de crises politiques entre les partenaires dans les années cinquante et soixante, car la modération ne résout pas tout. Par exemple laïques et religieux se sont fréquemment affrontés sur la question incroyablement épineuse de "Qui est Juif ?".

Comment concilier la conception laïque selon laquelle doit être considéré comme Juif celui qui s'associe librement au destin de ce peuple, et la conception religieuse selon laquelle n'est Juif que celui qui est de mère juive ou s'est converti au Judaïsme ? Mais ces crises politiques se résorbaient finalement après quelques semaines ou quelques mois, et l'arrangement entrait à nouveau en vigueur.

Quant aux ultra-orthodoxes, ceux que j'ai appelé les "Hommes en noir" dans un livre paru sur ce sujet en 1991 (Paris, Presses de Sciences po), les ultra-religieux regroupés dans le parti *Agoudat Israel*, je n'irai peut-être pas jusqu'à dire qu'ils étaient "consignés dans leurs casernes", mais ils avaient choisi en 1952 de se replier sur leurs ghettos volontaires de Bné-Brak et des quartiers nord de Jérusalem. Il s'agit d'une société indépendante, séparée, représentant environ 5% de la population du pays, entièrement soumise à ses maîtres. Or ses rabbins avaient jugé bon de commander à leurs ouailles de se replier, de croître et de se multiplier sans s'occuper de politique et du monde extérieur. En dehors d'une brève période qui a suivi la création de l'Etat, ils ne participaient à aucune coalition gouvernementale et ne gênaient personne. Pendant vingt-cinq années ils se sont tenus à l'écart, se concentrant sur le développement de leurs institutions, de leurs écoles et de leurs académies talmudiques. D'une démographie très dynamique, dotés de familles nombreuses, ils se développaient quantitativement et étendaient leurs quartiers. De plus, leurs jeunes avaient reçu de Ben Gourion lui-même l'autorisation de ne pas effectuer leur service militaire.

A mon sens, ce "statu quo" à l'israélienne pouvait largement être considéré comme un arrangement de type fédéraliste. En effet, il reposait sur ce que mon regretté ami, le professeur Daniel J. Elazar, définissait comme les deux principes-clés du fédéralisme: le principe de centralité et le principe d'autonomie. Tout d'abord, l'autorité de l'Etat central se trouvait préservée: l'ensemble des lois, l'appareil administratif, les réglements portant sur les institutions, les personnes et les biens étaient *uniformes*: le principe d'unicité de l'Etat, symbolisé par le terme hébreu *mamlakhtiout* forgé par David Ben Gourion, s'appliquait sans restriction à tous les citoyens de l'Etat d'Israël. L'impulsion, la direction, venait du centre, de l'Etat.

Mais d'un autre côté, le statu quo permettait à chaque communauté religieuse de vivre au mieux selon ses propres principes, sans se sentir contrainte et obligée par l'Etat, ou par les autres segments de la société civile. Les ultra-orthodoxes ont toujours eu le droit d'habiter dans des quartiers où ils pouvaient s'organiser selon leurs principes de vie : stricte observance des règles du chabbat et des fêtes juives, interdiction de circuler en voiture et fermeture des rues par des barrières le jour du chabbat, règles contraignantes concernant la tenue des femmes, etc... Mais c'est surtout dans le domaine de l'éducation qu'un arrangement de type fédéraliste était pratiqué. Dans le cadre d'un grand service relevant à l'échelon central du Ministère de l'Education, existaient trois secteurs autonomes: le secteur dit "d'Etat" (laïque), le secteur dit "religieux d'Etat" (c'est-à-dire sioniste-religieux), et le secteur dit "indépendant" (c'est-à-dire ultra-orthodoxe).

Or ce "vivre-ensemble" des laïques et des religieux, dont le maître-mot était, comme dans tout système fédéraliste, *modération*, a éclaté. C'est ce que beaucoup considèrent comme la tragédie de l'Etat d'Israël et le premier effet de ce *danger de paix* que j'évoquai plus haut.

Je crois que plusieurs dates fondamentales scandent cette rupture du "statu quo" et de la coexistence entre laïques et religieux : 1967, 1977, 1987, 1995 et 2003.

1967

C'est la première date cruciale, celle de la guerre des six-jours. Il s'agit certainement d'un tournant dans l'histoire de l'Etat d'Israël. La victoire quasi-miraculeuse de Tsahal après une période d'attente et d'angoisse mortelles; la reconquête inattendue des territoires de Judée-Samarie faisant partie de la Terre d'Israël promise par Dieu au peuple juif; la réunification de Jérusalem, avec la prise du quartier juif et du Mur du Temple; bref, ces événements ont d'un seul coup fait "basculer" le monde religieux dans un extrémisme nationaliste et religieux dont il était, auparavant, très éloigné. Les rabbins qui dirigeaient et orientaient le public sioniste-religieux l'ont guidé vers des options de plus en plus nationalistes : selon eux, aucun gouvernement juif ne pouvait être autorisé à négocier la moindre parcelle des Territoires avec l'ennemi, car il s'agirait d'une véritable rébellion contre Dieu lui-même... Le Parti National Religieux (P.N.R.), jadis le compagnon fidèle des travaillistes, le pilier du statu quo symbole de modération politique, est devenu un mouvement messianiste et extrémiste pour qui toute concession territoriale, même minimale, devenait tabou, une faute religieuse d'une gravité extrême. De parti politique situé au centre mou de l'échiquier politique israélien, le parti allait virer à droite, puis à l'extrême-droite de la scène publique. Le P.N.R. s'est jeté à corps perdu dans le processus de colonisation accélérée des territoires occupés, il a soutenu les jeunes colons venus s'installer en Judée-Samarie et à Gaza. La fin de cette course à l'extrémisme allait le situer, au fil des années, très à la droite du Likoud...

Il s'est agi non seulement d'une course à l'extrémisme politique mais également à l'extrémisme dans la pratique religieuse, qui a de plus en plus rapproché les sionistes religieux des ultra-orthodoxes. Les jeunes générations se sont mises à pratiquer les Commandements avec beaucoup plus d'empressement et de rigueur que leurs parents. Par exemple, l'option de la *yechiva*, l'académie talmudique, a remplacé chez beaucoup d'entre eux l'entrée à l'Université. Les jeunes femmes mariées portent la tête couverte, alors que bien souvent leurs mères allaient tête nue. Le Parti National Religieux a commencé à rivaliser avec les ultra-orthodoxes pour obtenir de nouvelles lois de coercition religieuse dans tous les domaines.

Bref, pour l'arrangement de type fédéraliste entre laïques et religieux, la guerre des six-jours, saluée comme un miracle sur le plan militaire, s'est révélée une catastrophe : elle a mis à mal le tissu social israélien, réduisant en miettes le centre mou, modéré et consensuel de la vie politique, suscitant de toutes parts fanatismes et forces centrifuges.

1977

Deuxième étape, la victoire du grand parti de droite nationaliste, le Likoud de Menachem Begin, lors des élections de 1977. C'est à ce moment précis que les ultra-orthodoxes de l'*Agoudat Israel*, ont décidé de quitter leurs ghettos volontaires et de "rentrer en société». Moyennant des subsides très importants de l'Etat et la promesse de lois de coercition religieuse, ils entrent dans la coalition gouvernementale de Menachem Begin. En fait, ils ne quitteront pratiquement plus aucune coalition gouvernementale, de droite comme de gauche, jusqu'à ce jour. Ils seront toujours là, demandant toujours plus de budgets pour leurs institutions, toujours plus de concessions à leur conception de l'Etat théocratique.

Les deux raisons de ce retour en société des ultra-orthodoxes, étaient d'ordre économique et politique. Sur le plan économique, les besoins des "hommes en noir" étaient et sont de plus en plus grands. Ayant cru et multiplié durant toutes ces années, ayant des masses de jeunes à loger, à éduquer et à nourrir, des institutions exceptionnellement nombreuses a financer, cette société avait besoin de la manne gouvernementale. Donner son appui aux coalitions du Likoud ou du Parti travailliste, c'était, d'abord, obtenir des fonds importants, que seul le budget de l'Etat pouvait fournir. Sur le plan idéologique, c'est un fait que sans devenir "sionistes", les ultra-religieux, jadis aliénés à l'Etat, sont devenus de plus en plus nationalistes. Ils se sont de plus en plus identifiés à l'Etat, à la nation, et aux objectifs politiques de la droite israélienne. Ce processus les a poussés vers une alliance étroite avec le Likoud, et ils sont devenus les supporters les plus actifs de Begin et d'Itshak Shamir, de Binyamin Netanyahou puis d'Ariel Sharon (avant de trouver ce dernier beaucoup trop…modéré !) Bien entendu, tout en "rentrant en société", les ultra-orthodoxes n'ont en rien renoncé à leurs privilèges, et en particulier à celui qui révolte le plus le public laïque, à savoir l'exemption de service militaire...

Quelques années plus tard, cette percée des ultra-religieux allait à nouveau être mis en évidence par le succès du nouveau parti *Shas*. Fondé par le grand-rabbin sefarade Ovadia Yosef, ce parti se donnait pour tâche de rassembler les Juifs religieux dits "orientaux". Il faisait appel aux masses traditionnelles, originaires des pays arabes, et n'allait cesser de progresser, devenant le troisième parti de l'Etat. Sous la houlette de son Maître, il n'hésitait pas à faire appel aux promesses de bénédictions et de guérison, aux amulettes, talismans et autres superstitions, offrant aux familles défavorisées des transports scolaires et des cantines gratuites, et profitant de cette stratégie sur le plan électoral. Bref, les partis ultra-religieux ont acquis une position de force dans la société israélienne, ce qui a contribué à dissoudre encore un peu plus les éléments du statu quo.

1987

La troisième date que je souhaiterais ajouter est 1987. A mon avis, il s'agit d'une date-clé de l'histoire récente de l'Etat d'Israël, et pas seulement parce qu'il s'agit de la date du début de la première intifada (dite "des pierres"), dont on sait l'énorme impact qu'elle a eu sur la société israélienne. C'est aussi cette année là, que paraît un livre qui a fait l'effet d'une bombe en Israël : il s'agit de l'ouvrage de l'historien israélien Benny Morris, sur l'origine du problème des réfugiés palestinien. Ce livre inaugure le phénomène des "Nouveaux historiens", que j'ai traité dans mon ouvrage *La Nouvelle histoire d'Israël* (Gallimard, 1998). Au delà du texte de Morris, le phénomène dit des Nouveaux historiens constitue la concrétisation de ce qui est en train de se passer, cette fois-ci *au sein du public laïque ou ultra-laïque*. Il s'agit de la remise en question, au-delà des grands mythes fondateurs de l'Etat, comme la guerre d'Indépendance de 1948, des cadres collectifs et des références juives de l'Etat d'Israël. Pour beaucoup d'observateurs de cette société, celle-ci est en train d'entrer dans une ère que l'on peut qualifier de "post-sioniste".

En effet, il serait faux et injuste d'affirmer que les coups portés à l'arrangement fédéraliste du statu quo n'ont été portés que par les cercles religieux extrémistes. Ils ont aussi été portés, dans les années quatre-vingt dix et au début des années deux mille, par les franges intellectuelles et émancipées de la bourgeoisie aisée de Tel-Aviv et de la plaine côtière. Le "post-sionisme" et l'utra-laicité pénètrent tous les milieux : universités, professeurs, chercheurs, étudiants, écrivains, poètes, artistes, journalistes, medias, faiseurs d'opinion, le grand quotidien *Haaretz*, etc... Réagissant surtout aux excès des partis religieux et aux exigences abusives de leurs rabbins, peut-être touchés par la vague post-moderniste, les laïques intransigeants n’acceptent plus l’arrangement du statu quo, concocté en son temps par David Ben Gourion. Ils n’acceptent plus le “minimum commun”, et soulignent le fait que la grande majorité des Israéliens se définissent comme des laïques, et veulent un Etat totalement détaché de la religion. Certains commencent même à revendiquer un “Etat-de-tous-ses-citoyens” au lieu d’un “Etat juif” ; beaucoup parlent d’abolir purement et simplement la Loi du Retour, qui réserve aux seuls Juifs le droit de s’installer en Israël et d’obtenir la citoyenneté; d’autres proposent encore de changer le drapeau de l’Etat, en adopter un graphisme où ne figurerait plus l’étoile de David ; certains demandent un nouvel hymne national, qui ne parlerait plus de “l’espoir juif vieux de deux mille ans” ; d’autres conseillent aux Juifs de la diaspora de s’occuper de leurs affaires et de cesser de donner de l’argent à Israël ; pour d’autres enfin, il est urgent que les jeunes israéliens cessent de se focaliser sur la Shoah, et commencent à s’intéresser aussi aux autres génocides dans le monde... Pour la première fois, aux élections de 2001, un parti politique laïque et anti-religieux, le Chinouy (Changement) s’est présenté et a obtenu un succès exceptionnel.

1995

Le 4 novembre 1995, le premier ministre de l’Etat d’Israël Itshak Rabin est assassiné par un jeune homme qui se déclare religieux, et qui affirme avoir commis son acte avec l’autorisation de rabbins extrémistes, afin de bloquer le processus de paix inauguré à Oslo. Ce crime, ajouté au fait que la population religieuse dont est issue l’assassin n’a pas vraiment fait son autocritique à la suite du meurtre, a encore plus éloigné les nationalistes religieux du reste de la population. Les efforts faits par certains pour tenter de rapprocher ces segments antagonistes de la société au cours des dix années qui ont suivi n’ont pas franchement réussi.

2003

C'est au cours de l'année 2003 que l'actuel premier ministre de l'Etat d'Israël, Ariel Sharon, a annoncé son intention de se retirer de la bande de Gaza, de démanteler les colonies juives qui y sont installées, et de remettre ce territoire aux Palestiniens. Pour l'ensemble de la population religieuse d'Israël, à de très rares exceptions près, il s'est agi ni plus ni moins que d'une déclaration de guerre à l'attachement des Juifs pieux à la Terre d'Israël. Pour les colons et l'extrême-droite religieuse, la bande de Gaza fait partie de la terre promise par Dieu à Abraham, Isaac et Jacob, et la décision du premier ministre ne peut être interprétée que comme un crime contre la volonté de Dieu lui-même. Là encore, même s'il existe des religieux qui acceptent le retrait, et même si bon nombre de laïques qui s'y opposent, il reste que le tissu de la société s'est trouvé une nouvelle fois violemment déchiré.

Au total, nous sommes de plus en plus loin des temps du "statu quo". D'un côté, on trouve une société religieuse (environ 25 % de la population), de plus en plus extrémiste dans son ethnocentrisme, son nationalisme, son particularisme, sa religiosité, et qui "évacue" toute espèce de tendance à l'universalisme et à l'altérité. C'est ce que certains résument par le symbole "Jérusalem". Et de l'autre, une population laïque, que symbolise "Tel-Aviv la libérée", de moins en moins attachée au patrimoine juif traditionnel, de plus en plus cosmopolite, de plus en plus avide de créer une société libérale à l'occidentale, une société individualiste où les maîtres-mots seraient : normalité et consommation. Ces laïques-là ne rêvent qu'à l'économie capitaliste et à la société d'abondance, ils recherchent avant tout le succès matériel, pensent Israël en termes d'autoroutes et de haute technologie.

Aujourd'hui, telles sont les questions lancinantes auxquelles l'Etat d'Israël est confronté. Comment reconstruire le tissu social? Comment ramener cette société vers son centre? Comment bâtir des ponts? Comment concilier à nouveau centralité et autonomie? Quelles nouvelles solutions fédéralistes peuvent-elles remplacer un statu quo dépassé? Comment repenser Israël ?

Nazione, Religione e identità : la percezione cristiana

Stefano CECCANTI

Sommario: 1. Le chiese cristiane diverse dalla cattolica: il ruolo anticipatore delle Chiese riformate; 2. La Chiesa cattolica alla base della terza ondata democratica: la fiducia nel pluralismo col Concilio Vaticano II; 3. Il parziale rilancio della visione tradizionale: per una "protezione" ecclesiastica delle democrazie; 4. Le ragioni del parziale *revirement* e le sue evidenti *impasses*; 5. I più recenti sviluppi; Bibliografia; Abstract.

1. LE CHIESE CRISTIANE DIVERSE DALLA CATTOLICA : IL RUOLO ANTICIPATORE DELLE CHIESE RIFORMATE

Questa esposizione si concentrerà sulla Chiesa cattolica, non solo e non tanto perché essa è la principale delle Chiese cristiane, dotata anche di una soggettività internazionale, quanto perché per ragioni diverse è quella che ha avuto il percorso più difficile nel rapporto col diritto delle moderne esperienze di democrazia pluralista.

La chiesa ortodossa, al di là del suo policentrismo, si è trovata quasi solo in situazioni estreme: o di rappresentare una piccola minoranza o una larghissima maggioranza (in Grecia e in alcune delle nuove democrazie dell'Est Europa) e quindi non è stata ancora in grado di produrre una riflessione consistente al di là dell'impostazione tradizionale di richiedere, ove in condizione di farlo, privilegi di status per la sua posizione di confessione dominante [Ceccanti 2001, 55]. Non a caso lo Stato più condannato dalla Corte di Strasburgo per violazione dell'articolo 9 sulla libertà religiosa è proprio la Grecia ortodossa, per la sopravvivenza di norme ispirate a un modello di tolleranza religiosa (una religione privilegiata, gli altri culti ammessi nella misura in cui non fanno concorrenza ad essa) più che di vera e propria libertà religiosa (che comporta in linea di massima un'uguaglianza di trattamento fra le confessioni, senza comunque impedire normative specifiche che tengano ragionevolmente conto del diverso seguito e delle diverse caratteristiche di ognuna di esse) [Ivi, 68 s., 207-213]. La Chiesa ortodossa, come dimostrano anche le vicende della stretta "sinfonia" tra essa e il potere politico in Russia, non è uscita dallo schema tradizionale "un roi-une loi-une foi", fortemente limitativa del pluralismo [Ivi, 95-109], tant'è che, come ha fatto Julia Kristeva, ci si può chiedere, senza essere deterministi, se ciò non sia legato a problemi teologici, e in particolare alla particolare visione del dogma trinitario che svaluta l'autonomia di Cristo (lo Spirito procede solo dal Padre a differenza del Credo cattolico, è il contenzioso del cosiddetto "Filioque") e quindi quella delle realtà temporali. Per Kristeva "mentre la 'e' cattolica (il que del Filioque-NdA) mette sullo stesso piano Padre e Figlio... aprendo la strada all'individualismo occidentale, l''attraverso' ortodosso suggerisce un delizioso ma pernicioso annullamento del Figlio e del credente. Così la rivolta non può che esprimersi attraverso la distruzione perché l'autorità divina non può essere discussa né criticata né negoziata" [cit. Ivi, 55].

All'estremo opposto si situa l'esperienza delle Chiese protestanti che, pur non priva di pesanti contraddizioni storiche, è però quella che per prima ha posto le premesse teologiche e culturali per il pluralismo religioso e politico, per la concezione dello Stato moderno in cui dentro una cornice segnata da regole condivise e da un minimo di valori comuni su cui esse si fondano è possibile concepire la compresenza di diverse nazioni, religioni, identità [cfr., *amplius,* Volpi 2001]. Il sacerdozio universale dei fedeli democratizza infatti la struttura ecclesiastica dall'interno e il libero esame delle scritture sviluppa l'autonomia dell'individuo: sono rimossi gli impedimenti fondamentali (la rigidità del principio di autorità, la sua tendenziale coincidenza col monopolio dell'interpretazione della Verità) al sorgere e al consolidarsi della sovranità popolare, del controllo di costituzionalità, del sistema moderno di pesi e contrappesi sia tra gli organi dello Stato sia tra centro e periferia [Rollet 2003, 75]. Ciò spiega la larga coincidenza tra prevalenza del protestantesimo e diffusione della democrazia fino alla seconda guerra mondiale, anche se la storia presenta indubbie contraddizioni dovute allo stretto rapporto tra Chiese protestanti e genesi degli Stati nazionali, nella dissoluzione del Sacro Romano Impero. Quella genesi ha favorito non solo una sorta di fusione della Chiesa dominante con lo Stato, con alcuni privilegi storici (oggi pressoché scomparsi, tranne nel vincolo di appartenenza stabilito per il Monarca), ma anche una sorta di rapporto simbiotico, acritico nei confronti del potere politico, che si è tradotto anche in consenso agli Stati autoritari sorti in modo formalmente legittimo dalla crisi di alcune democrazie, a cominciare da quella tedesca. Sono passati quasi settant'anni esatti dal profetico sinodo di Barmen, pur minoritario, della Chiesa confessante, che aveva rilevato in tempo quell'errore storico (maggio 1934). Nella Tesi II si condannava l'idea che a partire dalla distinzione Dio/Cesare si dovesse giungere ad un'autonomia dei governanti dalla morale, tale che nei loro settori di competenza "non sarebbero necessarie la giustificazione e la santificazione" di Dio; nella III la subordinazione del messaggio evangelico alle "convinzioni ideologiche o politiche di volta in volta dominanti"; nella V si condannava l'idea che la Chiesa dovesse divenire organo dello Stato [testi integrali a cura di Rostagno 1984, 79-86]. Come spiega il pastore Giorgio Peyrot chiarendo quell'impostazione teologica ed ecclesiologica, della distinzione di piani tra Dio e Cesare ma anche della diversità nell'atteggiamento verso Dio e verso Cesare, "La soggiacenza a Dio è completa, perenne, legata come è al senso del timore; mentre la sottomissione ai potenti di questo mondo è per un tempo soltanto, subordinata alla nostra posizione primaria verso Dio, unita com'è al solo senso di una resa di onore... Rendere onore ai pubblici poteri comporta invece soltanto rispetto, riguardo, considerazione per il ruolo esplicato dalle persone, per le funzioni svolte" [1984, 199]. Ovvero, come ha espresso con particolare forza Dietrich Bonhoeffer prima del suo martirio, invitando a far attenzione alla natura anche demoniaca del potere: "Il dovere sembra capace di fornire la guida sicura. Ma l'uomo del dovere alla fine dovrà compiere il proprio dovere anche nei confronti del diavolo" [1988, 61]. Dopo tali tragiche esperienze, possiamo dire che il ruolo teologico di anticipazione delle Chiese riformate si è potuto pienamente sviluppare, senza più il peso di quelle contraddizioni storiche.

2. LA CHIESA CATTOLICA ALLA BASE DELLA TERZA ONDATA DEMOCRATICA : LA FIDUCIA NEL PLURALISMO COL CONCILIO VATICANO II

"Noi siamo gli amici della vostra vocazione di ricercatori (...). Per voi abbiamo un messaggio ed è questo: continuate a cercare, senza stancarvi, senza disperare mai della verità! Ricordatevi la parola di uno dei vostri grandi amici, S. Agostino: 'Cerchiamo con il desiderio di trovare e troviamo con il desiderio di cercare ancora'".

Queste parole del messaggio del Concilio Vaticano II agli intellettuali, insistendo sulla ricerca quale trait d'union tra libertà e verità che configura, tra l'altro, una nuova visione del diritto (qui ci occupiamo solo del diritto posto dagli Stati, non di quello canonico, interno alla Chiesa), sintetizza le novità del Concilio Vaticano II che secondo le analisi motivate di Samuel Huntington, hanno costituito la principale spinta religiosa nella terza ondata di democrazie, sorte dalla rivoluzione portoghese del 1974 fino a quelle del 1989-1990 nel Centro-Est Europa [1995, in particolare pp. 99-108]. L'aggiornamento conciliare su diritto e democrazia fa perno su questo atteggiamento descritto nel Messaggio citato, non su una generica apertura al mondo, e si compendia in un trittico di documenti.

Con la Dei Verbum, il documento sulla rivelazione divina, emerge la consapevolezza della natura storicamente limitata e condizionata della percezione umana della verità e si afferma pertanto una visione dinamica della rivelazione, la cui comprensione "cresce e progredisce" in un circuito che, come enuncia il suo paragrafo 8 b, parte dalla "riflessione" e dallo "studio dei credenti" (vediamo qui il chiaro riavvicinamento alle Chiese riformate, come pure nella Lumen Gentium par. 10 e nella Presbyterorum ordinis par. 2 che introducono il tema del sacerdozio ministeriale all'interno del sacerdozio comune dei fedeli) [cfr., amplius, Dianich 1984, 64 ss.], passa attraverso l'"esperienza" storica laica e giunge infine alla "predicazione" dei vescovi.

Dalla Gaudium et Spes (il documento sulla Chiesa nel mondo contemporaneo), che insiste sull'autonomia da riconoscere giustamente alle realtà temporali, se ne ricavano le conseguenze storico-politiche. Quale può essere il contesto migliore in cui riflessione, studio, esperienza e predicazione – questo insieme di atti e di soggetti in cui si condensa l'esperienza umana, consentono alla percezione della verità di crescere e progredire, se non quello in cui la consapevolezza della dignità umana impone il rifiuto della coazione (par. 17), in cui i diritti spettano alla persona, che sia o no credente (21 g), in cui sia possibile concepire "in forma dinamica" il bene comune (74 g) e i valori perenni, come quello della famiglia, possano essere sviluppati ben distinguendo "realtà permanenti" e "forme mutevoli" (52 c)? Non a caso viene enunciata un'opzione preferenziale per la democrazia, in cui "la maggioranza dei cittadini è fatta partecipe della gestione della cosa pubblica in un clima di vera libertà" (31 e) e in cui, parafrasando quasi alla lettera l'art. 16 della dichiarazione dei Diritti francese del 1789, si realizzano "ripartizione delle funzioni e degli organi del potere" nonché "protezione efficace e indipendente dei diritti" (75 d). Con questa nuova comprensione, la Chiesa può ammettere, in modo liberatorio, che "molto giovamento le è venuto e le può venire perfino a motivo dell'opposizione di quanti l'avversano o la perseguitano" (44 c), può affermare il proprio 'disinteresse egemonico' con la disponibilità rinunziare a "privilegi", ancorché "legittimamente acquisiti, ove constatasse che il loro uso potesse far dubitare della sincerità della sua testimonianza o nuove circostanze esigessero altre disposizioni" (76 g), affidandosi con fiducia alla competenza, anche se non esclusiva, di un laicato in grado di assumersi "la propria responsabilità" e che abbia nei confronti del magistero dei vescovi un'"attenzione rispettosa", senza aspettarsi da esso né richiedergli una "soluzione concreta" ai problemi emergenti (43 b).

Con la Dignitatis Humanae (la dichiarazione sulla libertà religiosa) viene puntualizzato, in termini propriamente giuridico costituzionali, il ruolo minimo che deve esercitare il diritto, nell'impostazione complessiva della Gaudium et Spes, con accenti che in più punti richiamano direttamente il primo emendamento della Costituzione degli Stati Uniti d'America. Un conto è infatti affermare in libertà il "dovere morale dei singoli e della società verso la vera religione e l'unica Chiesa di Cristo" in cui si manifesta, pur in modo imperfetto fino al compimento del Regno, il massimo di verità possibile (1d), e un altro è affermare il ruolo del diritto, che deve tener conto della legittima richiesta degli uomini contemporanei di non "essere oppressi da misure coercitive" (1 a). Ne consegue il favor libertatis, per cui "nella società va rispettata la norma secondo la quale agli esseri umani va riconosciuta la libertà più ampia possibile, e la loro libertà non deve essere limitata se non quando e in quanto è necessario" (7 c), e l'incompetenza dello Stato in materia religiosa (6 e), anche nei confronti di coloro che discutibilmente, ma legittimamente, "non soddisfano all'obbligo di cercare la verità e di aderire a essa" (2 b), con un ristretto potere di intervento riconosciuto allo Stato di limitare tale libertà al fine di tutelare l'ordine pubblico (come in molte Costituzioni europee a cominciare da quella italiana), "parte fondamentale del bene comune", ma concepito in modo ben più restrittivo di quest'ultimo (7 c). Non tale, comunque, da mettere in discussione "l'immunità dalla coercizione esterna" (2 b), il pilastro fondamentale senza cui non vi sarebbe una democrazia liberale, e quindi il contesto propizio perché la ricerca possa collegare libertà e sviluppo della comprensione della Verità.

La precedente dottrina della indifferenza rispetto alle varie "forme di governo" (nozione corrispondente a quelle che nella dottrina giuridica italiana sono le "forme di Stato"), affermata solennemente sin dall'enciclica immortale Dei di Leone XIII (1885), aveva avuto il merito storico di superare l'indissolubilità del legame tradizionale tra il Trono e l'Altare [Di Rovasenda 1979, 24 s.]; tuttavia, legandosi ad un'autocomprensione della Chiesa come 'società perfetta' l'indifferenza di principio finiva per tradursi in atteggiamento pratico di maggiore o minore favore accordato ai regimi di qualsiasi natura nella mistura in cui riconoscessero spazi alla Chiesa cattolica. Ci si esponeva perciò alle nuove strumentalizzazioni dei regimi autoritari, i quali, potendo garantire posizioni di privilegio alla Chiesa spesso superiori a quelli delle democrazie, per la dottrina previgente al Vaticano II erano da preferire.

In termini storici i documenti del Vaticano II sono il riconoscimento di validità teologica ex post dei frutti migliori del costituzionalismo occidentale, unificati nella persona di colui che ricevette da Paolo VI nelle proprie mani il messaggio agli intellettuali, Jacques Maritain. Unificate, perché Maritain è a cavallo tra due esperienze storiche differenti, ma comunicanti: la libertà anglo-americana, aliena dalle rigidità giacobine, del periodo dell'esilio bellico da antifascista negli Usa, e l'esperienza delle Democrazie cristiane europee sorte in alternativa al clerico-fascismo (Maritain era dal '37 in Europa soprattutto l'uomo dell'obiezione di coscienza al connubio franchista spagnolo, benedetto dalla maggioranza dei vescovi con l'intollerabile dizione di "Guerra giusta"se non talora persino con quella di "Guerra santa") e in competizione con il marxismo, 'ultima eresia cristiana', secondo la sua definizione che legittimava la collaborazione senza confusione, a differenza della rigida barriera posta a destra [cfr., amplius, Rollet 2003, 113-127]. Simmetricamente, dal suo punto di vista, era perfettamente comprensibile lo choc del Generale Franco, il quale "non poteva concepire che la Chiesa che aveva benedetto la sua crociata nella Guerra civile... ora si opponesse alla sua dittatura. Quasi un quarto di secolo dopo quella benedizione nel carcere di Zamora – utilizzata specialmente per il clero che contestava il regime – c'erano circa cinquecento sacerdoti imprigionati" [Rojas 2003, 168].

Significava riconoscere ex post anche le ragioni di Alcide de Gasperi contro quelle clerico-moderate dominanti nel mondo cattolico durante la Guerra Fredda che avrebbero voluto superare qualsiasi barriera di alleanza a destra [Scoppola 1991 e Riccardi 2003], quelle dei cattolici della Resistenza francese contro i Vescovi massicciamente allineati al regime di Vichy (che Maritain, ambasciatore di Francia presso la Santa Sede, si operava a far sostituire), dei cattolici americani invisi alla Curia perché convinti, come il principale estensore della Dignitatis Humanae, il gesuita John Courtnay Murray, non a caso condannato prima del Concilio, che non si dovesse tollerare la democrazia come un male minore, come una mera ipotesi rispetto all'ideale, alla tesi massimale, dello 'Stato cattolico'. Come scriveva Murray al cardinale Spellmann, durante i lavori del Concilio (18 novembre 1963): "la Chiesa cattolica negli Stati Uniti non 'tollera' il sistema costituzionale americano (sarebbe un'assurdità). I vescovi americani e i fedeli americani approvano positivamente e sostengono il primo emendamento e la sua clausola sulla libertà religiosa. Non la considerano come una 'ipotesi' opposta a una 'tesi'" [cit. in Gonnet 1994, 345].

Ciò non significa, evidentemente, dogmatizzare la lettera dei documenti conciliari o ritenerli del tutto risolutivi ai fini delle problematiche successive: ad apparire valido è soprattutto il metodo di lettura della realtà, di tipo induttivo, e la ricerca di un criterio, di un discernimento che non prescinda da essa, che non vi guardi soltanto per applicarle soluzioni 'pure' e decontestualizzate.

3. IL PARZIALE RILANCIO DELLA VISIONE TRADIZIONALE : PER UNA "PROTEZIONE" ECCLESIASTICA DELLE DEMOCRAZIE

Negli anni recenti, alcuni documenti magisteriali, in particolare l'enciclica *Veritatis Splendor* – si pensi al par. 34 che enuncia che "la coscienza ha dei diritti perché ha dei doveri", al par. 101, in cui si denuncia "il rischio dell'alleanza fra democrazia e relativismo etico", e al par. 60 sulla necessità di obbedire alla "norma oggettiva" –, la *Evangelium Vitae* – che ribadisce quel rischio (par. 19 s., 69 s.), nonché quella necessità (par. 60), e che contro di esso rilancia con forza l'obiezione di coscienza (par. 73) [vedi i rinvii puntuali e la ricostruzione complessiva in Berlingò 1999] –, nonché alcune prese di posizione del magistero ordinario, le ultime delle quali saranno trattate oltre, hanno riproposto un nesso stringente tra libertà e verità, espungendo, o comunque comprimendo significativamente, il tema della ricerca e quindi riproponendo un ruolo più marcato del diritto a difesa della verità, pur senza rilanciare la teoria dello Stato cristiano né regredire all'idea di tolleranza religiosa.

Questa impostazione è stata puntualmente criticata come regressiva rispetto all'impostazione conciliare da vari settori e in particolare da uno dei massimi giuristi europei, allievo di Maritain e di Norberto Bobbio, Gregorio Peces Barba [1995 e 1996] e nelle conclusioni del citato volume di Samuel Huntington [1985, 297].

Simmetricamente, c'è stato invece chi, come B. Dufour, sulla rivista "Communio" con uno scritto così ben motivato (dal suo punto di vista) e sintonico col nuovo pontificato da costituirne una sorta di interpretazione autentica in questa materia, ha elogiato questo parziale mutamento, addebitando al Concilio e alla sua ricezione negli anni immediatamente seguenti, sulla scia di un eccesso di condiscendenza verso le democrazie occidentali e di quella americana in particolare, la colpa di aver sottovalutato i rischi dell'alleanza tra democrazia e il relativismo etico [1995]. Del resto è noto che la rivista "Communio" si propone più generalmente di supportare interpretazioni 'neutralizzanti' degli aspetti più marcati delle novità conciliari, sulla base di una lettura sistematica che tende a inglobarle in continuità col magistero precedente, valorizzandone le costanti e svalutando di conseguenza i rilievo quantitativo e qualitativo delle discontinuità apportate. Per Dufour la particolare interpretazione del Vaticano II sostenuta dal nuovo pontificato si baserebbe sulla "tensione escatologica" che impone alla Chiesa, per essere fedele alla sua missione, di ricordare ai legislatori che essi non possono "considerarsi giudici definitivi e universali", non appartenendo "all'uomo di separare il buon grano dalla zizzania" [1995, 109]. Tuttavia si può replicare che la tensione escatologica coinvolge anche la Chiesa, relativizza anche il suo ruolo e i suoi giudizi, tant'è che essa, ben distinta dal Regno di Dio, è con modestia definita in apertura della Costituzione dogmatica conciliare *Lumen Gentium* al n. 1 "segno e strumento dell'intima unione con Dio e dell'unità di tutto il genere umano". Al di là di quel che la Chiesa dice di se stessa, come ricorda ulteriormente Peces-Barba, un conto è affermare giustamente che "nessuna posizione può, se trionfa con la maggioranza, attribuirsi il fatto di esprimere la verità unica", rifiutando il "positivismo ideologico" antipluralista (o la 'democrazia totalitaria' come ha detto più volte l'attuale pontefice), un altro conto è dedurne che "la verità possa venire da una minoranza religiosa o filosofica, che pensando di esprimere il monopolio della verità possa imporsi alla maggioranza" [1996, 87].

Per comprendere meglio questa parziale riproposta del magistero precedente occorre chiarire, sia pure brevemente, i termini della posizione preconciliare, a modo di trittico logicamente corrispondente ai documenti conciliari prima esaminati:

(1) Al cuore dell'impostazione tradizionale stava l'idea che il magistero della Chiesa, 'società perfetta', possedesse l'interpretazione pressoché esatta non soltanto della Rivelazione in senso stretto, ma anche "del bene e del male nell'uomo, nel senso completo, complessivo, quasi come un alone dentro il quale la parola rivelata sta e vive e dal quale non può essere isolata", cioè della legge naturale [Dianich 1990, 15]. Di conseguenza, il magistero non poteva non dettare indirizzi anche al legislatore civile, il quale, come del resto la stessa società civile, non poteva essere considerato capace di consistenza etica autonoma a causa del peccato. Lo conferma autorevolmente e in modo del tutto esplicito il celebre trattato sulla Chiesa del cardinale Giuseppe Siri, una delle più autorevoli esposizioni del Magistero pre-concialiare: "l'azione magisteriale della Chiesa è ampia quanto la legge morale che ne è oggetto, ossia si estende quanto l'azione libera di qualunque uomo. Anche dei non cristiani, poiché essa detiene la prima legge di Dio e la sua infallibile interpretazione; quella legge appunto che vale per tutti gli uomini e che assorbe e canonizza il diritto di natura". [1944, 307].

(2) Ne conseguiva che la figura storica ottimale non potesse che essere quella dello 'Stato cristiano', dello Stato che riconoscesse il massimo spazio possibile all'autorità d'interpretazione del magistero, mentre la Chiesa, come già accennato in precedenza, non considerava rilevanti le altre caratteristiche della forma di Stato, a cominciare dalla sua democraticità o meno. In astratto, quindi, l'atteggiamento nei confronti delle forme di Stato era, sin da Leone XIII, di neutralità. In concreto, però, quello schema finiva per condurre quasi naturalmente a privilegiare i compromessi con gli Stati autoritari di destra, più disponibili a contraccambiare il consenso ecclesiastico con la riverenza formale, e alcuni privilegi, a un'istituzione imperniata sull'ordine, piuttosto che a privilegiare la libera concorrenza delle posizioni nel quadro dello Stato democratico che meno si prestava a detti privilegi (dal concordato italiano del '29 a quello portoghese del '40 a quello spagnolo del '53). Del resto, se l'eticità stava tutta dalla parte dell'istituzione e il peccato tutto nella società civile ad essa esterna, la tutela delle posizioni ecclesiastiche finiva per coincidere di fatto col bene comune. Anche i possibili conflitti coi regimi autoritari avvennero, per lungo tempo, dentro questo schema: come notarono alcuni dei dirigenti popolari antifascisti spinti

all'esilio nel clima di intese fra Chiesa e Stato fascista sfociato nel Concordato del '29, le proteste della Santa Sede per gli scontri del '31 tra il Regime e le associazioni giovanili cattoliche non ponevano affatto la richiesta del rispetto di un generale diritto di associazione, ma quello del rispetto delle garanzie concordatarie. Le associazioni cattoliche erano difese perché cattoliche, non perché associazioni;

(3) Ne risultava che non fosse certo ammissibile un diritto naturale dell'uomo alla libertà religiosa, ma, caso mai, una limitata tolleranza religiosa per chi decideva di perseverare nell'errore, essendo soltanto la Verità ad avere diritti.

La posizione che emerge dai recenti documenti magisteriali che ho citato, autorevolmente supportata dalla rivista "Communio", non segna affatto un mero ritorno a questo trittico tradizionale nella sua interezza. Sia il secondo che il terzo elemento ('Stato cristiano' e 'tolleranza religiosa') sono del tutto assenti e anzi, su questi aspetti, c'è una chiara continuità col Vaticano II, nell'opzione preferenziale per la democrazia e per la libertà religiosa. C'è però una maggiore vicinanza al primo elemento del trittico tradizionale che non a quello della *Dei Verbum* 8 b: una visione più statica della Rivelazione e della sua interpretazione magisteriale fino ad abbracciare la legge naturale. Non si tratta quindi di una smentita del Concilio Vaticano II, ma di una sua interpretazione in chiave riduttiva delle novità.

Non si tratta di una assoluta novità. C'è una notevole continuità con le posizioni sostenute dai vescovi polacchi al Concilio, anche se in quella sede la loro impostazione non prevalse. Essi si saldarono con le posizioni americane e con quelle europee della maggioranza conciliare nel negare allo Stato un ruolo preponderante nella regolazione delle questioni religiose, ma non in nome della fiducia per la democrazia che animava Courtnay Murray, il principale estensore del documento sulla libertà religiosa, quanto piuttosto per il timore che quel ruolo, rivendicato dalla minoranza tradizionalista pensando alle protezioni ricevute dai regimi autoritari (ancora vivi e vegeti in Spagna e Portogallo, traballanti proprio dopo e a causa del Vaticano II), potesse essere utilizzato a propria giustificazione dai regimi comunisti per limitare il ruolo della Chiesa cattolica.

La linea costante dell'episcopato polacco, pur giungendo spesso ad analoghe conclusioni pratiche, si basava sul concetto per cui "soltanto la verità rende l'uomo libero e soltanto la responsabilità, intesa come assunzione del dovere da parte di una coscienza rettamente formata, qualifica effettivamente la libertà", senza marcare la distinzione tra dovere morale e ruolo più limitato del diritto [Scatena 2001, 160]. Siamo decisamente lontani dall'impostazione complessiva del testo finale della *Dignitatis Humanae*, nonostante la presenza in essa di alcuni brani oggettivistici, inseriti per limitare il dissenso tradizionalista che tuttavia, in quella collocazione sistematica, non intaccano il primato del contributo dell'episcopato americano e di Murray [Scatena 2000]. Non a caso il cardinale Kasper ha sottolineato che "Il concilio ha realizzato, soprattutto nella Dichiarazione sulla libertà religiosa, pur nella piena garanzia di continuità magisteriale, un significativo scambio di paradigma. Ha accettato in linea di massima i processi moderni di libertà e si è posta sul terreno degli ordinamenti di libertà creati dall'illuminismo politico" [1995, 42].

Nell'impostazione americana, sostanzialmente prevalsa, la libertà religiosa era un concetto eminentemente giuridico-costituzionale, l'affermazione della libertà sotto un governo limitato; in quella polacca, un concetto eminentemente teologico-morale, prioritario rispetto ai nodi giuridico-costituzionali. Due approcci avvicinabili nella pratica per moltissimi aspetti, entrambi diversi dalle visioni tradizionalistiche, ma non equivalenti.

Del resto una linea analoga, un'altra opinione concorrente potremmo dire, era stata più ampiamente e coerentemente sostenuta dai vescovi polacchi sulla *Gaudium et spes*, convergente sì con la maggioranza conciliare su molte conclusioni pratiche, sull'opzione preferenziale per la democrazia, ma dissonante rispetto alle motivazioni. Rispetto allo schema di Mons. Guano del 1964, ampiamente ripreso nel testo finale, che parte da una lettura induttiva della realtà, dalle domande dei contemporanei, per passare al giudizio e quindi alle implicazioni pratiche, secondo le esperienze più positive di dialogo col moderno delle nuove forme di Azione Cattolica di ambiente e di pastorale della cultura (vedere-giudicare-agire secondo il trinomio del cardinale Cardjin, fondatore della Joc, del movimento degli operai cristiani; ma a esiti analoghi conduceva anche la sensibilità montiniana), lo schema alternativo dei vescovi polacchi partiva invece, classicamente, dai "fatti primari" che "determinano l'esistenza della Chiesa", per passare ad affrontare "i problemi maggiori del nostro tempo, rivolgendosi a fedeli e non fedeli sulla base del diritto naturale".[Acerbi 1979, 220].

C'è una differenza di linguaggio (pastorale-induttivo a tre tempi, vedere-giudicare-agire per la maggioranza conciliare; dottrinale-deduttivo a due tempi, dottrina-applicazioni per i vescovi polacchi) che tradisce due diversi tipi di interlocutori.

Nel primo caso, la preoccupazione è rivolta all'opinione pubblica democratica. L'intento è di sincronizzarsi con la sua aspirazione alla libertà e di esercitare un ruolo critico all'interno di essa. Basti citare due interventi emblematici del dibattito conciliare, anche se non privi di una certa cautela per evitare di contrapporsi esplicitamente al magistero passato, ripresi in questo senso da Acerbi: "la dichiarazione sull'esercizio libero della religione nella società è assolutamente necessaria nelle circostanze odierne. Se non fosse promulgata, la Chiesa sarebbe condannata nel foro della opinione pubblica come se fosse contraria alla libertà religiosa" (cardinale Krol); "una cosa è di importanza somma. Attraverso questa dichiarazione la Chiesa cattolica deve mostrarsi a tutto il mondo d'oggi come una protagonista della libertà, umana e civile, specialmente in materia religiosa" (cardinale Cushing) [Ivi, 261].

Nel secondo caso la democrazia da privilegiare suppone un ruolo maieutico dell'istituzione ecclesiastica, in nome del suo ruolo di lettura del diritto naturale, di cui il diritto positivo deve essere ampia e fedele positivizzazione. Così come l'identità della Polonia è protetta di fronte a un regime socialista dal Magistero, che tutela con la sua azione cristiani e non, anche in un migliore quadro di garanzie quale è realizzabile in una democrazia ci si può salvare dal relativismo etico soltanto grazie a un analogo ruolo di tutela dell'istituzione ecclesiastica, quasi una sorta di "corte costituzionale magisteriale" fondata sul diritto naturale. Il pluralismo di nazioni, religioni, identità resta riconosciuto, ma è la Chiesa cattolica a ordinarlo, a "rivelare" la sua struttura interna, secondo la propria lettura della legge naturale.

Che uno scarto vi sia stato è comunque innegabile. Anche in questo caso, come in quello tra pre-Concilio e Concilio narrato con lo stupore di Francisco Franco, la discontinuità è più facilmente inquadrabile con un esempio storico, sempre relativo alla Spagna. Il Cardinale Tarancon, primate di Spagna ed uomo chiave nella delegittimazione del regime franchista, in stretto raccordo con Paolo VI, al momento di prendere possesso della sede di Madrid, il 18 gennaio 1972, aveva solennemente detto, rifacendosi ai documenti conciliari: "Tradizione di secoli ha prodotto una specie di simbiosi fra ciò che è religioso e ciò che è patriottico, ciò che è sociale e ciò che è ecclesiastico... Gli uomini, anche in Spagna, hanno preso coscienza dell'autonomia dell'ordine temporale e non ammettono eccezioni in questi campi per motivi religiosi" [cit. in Paronetto Valier 1996, 71]. Ora il medesimo Tarancon, proprio per aver seguito questo medesima linea, fu quanto mai sconcertato fino a uscirne piangente per la dura rampogna ricevuta in udienza privata da Giovanni Paolo II, riportata nel dettaglio dal giornalista italiano Massimo Olmi, amico di Tarancon, con particolari tali che solo il medesimo poteva avergli fornito ("Lei ha permesso che nella nuova Costituzione non si facesse da nessuna parte il nome di Dio, così come ha permesso che la religione cattolica non vi figurasse come religione ufficiale dello Stato spagnolo") [cit. in Olmi 1986, 102]. I due grandi avversari, Franco e Tarancon, entrambi spiazzati dai successivi mutamenti della Chiesa!

4. LE RAGIONI DEL PARZIALE *REVIREMENT* E LE SUE EVIDENTI *IMPASSES*

Se la ricostruzione di alcune tendenze recenti può essere relativamente agevole, più problematico è invece coglierne le ragioni e le ulteriori prospettive.

Normalmente le reazioni difensive, di ripiegamento parziale sulle identità tradizionali, derivano da *shock* per esiti imprevisti delle aperture tentate e non del tutto riuscite.

Probabilmente gli aspetti da cogliere sono due. Il primo è quello dei riflessi *ad intra* di quella valorizzazione della ricerca, della democrazia e della libertà che il Concilio aveva riconosciuto *ad extra*. Come avevano dal loro punto di vista coerentemente stigmatizzato i tradizionalisti, *tout se tient*: quei riconoscimenti avrebbero necessariamente portato ad analoghe richieste interne alla Chiesa, mettendo in crisi il diritto canonico consolidato, la forza del principio di autorità nella vita interna della Chiesa, dalle forme tradizionali del primato pontificio al ruolo del sacerdozio ministeriale, alle modalità di formazione delle decisioni sulle materie coinvolgenti il laicato. Questa sfida in un'istituzione bimillenaria poteva ben difficilmente essere accolta in tempi brevi con soluzioni al tempo stesso innovative ed equilibrate, in grado di recepire le istanze di libertà senza mettere in pericolo l'esistenza e la funzionalità dell'istituzione.

Il secondo è l'effetto di spiazzamento per ulteriori novità *ad extra* non previste nella loro radicalità. Infatti nell'immediato postconcilio varie spinte, a cominciare dalla rivoluzione dei costumi, con la possibilità di scindere la sessualità dalla riproduzione, si sono rivelate problematiche per la Chiesa cattolica, che è stata sorpresa dai rapidi mutamenti delle legislazioni civili in questi delicati ambiti di vita (generalizzazione di normative sul divorzio, depenalizzazione parziale dell'aborto, regolazione di forme di convivenza diverse dal matrimonio, parziale liberalizzazione dell'accesso alle tecnologie riproduttive, ecc.). In realtà esse hanno finito spesso per ratificare più che accelerare i mutamenti intervenuti, dei quali non vi era però piena coscienza (basti pensare alla sorpresa dell'episcopato italiano per i risultati, in realtà prevedibili, del referendum sul divorzio del 1974 e dello stesso atteggiamento dei praticanti).

La vicenda dell'enciclica *Humanae Vitae*, ben prima quindi dell'inizio dell'attuale pontificato, ma in cui l'attuale pontefice ha giocato un ruolo molto significativo, si pone al centro di entrambi gli *shock* e segna un improvviso ritorno del linguaggio dottrinale binario rispetto a quello pastorale ternario, il quale ultimo era stato individuato dal Concilio non già come un grado minore di aderenza alla dottrina, ma come modo di presentare credibilmente la dottrina nel contesto contemporaneo. L'accettazione del punto di vista largamente minoritario nella commissione preparatoria di quell'enciclica segna una discontinuità importantissima nell'*imprinting* della ricezione del Concilio, rendendo difficili gli sviluppi più coerenti con le novità quell'evento, come segnala con precisione nei dettagli l'ex vicepresidente della Conferenza Episcopale Francese, monsignor Gabriel Matagrin, in uno dei libri più illuminanti degli ultimi anni dal punto di vista storico, teologico e anche giuridico della Chiesa tra Concilio e postconcilio [2000, 229-250 e 424]. Tra l'altro Matagrin identifica nell'attuale pontificato e negli episcopati polacco e italiano, che ne sarebbero da tempo gli interpreti più pronti, una linea che intenderebbe "progettare un regime politico che riconoscerebbe il primato della Chiesa" [363], risentendo eccessivamente dello scontro storico col "totalitarismo marxista" [367] più che operare "attraverso la formazione delle coscienze" [220], la quale invece sarebbe più confacente, per Matagrin, all'ecclesiologia conciliare e a un contesto storico in cui, sulla base di una lettura legata al pensiero di Emmanuel Mounier, "cristiani e non cristiani debbono inventare insieme le grandi linee di una cultura che sia rispettosa dell'uomo, ma che è inedita e il cui volto non è conosciuto in anticipo" [225]. Che quello dei temi dell'*Humanae Vitae*, della perdita di controllo della Chiesa sulla sessualità femminile, con l'emergere di una spinta moderna alla "maternità qualitativa", selettiva, di fronte alle nuove possibilità di separare la sessualità dalla procreazione, lo dimostra lo scritto citato, anche qui molto istruttivo, di Dufour che cita, come unico esempio di contrasto quasi irriducibile con le democrazie occidentali, la linea da esse tenuta su contraccezione e aborto nella Conferenza internazionale del Cairo della metà degli anni '90 su "Popolazione e sviluppo" [Dufour 1995, 96].

Eppure i nodi irrisolti tornano fatalmente al pettine. Se la prima parte dell'attuale pontificato era stata segnata dall'efficace *pars destruens* nei confronti dei moribondi regimi dell'Est europeo, la seconda ha dovuto fare i conti coi problemi derivanti con una possibile *pars construens* che si è rivelata ben più difficile, nonostante che l'euforia per la caduta del comunismo ne avesse sul momento favorito la riproposizione enfatica [Galli 1990]. L'idea di una democrazia 'ecclesiasticamente protetta'non si è rivelata feconda: essa non ha favorito né la nascita di democrazie cristiane laiche, come nell'immediato secondo dopoguerra, né un efficace presenza di *leaders* cattolici all'interno di altri partiti anche laddove la presenza sociale della Chiesa di Roma e il ruolo positivo nella transizione erano più marcati; ha al contrario determinato una contro-reazione di tipo laicista, nonostante i grandi meriti pregressi, la quale è stata spesso uno dei fattori di rilegittimazione dei partiti ex-comunisti a cominciare proprio dalla Polonia [Drweski 2001]; non ha frenato, se non momentaneamente, legislazioni di tipo permissivo negli ambiti di vita 'eticamente sensibili', spesso ancor più marcate di quelle esistenti nelle democrazie occidentali criticate per il relativismo etico.

Peraltro K. Woycicki, un importante cattolico liberale polacco, pur essendo anche amico personale del pontefice, a dieci anni di distanza, ricorda invece i tentativi falliti di modificare per tempo dall'interno, sin dagli anni '60, l'impostazione della Chiesa polacca, quando essa non intese modificare la propria impostazione tradizionale per far meglio fronte al Regime, e l'inevitabile disfatta di quel modello una volta eclissatosi il nemico: "Finché il cattolicesimo polacco si trovava in prima linea nella lotta contro il comunismo (...) il nemico comune univa tutti (...). Un enorme pericolo per il cattolicesimo polacco è che vasti settori di esso vengano conquistati da tendenze nazionaliste, antimoderniste e fondamentaliste. Ma questo è più un problema interno della Chiesa e della sua gerarchia che un problema capace di dominare la vita pubblica e politica polacca. Più il conservatorismo cattolico sarà aggressivo più diverrà minoritario", [2000, 92-94]. Viceversa, come rivela lo scritto di Dufour, nell'immediato post 1989 Giovanni Paolo II, convinto dell'esportabilità del modello polacco così come inteso allora, con un ruolo marcato della Chiesa a protezione della nascente della democrazia, ha proprio per questo criticato le democrazie occidentali ribadendo il nesso stringente tra libertà e verità, che il Concilio avrebbe sacrificato essendo "una reazione al totalitarismo piuttosto che al liberalismo" [1995, 91-92]. La linea dei vescovi polacchi, rimasta minoritaria al Concilio, in quanto timorosa di una canonizzazione delle esperienze occidentali, ma concorrente nell'esito finale di approvazione del testo, poteva servire ora a un affinamento della sua interpretazione. In realtà, come ricorda Woycicki, nella transizione alla democrazia "la società strumentalizzava la religione resistendo alla dittatura comunista, ma i processi di laicizzazione erano non meno reali che nei paesi occidentali" [2000, 92]; resisi improvvisamente conto del fenomeno, i vescovi hanno reagito in modo tradizionalista, persino dichiarandosi "favorevoli all'ingresso della Polonia nell'Unione europea solo dopo lunghe esitazioni" [Ivi, 93], paradossalmente trascinati dai postcomunisti.

Da qui le oscillazioni tipiche di un periodo in cui le coordinate di fondo si rivelano obiettivamente incerte: per un verso alcune puntualizzazioni restrittive di singoli documenti e atti del magistero ordinario già segnalati, per altro verso atti che invece segnalano una ripresa marcata dello spirito dell'evento conciliare, dagli incontri di Assisi, al di là delle frontiere dello stesso ecumenismo tradizionale, dalla richiesta giubilare di perdono, alla disponibilità a rimettere in discussione le forme storiche del primato petrino. Questi ultimi atti non si inquadrano bene nel *revirement* dottrinale prima segnalato; al di là dei loro aspetti pratici e delle specifiche motivazioni di ciascuno essi infatti si rifanno per la loro radicale novità alla dinamica di ricerca sollecitata dal Messaggio del Concilio agli intellettuali e da *Dei Verbum* 8 b. A riprova di ciò basti vedere le legittime e coerenti manifestazioni di dissenso dei settori ecclesiastici che avevano supportato quel *revirement* e che hanno colto una ripresa di rapporto forte con l'evento conciliare, soprattutto in occasione del "mea culpa" del Giubileo, il quale, mettendo in discussione errori del passato finiva di fatto per relativizzare anche nel presente le prese di posizioni magisteriali nell'amplissimo ambito non legato all'infallibilità, compreso quello socio-politico. Se infatti il punto-chiave del ridimensionamento delle novità conciliari consisteva nello stemperarle all'interno del magistero precedente, sopravvalutando le continuità e sminuendo gli scarti, nessuna di queste ultime storiche aperture aveva in realtà precedente alcuno, era presentabile in continuità con analoghi atti precedenti, soprattutto quella solenne della richiesta di perdono, nemmeno nello stesso Vaticano II. Quasi che, come in un moto pendolare, dopo aver limitato i rischi di tenuta dell'istituzione, si dovesse riaprire una nuova fase di sperimentazioni ardite, anche se non azzardate.

Sulla frontiera del diritto questo richiede forse di ritrovare un punto di partenza preciso nella letteralità del già richiamato brano di *Gaudium et spes* 43 b: affidarsi con fiducia da parte della Chiesa alla competenza propria, anche se non esclusiva, di un laicato in grado di assumersi "la propria responsabilità" e che abbia nei confronti del magistero dei vescovi un' "attenzione rispettosa" senza attendere né richiedere ad esso una "soluzione concreta" ai problemi emergenti (43 b).

È invece concettualmente inadeguato all'oggi della Chiesa e delle nostre democrazie, alle possibilità di corretta comprensione da parte di quella gran parte dell'opinione pubblica che ricerca attraverso il diritto un ruolo di 'moralità minima condivisa', di equilibri ragionevoli tra libertà e responsabilità (senza rinnegare comunque l'acquisizione liberale della natura fondamentalmente procedurale della democrazia), immaginare che spetti all'episcopato il ruolo di 'tutela della democrazia', di precisazione quasi sotto dettatura al legislatore degli elementi desumibili univocamente dal diritto naturale da positivizzare in una sorta di prendere o lasciare. È l'intelligenza creativa e anticonformista di Maritain, al di là degli aspetti inevitabilmente transeunti della sua impostazione, che ha ricevuto quel messaggio del Concilio, non chi si è attenuto alla rigida ripetizione delle apparenti certezze tradizionali, di letture del diritto naturale inevitabilmente condizionate dalla storia, anche se non del tutto da essa determinate.

Nella Settimana sociale dei cattolici del 1945 su "Costituzione e costituente", in cui, la relazione di mons. Antonio Lanza, arcivescovo di Reggio Calabria, aveva definito, sulla base del diritto naturale, indisponibile per il legislatore costituente il carattere "gerarchico" del rapporto uomo-donna nel matrimonio [1946, 227], l'allora Presidente del Consiglio Alcide de Gasperi invitò saggiamente a non immaginare il ruolo del credente legislatore (che del resto non è chiamato a rappresentare i soli credenti e che agisce istituzionalmente libero da mandato imperativo non solo rispetto al suo partito ma anche rispetto alle autorità ecclesiastiche) in un' "atmosfera ossigenata" da "grande ascensione montana", ma nella logica di "fissare una pratica di convivenza civile che tiene conto delle opinioni altrui e che deve cercare una via di mezzo fra quelle che possono essere le aspirazioni di principio e le possibilità di azione" [1946, 315]. Lì si colloca la responsabilità tipicamente laicale e forse da essa bisognerebbe ripartire per evitare anomale forme di supplenza in cui l'autorità ecclesiastica non solo, come è doveroso, richiama le posizioni del Magistero, anche sulla base del diritto naturale, ma si fa anche carico in via sostanzialmente diretta (al di là della interposizione formale di gruppi di pressione da essa dipendenti, versione aggiornata dei Comitati civici italiani di Luigi Gedda) anche della mediazione legislativa di quelle posizioni.

5. I PIÙ RECENTI SVILUPPI

Il pendolo nell'ultimissima fase del pontificato sembra nuovamente andare in senso restrittivo. I due recenti documenti del 2003 della Congregazione per la dottrina della Fede sulle responsabilità dei cattolici nella vita politica e sul riconoscimento legale delle unioni tra persone omosessuali, pur riconfermando alcuni punti-chiave dell'insegnamento conciliare, esprimono vari aspetti di un atteggiamento sostanzialmente difensivo rispetto al pluralismo delle società contemporanee, non ben distinto dal relativismo culturale. Vi si afferma infatti: "è oggi certo verificabile un certo relativismo culturale che offre evidenti segni di sé nella teorizzazione e difesa del pluralismo etico che sancisce la decadenza e la dissoluzione della ragione e dei principi della legge morale naturale" [2003 a, 72], quando, com'è noto, il rispetto e la valorizzazione per il pluralismo non coincide affatto col relativismo, che ne è semmai una deviazione semplicistica. Ciò comporta come conseguenza pratica una visione meramente riduttiva delle intese legislative per le quali, anziché valorizzare il ruolo attivo e propositivo dei cattolici impegnati in politica, se ne limita la funzione ad una sorta di "riduzione del danno"provocato dal dover tener conto di altre visioni, viste come aprioristicamente lontane dalla retta comprensione della "legge morale naturale" [Ivi, 73] e affermando perentoriamente che sulla "retta concezione della persona.. l'impegno dei cattolici non può cedere a compromesso alcuno" [Ivi, 72]. Affermazioni rivelatrici di problemi complessivi ancora irrisolti dato che, come ha rilevato un acuto osservatore svizzero, Alberto Lepori, ove prese strettamente alla lettera "ogni discorso politico al di fuori del cattolicesimo diventa praticamente impossibile" e si rischia così di "fare dell'ostruzionismo, col rischio spesso di non giungere a nessuna soluzione praticabile" [2003, 29]. Anzi, con una selettività non ben argomentata, si distingue un nucleo duro di materie che per loro natura "non ammettono deroghe, eccezioni e compromesso alcuno", le prime delle quali sono però chiaramente identificabili in prese di posizioni puntuali ("aborto..eutanasia" con divieto di legalizzazione, "diritti dell'embrione umano" da riconoscere, "famiglia fondata sul matrimonio monogamico tra persone di sesso diverso", unica a meritare un "riconoscimento legale", "libertà di educazione" per le scuole cattoliche) mentre le seconde si traducono in principi direttivi più generici ("tutela sociale dei minori...moderne forme di schiavitù...libertà religiosa...economia che sia al servizio della persona"), fino a parlare della pace, dove le possibilità di mediazione sono le più elevate giacché solo per essa si invita a tener presente quella "complessità delle ragioni in questione" (Ivi, 72-73), che sembra invece tipica dell'intera responsabilità politica contemporanea. Almeno secondo quanto indicava già Jacques Maritain ne "L'Uomo e lo Stato", per il quale un eccesso di proibizioni legislative pur ben fondate in astratto potrebbe mettere in pericolo il bene comune, se si ignorasse concretamente "il gran numero d'individui la cui forza morale non è all'altezza di mettere in atto la tale o la talaltra proibizione" [1981, 202] giacché il pluralismo, la sua difesa e valorizzazione, non è una necessità negativa a cui rassegnarsi, non è legato al relativismo, ma è un dato costitutivo del bene comune: la "proibizione sarebbe in discordia col codice etico di comunità di cittadini la cui lealtà verso la nazione e fedeltà verso il proprio credo morale, per quanto imperfetto possa essere, importano soprattutto al bene comune" [Ivi].

In fondo sembra riproporsi, nonostante il Concilio Vaticano II, quella mentalità denunciata da Maritain a Léon Blum al momento della pura e semplice conferma del Concordato del 1929 nella nuova Italia repubblicana, per la quale la Chiesa cattolica "ha come abitudine quella di difendere fino allo stremo le posizioni giuridiche che occupa, anche se non ignora che esse dovranno un giorno essere abbandonate" [in Margotta Broglio 1989, 887]. Chissà se il nuovo pontificato che obiettivamente non appare lontano non supererà definitivamente questo atteggiamento preoccupato per il pluralismo esterno e interno alla Chiesa.

BIBLIOGRAFIA

AA.VV., 1983 *Tutti i documenti del Concilio*, Uciim-Massimo, Milano-Roma

ACERBI A. , 1979 *La Chiesa nel tempo*, Vita e Pensiero Milano

BERLINGÒ S., 1999 *"Continuo" e "discontinuo" cattolico a proposito della libertà religiosa: dalla Dignitatis Humanae al magistero di papa Wojtyla*, in Studi in onore di Piero Bellini, I, Rubbettino, Soveria Mannelli, pp. 75 ss.

BONHOEFFER D., 1988 *Resistenza e resa. Lettere e scritti dal carcere*, Paoline, Milano

CECCANTI S., 2001 *Una libertà comparata. Libertà religiosa, fondamentalismi, società multietniche*

Congregazione per la dottrina della fede, 2003 a *Nota dottrinale circa alcune questioni riguardanti l'impegno e il comportamento dei cattolici nella vita politica*, 16 gennaio, in http://www.vatican.va/roman_curia/congregationis/cfaith/doc_doc_index_it.htm

2003 b *Considerazioni circa i progetti di riconoscimenti legali delle unioni tra persone omosessuali, 31 luglio*, in http://www.vatican.va/roman_curia/congregationis/cfaith/doc_doc_index_it.htm

DE GASPERI A., 1946 *La luce del pensiero cristiano nella vita politica*, in Aa. Vv., Costituzione e costituente, Icas, Roma, 1946, p. 315.

DIANICH S., 1984 *Teologia del ministero ordinato. Una interpretazione ecclesiologica*, Paoline, Milano
1990 *Riflessioni teologiche sulla democrazia*, in "Il Margine" n. 6, pp. 13 ss.

DI ROVASENDA E., 1979 *Il magistero sociale-politico dei Papi dall'enciclica 'quanta Cura' alla vigilia del Concilio Vaticano II*, in AA.VV., Cattolici e politica in un mondo diviso, Ave, Roma

DRWESKI B., 2001 *L'Eglise dans une Pologne désenchantée*, in "Le courrier des Pays de l'Est", n. 1017, 17 ss.

DUFOUR B., 1995 *La Déclaration Dignitatis Humanae trente ans après sa promulgation. Glissement et renversement*, in "Communio" n. 6, pp. 89 ss.

GALLI C., 1990 *Autorità cattolica e ragione moderna*, in "Biblioteca della Libertà", n. 110, pp. 61 ss.

GONNET D., 1994 *La liberté religieuse à Vatican II. La contribution de John Courtnay Murray*, Editions du Cerf, Paris

HUNTINGTON S., 1995 *La terza ondata. I processi di democratizzazione alla fine del XX secolo*, Il Mulino, Bologna

KASPER W., 1995 *Chiesa e libertà*, in "Il Regno documenti" n. 1, pp. 39, ss.

LANZA A., 1946 *Estensione e limiti del potere costituente*, in Aa. Vv., Costituzione e costituente, Icas, Roma, 1946, p. 221 ss.

LEPORI A., *Due recenti documenti della Congregazione per la dottrina della fede*, in "Appunti di cultura e di politica", n. 5/2003, pp. 28 ss.

LOMBARDI G., 1991 *Persecuzioni, laicità, libertà religiosa. Dall'Editto di Milano alla "Dignitatis Humanae"*, Studium, Roma

MARGIOTTA BROGLIO F., 1989 *Ancora sull'art. 7 della Costituzione: un progetto di Jacques Maritain per l'internazionalizzazione dei patti lateranensi e propositi della Santa Sede per l'ampliamento della Città del Vaticano (1944-1948)*, in Studi in onore di Lorenzo Spinelli, Mucchi, Modena, Vol. I, pp. 851 ss.

MARITAN J., 1981 (ed. originale 1951) *L'uomo e lo Stato*, Vita e Pensiero, Milano

MATAGRIN G., 2000 *Le chêne et la futaie*, Bayard Presse, Paris

OLMI M., 1986 *La Spagna dieci anni dopo*, Edizioni Lavoro, Roma

PARONETTO VALIER M., 1996 *Paolo VI e la Spagna*, pp. 71 ss.

PECES BARBA G., 1995 *Etica, poder y derecho. Reflexiones ante el fin de siglo*, Boletin Oficial del Estado – Centro de estudios polìticos y constitucionales, Madrid
1996 *La democracia en Espana. Experiencias y reflexiones*, Temas de Hoy, Madrid

PEYROT G., 1984 *Chiesa e Stato. I ruoli rispettivi della Chiesa e dello Stato*, in S. Rostagno (a cura di) 1984, pp. 191 ss.

RICCARDI A., 2003

ROJAS C., 2003 *Diez crisis del franquismo*, La Esfera de los libros, Madrid

ROLLET J., 2003 *Religione e politica. Cristianesimo, Islam e democrazia*, Città Aperta, Troina (Enna)

ROSTAGNO S. (a cura di), 1984 *Tra la croce e la svastica. Il messaggio di una Chiesa confessante per il nostro tempo (Barmen 1934-84)*, Claudiana, Torino

SCATENA S., 2000 *La libertà religiosa: momenti di un dibattito dalla vigilia del concilio Vaticano II all'inizio degli anni'90*, in "Cristianesimo nella storia" n. 21, pp. 587 ss.
2001 *Liberté religieuse et modernità politique*, in "Raisons politiques" n. 4, pp. 156 ss.

SCOPPOLA P., 1991 *La Repubblica dei partiti*, Il Mulino, Bologna

SIRI G., 1944 *La Chiesa*, Studium, Roma

VOLPI M., 2000 *Libertà e autorità. La classificazione delle forme di stato e delle forme di governo*, Giappichelli, Torino

WOYCICKI K., 2000 *Polacco=cattolico, ambiguità di uno stereotipo*, in "Limes" n. 1, pp. 92 ss.

ABSTRACT

Le Chiese protestanti sono state le prime nel cammino verso le democrazie pluralistiche, che negli Stati moderni ha portato a riconoscere varie nazionalità, religioni e identità parziali, in una cornice di regole e di valori minimi comuni. La Chiesa cattolica col Concilio Vaticano II ha inserito forti elementi di discontinuità rispetto al magistero precedente seguendo quel medesimo cammino e facendo tesoro delle proprie esperienze positive del periodo precedente, da quella americana a quella delle democrazie cristiane europee, in uno schema teorico che parte da una visione aperta della Rivelazione, passando per un'opzione preferenziale per la democrazia e giungendo ad una valorizzazione positiva della libertà religiosa. In anni recenti l'attuale pontefice ha in più occasioni segnato, con alcuni interventi magisteriali, supportate da interpretazioni "continuiste" del Vaticano II col magistero precedente, e in continuità con la linea dei vescovi polacchi in Concilio, un parziale "revirement" rispetto a quella discontinuità, in un quadro teorico in cui spetterebbe alla gerarchia ecclesiastica far valere i diritti della verità, attraverso una sicura individuazione del diritto naturale da trascrivere nelle legislazioni positive. Una sorta di "democrazia ecclesiasticamente protetta", che è apparsa forte nella prima parte del pontificato, ma che si è rivelata poi inefficace. Ne emerge la possibilità e la necessità di una ripresa delle novità conciliari a partire dalla valorizzazione di un ruolo più attivo della responsabilità del laicato cattolico impegnato in politica.

The Alternatives : Other Institutional and Procedural Tools for Conflict Management

"The Alternatives : Other Institutional & Procedural Tools for Conflict Management"

Liah GREENFELD

Consideration of the American case in the framework of this conference presupposes a) that the United States, being, like Switzerland, a federalist structure, represents, like Switzerland, a federation of ethnic communities; b) that ethnic diversity normally leads to conflict, and therefore must be a constant possibility in a nation such as the United States, composed of numerous ethnic strands; c) that the fact that ethnic conflict rarely surfaces in the United States is, like in Switzerland, attributable to the federalist institutions and procedures. These presuppositions are wrong. The general absence of ethnic conflict in the United States is not a result of skillful conflict management; rather, it reflects the open, fluid, and individualistic nature of American society and its national consciousness which, despite the vociferous "multiculturalism" of the academy, denies ethnic differences cultural significance.

A. Despite the extreme diversity of ethnic origins among Americans, perhaps equaled only by the diversity of origins among Israeli Jews and Australians, ethnic considerations of whatever kind are absolutely foreign to the federalist tradition and institutions of the United States. The nation had been conceived as a federation of self-governing communities of individuals, with no account taken of the ethnic composition of these communities, and federal structure has always remained a mechanism for the protection of the rights of individuals, rather than groups. During the first century of the national history, especially in the original states along the Atlantic coast, it is true, these self-governing communities of individuals developed fierce particularistic loyalties and, for all intents and purposes, became groups to which rights of individuals within them were considered subservient. These particularistic loyalties were at first innocuous and not only coexisted peacefully with, but reinforced the sense of general (or federal) national commitment. But with the acquisition of new territories and the declaration of California a free state after the end of the Mexican War they congealed around the contentious issue of slavery, which was, paradoxically, the issue of the interpretation of American liberty, and undermined the national commitment, putting the existence of the nation itself in grave danger. After the Civil War – by far the greatest conflict in the history of the United States to date, and entirely unconcerned with ethnic differences – the states were no longer admissible objects of ardent civic loyalty which could in any way compete with the loyalty to the national whole, and in general dual loyalties were no longer tolerated. Federalism, more than ever before, became an institutional mechanism for the protection of individual rights.

It so happened that precisely as the Civil War put an end to state particularism, the salience of ethnic differences in the United States vastly increased. The increase in ethnic diversity itself was not the sole reason for that. Ethnic diversity characterized the American society from the 18th century. It did not go entirely unnoticed. Franklin, for instance, lamented it, in "Observations Concerning the … Peopling of Countries" asking rhetorically (and perhaps part in jest):

"Why should the Palatine boors be suffered to swarm into our settlements and, by herding together, establish their language and manners to the exclusion of ours? Why should Pennsylvania, founded by the English, become a colony of *aliens*, who will shortly be so numerous as to Germanize us instead of us anglifying them, and will never adopt our language or customs any more than they can acquire our complexion?" The problem of complexion provoked in this patriot a further consideration in support of uniformity: "The number of purely white people in the world is proportionally very small," he argued. "All Africa is black or tawny; Asia is chiefly tawny; America (exclusive of newcomers), wholly so. And in Europe, the Spaniards, Italians, French, Russians, and Swedes are generally of what we call a swarthy complexion; as are the Germans also, the Saxons only excepted, who, with the English, make the principal body of white people on the face of the earth. I could wish their numbers were increased. And while we are, as I may call it, scouring our planet by clearing America of woods, and so making this side of our globe reflect a brighter light to the eyes of inhabitants in Mars or Venus, why should we, in the sight of superior being, darken its people? Why increase the sons of Africa by planting them in America, where we have so fair an opportunity, by excluding all blacks and tawnies, of increasing the lovely white and red? But perhaps I am partial to the complexion of my country, for such kind of partiality is natural to mankind."

But neither was it a matter that forced itself on – or even presented itself to – public attention. For Americans of English extraction ethnicity was not an issue, for it never became one in England. Since the beginning of the English *national* history Englishmen accepted any person born in England, no matter of what extraction, as a member of the nation and were quite ready to accept as such all those born elsewhere who wished to be considered English and had the interests of England at heart. Defoe's celebration of an immigrant of mixed origins as a "true-born Englishman" was only one of many expressions of this voluntaristic attitude. And, while Americans who hailed from elsewhere were more aware of the essential Englishness of their new country, than were, by and large, English Americans, they saw this Englishness as a national *American* characteristic and appropriated it as part and parcel, in effect the very core, of their American identity. The first American to broach the question what does it mean to be one was J. Hector St. John de Crevecoeur, an immigrant from France, who, in his *Letters from an American Farmer*, while attempting to answer it, guessed at the likely thoughts of a visitor from England: "He must greatly rejoice that he lived to see this fair country discovered and settled; he must necessarily feel a share of national pride…[He must say to himself:] 'This is the work of my countrymen… They brought along with them their national genius, to which they principally owe what liberty they enjoy and what substance they possess.' Here he sees the industry of his native country displayed in a new manner…"

What was new in the post-Civil War period, was therefore not so much the greater degree of ethnic heterogeneity of the immigration, its ethnic composition, in which East- and South-European elements came to predominate over West- and North-European ones, or even its colossal size, but the fact that in the last half of the 19th century the cultural significance of ethnicity (the way it was understood) changed both in the countries from which the immigrants were coming and in the United States.

B. In general, "ethnicity" is nothing more than an umbrella term for ascriptive characteristics, that is characteristics, independent of one's will and acquired by the accident of birth, from the color of one's eyes, the hue of one's skin, the texture of one's hair – or one's physical type more generally – to one's language or the manner of speaking it, or even the language of one's ancestors, one's religion or the religion of one's ancestors, one's or one's ancestors' presumed connection to a certain territory, customs, dietary requirements or habits, and the like. Since some easily visible ascriptive characteristics (such as eye- or hair-color, for instance) differ even in a smallest community, ethnic diversity, as a matter of fact, is a ubiquitous feature of human societies. However, in most of them ethnic differences have had little, if any, significance and no impact on social relations, be they conflictual or consensual, beyond the strictly personal level.

In the past characteristics acquired by birth which were considered significant were those that were believed to be providential, rather than accidental: i.e., belonging or not belonging to a particular legal estate. One carried one's social status, and therefore actual position and role in life, in one's blood – the fact that a certain person was born into a princely family or into a peasant's had nothing accidental in it, for every person was "called" by providence, and so was by his very nature, either a prince or a peasant. These significant ascriptive characteristics were cultural, but most cultural characteristics, such as language and, especially, religion, were not ascriptive, even if acquired at birth, because it was believed that language could be learned, while one's religion, whatever was the religion of one's ancestors, was fundamentally a matter of personal responsibility. It is true, that the social ascendancy and less then orthodox Christian practices of the recently and forcibly converted Jewish population in the Spain of their most Catholic majesties of Castille and Aragon, barely free from the Moslem rule, caused resentment among the older Christian nobility and led to the talk of "limpieza de sangre" as a criterion of the sincerity of faith. But this was an exception, for in Christian Europe religion – the sphere of the soul – was least of all a function of blood and could not be transmitted through bodily fluids. It is only our, modern and materialistic, age that came to see it as such, as it did other cultural attributes, such as language. And it was this age which first thought of "ethnicity" as a culturally significant category – the category for cultural characteristics acquired by birth – and that turned ethnic diversity (that is, diversity of ascriptive characteristics) into a social problem and a source of political conflict.

Like modernity in general, this changed attitude to ethnicity was a product of nationalism. Nationalism is the cognitive framework, or broad worldview, which emerged in early 16th century England and became the cultural foundation of modern society, economy, and politics. At its core lies the image of reality whose significant unit is the "nation" – that is a mass of population, whether a few thousand or several billion strong, which is regarded as sovereign and as a community of equals. It logically follows from the idea of an earthly population (rather than transcendental forces and their divinely appointed representatives) as the bearer of sovereignty that this image is essentially secular: it is focused on this world and represents it as ultimately meaningful. The philosophical materialism underpinning modern attitudes in virtually every sphere of social existence, in turn, logically follows from this endowment of the mundane with ultimate meaning. The concept of the "nation" presented above allows for a number of interpretations of popular sovereignty and equality, depending on whether the nation is defined in composite terms (namely, as an association of individuals) or in unitary terms (as a collective individual) and whether membership is believed to be in principle voluntary or innate. In the latter case, nationality itself is perceived as an ascriptive characteristic, acquired by birth, like physical type or sex, and transmitted by blood, i. e. genetically; in other words, nationality is viewed as ethnicity and we are faced with ethnic nationalism. Such perception, on the one hand, obscures the cultural and historical, thus *constructed*, nature of nations and national membership, while, on the other hand, it dramatically increases the cultural significance of ethnicity, and therefore its importance as a social and political force. It is as an element of *ethnic nationalism* that ethnicity becomes a source of identity and the foundation on which people base their attitudes to and relations with others. Before there was nationalism these attitudes and relations were based on one's and others' cultural attributes, for which one was considered to be personally responsible, either as a result of one's choice (as in the case of religion and language) or as a result of divine calling which it was one's duty to heed (as in the case of one's social position). In the framework of ethnic nationalism, one's social relations and attitudes became the function of pure – biological – accident.

Because ethnic identity (i.e. an identity based on ascriptive, accidental characteristics, acquired by birth) elevates purely biological features, such as physical type, to the level of cultural attributes and reduces cultural attributes, such as language and religion, to the level of purely biological features, distinctions between cultural identity groups necessarily turn into essential differences, similar to differences between people with incompatible blood types or even those between different biological species. They establish between such groups relations of insurmountable foreignness. The fact that experience of intermarriage and the production of robust progeny of mixed ethnicity (*mixed bloods* – what an eloquent expression of the cultural significance of biology!) systematically contradicts the assumption of such foreignness does little to undermine it, because, as is well known, even most intolerant people are remarkably tolerant of contradictions. With the social situation defined in this manner, consensus easily breaks along ethnic lines, competition over scarce resources (status, wealth, and political power) is likely to be seen in terms of ethnic rivalry, and coexistence of several ethnic groups, or ethnic diversity, as a result, comes to be perceived as a natural ground for conflict, always ready to erupt and contained only thanks to wise conflict management.

The political importance of ethnicity depends not on the measure of ethnic diversity within a community, but on the significance assigned by the culture to ethnic differences. In nationalisms which regard membership as in principle voluntary ethnicity plays little role. Israel, whose Jewish population is one of the most ethnically diverse communities in the world is a case in point. (Its characterization as both Jewish and extremely diverse should surprise no one: after all it surprises no one that almost all of the extreme ethnic diversity in the United States is concentrated within the population which is Christian by religious origin.) Israel is an open society. The fact that nationality in it is (for historical reasons) identified with religion reinforces its openness, for a religion accepting converts throws the gates of the political community open to people of any origin. The Law of Return brought together in one very small society people of every possible complexion, from pale blue-eyed blonds of Northern Europe to ebony-colored Ethiopians, of physical types as varied as in the United States, of languages as numerous and cultural traditions (namely, family customs and rituals, cuisines, ideas on what constitutes the good life, etc.) as diverse, and of different religious orientations. The majority of Israeli population are atheists, i.e., they are not Jews, if Judaism is defined as a religion. But they are a part of the Jewish community, according to the religious law, because they are descendents of a line of Jewish women. Many of them, especially since the collapse of the Soviet Union, are Christians, i. e., obviously not Jews, according to the religious law, and still are a part of the Jewish community, because the secular Law of Return applies to every person with at least one Jewish grandparent of whatever sex. The newcomers may keep apart or be kept apart by the circumstances, but their children intermix in the army, if not before, intermarry at a very high rate, and in the second generation form one common ethnicity of native-born Israelis or Sabras, different from the ethnicities of their immigrant parents. Conflicts in the Israeli society, which may be perceived as ethnic because, for instance, parties to them sport different skin color or practice different marriage customs, are in fact conflicts between different waves of immigration, the old-comers defending their hard-earned privileges, the new-comers fighting for theirs, which have nothing to do with the nature of anyone's ethnicity. Israel is a multiethnic society, which makes no fuss over its "multiculturalism." It is different in the United States.

English nationalism, from which American nationalism developed, defined membership in the nation in strictly voluntary, i.e., civic, terms. But already one of the two nationalisms that developed on the continent in the course of the 18th century, the Russian, was an ethnic nationalism. The only ethnic nation which was a source of a sizeable immigration to the United States before the Civil War, however, was Germany, and German immigrants, indeed, had a perceptibly harder time adjusting to their new society than others, for instance, the French; German immigrants were made unassimilable by their national identity; they tended to feel foreign, and many of them, after not very eagerly trying to blend in, decided that they don't like America, after all, reasserted their Germanity, and returned home. Many others remained, but remained German in America, keeping all the cultural baggage they believed they carried in their blood and transmitting it to their children – among the pre-Civil War immigrants theirs was a singular case.

After 1848, however, nationalism spread throughout Europe like wildfire, and most of post-1848 nationalisms were ethnic. Therefore, the great majority of people arriving in the United States in the last quarter of the 19th century were already members of nations whose cultural identity was believed to be innate (if not by themselves – for in their mass the immigrants were too busy to engage in deep introspection – then by the intellectuals among them). At the very same time American intellectuals, usually White Anglo-Saxon Protestants, in large numbers, began traveling to Germany for their university studies, making German scholarship, especially in history, philosophy, and what would soon be called "social sciences" the absolute model for the respective American disciplines. The ideas which prevailed in Germany of the day were those of ethnic nationalism elevated to the status of science (whether the history of Treitschke, the *Nationaloekonomie* deriving from the views of List, or the social philosophy of *Kathedersozialisten*). As a result, American academics, incongruously, imagined social reality (namely, politics, economic processes, social relations) in the quasi-biological terms of ethnic nationalism and nationality in terms of ethnicity. The fact that President Wilson, the author of the idea of "national self-determination," was among the first political scientists in the United States demonstrates how profound the implications of the German formation of American professors were.

The coincidence of these two developments: the mass immigration from ethnic nations and the derivation of American social science thinking from ethnic nationalism rendered the American society, on the whole, accepting of the residual, ethnic, loyalty to their old world origins among its newer citizens, which coexisted with the national loyalty to the United States, and made hyphenated, ethnic Americans a permanent feature of the national scene. But this very tolerance in the context of the individualistic and voluntary American nationalism simultaneously trivialized ethnicity to such an extent as to deprive it of all of its potential influence on social and political relations. In the United States ethnic diversity is both glorified and deprived of cultural significance.

American multiculturalism, paradoxically, is a proof of absolute deculturalization of ethnicity in the United States, its reduction to purely biological, accidental, and ascriptive attributes, for which the individual bears no responsibility whatsoever and which, therefore, according to the stringently individualistic American ethic, cannot be judged. The paradigmatic example of American multiculturalism is the set of six basic "Crayola" crayons for young children, which is called "Multicultural Crayons." Culture here is identified with color, of one's skin, as the drawing on the box suggests, that is, with a physical, genetically transmitted, and morally indifferent characteristic. Indeed, race as marked by skin color is the only element in the indigenous American experience to which the great majority of Americans can meaningfully apply the term "ethnicity." As a result, the concept, for which "ethnic culture" or simply "culture" are conventional substitutes, is generally understood as race. But the word "race" is banned (?) from the polite discourse as both unscientific (physical characteristics, we have learned, tell us nothing about people's moral and intellectual qualities, which are the only ones that matter, and therefore, should not be focused on) and suggestive of improper attitudes. Therefore, when Americans want to say "race," they say "(ethnic) culture." A society in which one meets people of several races becomes a "multicultural," ethnically diverse society.

This well-meaning conceptual confusion on the popular level is perpetuated by the conceptual confusion reigning among American social scientists, who hold on to the notions brought home by the Germany-returned intellectuals of the turn of the twentieth century, treat "culture" as a residual category for anything not sufficiently understood, and, generally, abstain from defining their terms. In 1924, in Culture and Democracy in the United States, Horace Kallen wrote: "Behind [the individual] in time and tremendously in him in quality are his ancestors; around him in space are his relatives and kin, carrying in common with him the inherited organic set from a remoter common ancestry. In all these he lives and moves and has his being. They constitute his, literally, natio, the inwardness of his nativity." America, he said, was a "nation of nationalities," a union less of states, than, in the words of Michael Walzer's 1990 commentary, "of ethnic, racial, and religious groups." Kallen's "organic sets," explains Walzer, are "cultural, not biological." But how can we equate ethnic, racial, and religious groups, unless they have some fundamental principle in common? And, since race is fundamentally physical and genetic, we must assume that it is similar physical or biological quality which makes ethnicity and, especially, religion genetically transmitted too, which allows us to place it in the same category with race. Indeed, it is hard to imagine how else but genetically would one contain one's ancestors in oneself, "carrying in common [with relatives and kin] the inherited organic set from a remoter common ancestry." It is this sort of thinking which underlies the multicultural educational policies in the United States, which encourage teachers to devise assignments requiring students of an elite middle school in the vicinity of Harvard University to "describe the values of their people." The youngsters, returning home with heavy hearts, know only too well that describing the values of liberal democracy won't do the trick, for it is presumed that the American people is not a natural community whose members must all be blood related (for isn't that the case in nations such as Germany or France, where everyone is inherently German or French, religions such as Judaism or Islam, where everyone is inherently Jewish or Muslim, and continents such as Africa, where everyone is black?) and, therefore, not a real people. Instead, they have to undertake an ethnographic research into the culinary customs of the country, or more likely one of the countries, from which their ancestors happened to immigrate, and vaunt, with as much enthusiasm as they can muster, the virtues of kielbasa or haggis.

Teenagers, as most parents would immediately recognize, tend towards culinary conformism, in the United States generally preferring all-American hamburgers to ethnic dishes, however delectable; thus, perhaps, "multiculturalism" is a greater burden for them than for other age groups. In general, however, it is a very light fare and easy to stomach. For in America, in fact, hard as it may be to believe, culinary diversity lies at the very heart of ethnic diversity, constituting the essence of ethnic culture. Ethnically, Americans are all followers of Feuerbach: they are what they eat. It all boils down to chicken soup, minestrone, and avgolemono. It is quite remarkable how much is invested in "the bread alone," so to speak. It is virtually impossible today to free oneself from hyphenation; it is not only schoolchildren who cannot identify as "Americans" tout court: the United States Census Bureau insists on everyone acknowledging an ethnicity. Its officials still (or, maybe, again) agree with Kallen that "whatever else [an American] changes, he cannot change his grandfather." Perhaps not, says Walzer, disagreeing, "but he can … reject [the grandfather's] customs and convictions." In fact, nothing less is required, and such rejection of customs and convictions – i.e. of cultural traditions – implies much more than the adoption "of a new 'life-style'."

To become an American one has to forswear (?) allegiance to all other sovereigns but the people of the United States and "to commit [oneself] to the political ideology, centered on the abstract ideals of liberty, equality, and republicanism." (Pledge?) This alone is enough to undermine "multiculturalism." For one cannot say that while sharing these ideals, Americans in their daily lives are nevertheless guided by traditions which disregard them and hold other values as supreme. It simply would not do to claim that liberty, equality, and republicanism apply only in politics, while in other spheres of life other ideals hold sway, to characterize, in other words, "the oneness" of Americans, what they have in common, as political, and their "manyness," what makes for their diversity, as cultural. We know very well that values of liberty and equality form the foundation of the American family, of the relations between the sexes, of the relations between parents and children, of the economic process, of the ever simmering social conflicts and of their resolutions, of the developments on American campuses and more generally and much more profoundly of the life of the mind in America. Only a complete misunderstanding of the nature of human reality – namely, of the fact that all of it is essentially cultural, that politics, as well as economies and social relations, are culturally constructed, and that one's identity is one's culture – political, economic, social – in a microcosm – only a complete misunderstanding of these fundamentals can lead one to the conclusion that "these abstract ideals [liberty, equality, and republicanism] made for politics separated not only from religion but from culture itself, or, better, from all the particular forms in which religious and national culture was, and is, expressed."

Do the sovereigns, allegiances to whom one must forswear, committing oneself to the ideals of liberty, equality, and republicanism, include His Holiness the Vicar of Christ in Rome? Certainly they do. That's why American Catholics (not Catholic-Americans, by the way) are up in arms against their Church, whose hierarchy, supported by the Pope, is unwilling to recognize sexual harassment – a concept which can be understood only in the context of the abstract ideals of liberty, equality, and republicanism – as a cardinal sin. Do these rejected sovereigns include the Lord God himself? Of course, they do. American Protestants protest only as Americans, against the injustices of the secular, political world, as Protestants they live on terms of the most intimate friendship with their Catholic and Jewish fellow-nationals, all three communities simply could not be more tolerant towards each others' beliefs, as they are also towards wicca, voodoo, and other less common forms of so-called "spiritualism." Who are they to tell others which God to worship and which Truth to believe: in accordance with the only truths Americans believe to be self-evident, all gods are created equal. Religion is understood as a style of life, a social club in which one chooses (for reasons of convenience more than anything else) to spend one's leisure, and in the end all that distinguishes a good American of one faith from a good American of another is when and what one prepares for one's holiday meals.

Unintentionally and effortlessly – in fact despite the intention and effort to achieve the contrary – religion is stripped of all its moral and vital significance. Its influence is reduced to deciding when to take a day off work and which groceries to buy. And religion is, doubtlessly, the most important of the cultural traditions affecting one's identity – if it affects one's identity – and the hardest to reject. Language, the other main ingredient of "ethnic culture" offers no resistance at all. How many Italian-Americans speak Italian? How many Polish-Americans know any Polish? How many of them in their lifetimes think of learning these ancestral tongues? The answer is, very few. In this context, too, it is chiefly the diet that establishes one's ethnic affiliation. American "multiculturalism" thus is very much like Ford's reaction to the suggestion to produce Model T in various colors: "You can have any color, so long as it is black." Similarly, in regard to the cultural – ethnic – diversity in the United States, the unspoken rule is: "You can uphold any values so long as they are American, practice any religion, so long as it is American, and speak any language, so long as it is American." You can have any ethnicity, in short, so long as it is American. And apart from that, you can eat whatever you like.

The by and large peaceful coexistence of ethnic, i.e., cultural, groups in the United States, therefore, is not an achievement of skillful conflict management, but a reflection of the plain fact that this huge and open society on the deep level, behind its surface of diversity, represents one cultural community, that, despite its population's looks which suggest great heterogeneity, it is based on a fundamental consensus regarding all the important existential questions. The only rift in the American society which could ever be described as ethnic, because it arose of differences acquired by birth and, though obviously culturally interpreted, not culturally constructed, was in fact based on race. Indeed, for a long period, perhaps lasting throughout the 19th century, in the relations between the white and the black populations, in particular, there was a presupposition of that essential, insurmountable foreignness, which is characteristic of our attitude to other species of life and of the relations between ethnic communities and nations in the framework of ethnic nationalism. This presupposition of foreignness reflected the suspicion (which itself very soon came under suspicion, leading to agonizing re-examination and self-searching among the white elite, to the abolitionist movement, and, finally, to the decisive excoriation of all references to race from the collective imagination of – white – Americans) that the descendents of African slaves were not quite those men who were created equal, that they were in actual fact a different species of being. After all, they differed so markedly, arriving on the slave ships naked and terrified, both in physical appearance and behavior from the mankind that white Americans knew either in the old world (in Europe and Asia) or in the new one (among American Indians). So Jefferson concluded that they did not have the full set of faculties that made one human – that is, were intellectually inferior; and for statistical purposes one black man was counted as ¾ of a white man. It should be remembered that precisely the same reasoning was applied to white women: they, too, were physically different from men and, on the whole, behaved differently. Their different behavior was believed to be a function of their different bodies, reflected in and mediated by the qualities of their minds. A woman, being a different sort of animal, could not be expected to be as reasonable, as intelligent as a man, and therefore could not be trusted to decide for oneself, to participate in the political process, and had to be taken care of, like a slave or a child. In both cases, that of black slaves and that of women, ascriptive biological characteristics for which the individual bore no responsibility whatsoever were made the sole basis of the individual's social position and ultimate destiny. But in neither case we are dealing with the phenomena of ethnicity and ethnic identity, and in neither case the relations between thus defined social categories were regulated by federal mechanisms.

Race was banished from the worldview of white Americans; only black people can now mention it and use it as an explanatory concept with impunity. Similarly, no man goes unpunished if he suggests or just raises a question in regard to women's intellectual faculties and their ability to do everything men do at least as well. At the same time, it is quite acceptable for women to brag that anything men can do they can do better and in general undermine the strong sex with their socially validated contempt and derision. American society is guilt-ridden for ever doubting the central tenet of its secular faith: that all human beings are created equal, and allowing the experience of mere physical differences to mislead it into conceiving socially unequal categories. For this reason, purely physical characteristics are considered today the only legitimate ground for special privileges, reverse discrimination proving the most symbolically effective way, however irrational, to expiate the national sin. Policies of affirmative action and equal opportunity, which make sure that a person with an admixture of black or American Indian genetic material has better chance to get accepted into a college or hired than a person of equal merit without such admixture, a woman has a better chance than a man with similar qualifications, may appear as a device for conflict management, but they play no such role in fact. There is no possibility of restitution for those who were hurt by discrimination in the past: it is not the same individuals, and not even their direct descendents, who profit from the reverse discrimination in the present; the individuals who suffer from the reverse discrimination are not the ones, and not the direct descendents, who have inflicted the hurt – no justice is served by making them suffer. It would be natural for these new victims to become disaffected, bitter, and turn against the physically marked groups to whose benefit ostensibly their personal welfare is sacrificed or against the society demanding such sacrifice as a whole. These policies, then, far from managing conflict, may be a source of it. But the symbolic logic behind them, the beautiful symmetry in the fact that those who benefit today are in some – physical – way like those who were discriminated against in the past and those who are being discriminated against in the present are like those who were responsible for the past discrimination, appeals to those who are not involved in the process directly, it satisfies the by-standers' desire for consistency, making it seem that the society which sinned was brought a full circle to the very source of its goodness, that it has atoned for its sin and is made good again.

There are no conflicts between women as a group and men as a group for the obvious reasons that the sexes do not constitute groups, but are merely abstract categories. Nevertheless the "women's card" is often used in political competition and has been known to win hearts, of men as well as women. A skillful use of this card is more likely to kindle a conflict, rather than manage it, but, again, such ideologically fanned conflict is unlikely to be one between people distinguished by the nature of their bodies. In contrast, break-down lines in spontaneous conflicts often coincide with racial distinctions, both because of the coincidence of physical characteristics, such as skin color, etc., with waves of recent immigrants, who usually find themselves on one side in these conflicts, and because of the persisting phenomenon of black underclass, which usually finds itself on the other side. The appeal to ethnic, ascriptive identity in such cases has the effect of making the existing rifts more profound, in fact conceptualizing, rationalizing, and therefore institutionalizing them.

Most conflicts in the United States, whether or not they are framed in ethnic terms, result from the systemic pressures of modernity, so heavy in this most open of nations, in particular the pressure of the demand for equality, which on the one side produces ambition and envy (the desire to become equal to the best and the desire to defend oneself from a sense of inferiority, respectively) and on the other threatened superiority (the fear of becoming equal to those socially, economically, politically below oneself, to be downwardly mobile). While constant, these conflicts are generally kept low-grade because social mobility which keeps families continuously rotating among social positions precludes the formation of the core of committed activists and of the pool of ever available recruits. It is the natural dynamics of American society, an expression of the profound individualism and voluntarism of its national consciousness, which manage conflict in the United States, not specially designed institutions and procedures. One cannot reproduce a culture by decree, which makes this great nation not a very realistic model for such conflict-torn regions such as the Middle East. But one can use the lessons its experience teaches to understand what ethnicity is and what it is not and which conditions one can – or cannot – expect ethnic coexistence, even in a federal framework.

A Confederal Solution to a Problem

The Case of Serbia and Montenegro

Dragoljub POPOVIĆ

1. SHAPES OF A PROBLEM

Montenegro and Serbia emerged as modern states in the 19th century. It was a result of a struggle for independence against the Turkish Empire. Throughout the 19th century there had been no common frontier of the two countries, for some parts of territory dominated by the Turks remained between them as long as in 1912.

Although the two countries had achieved home rule a long time before that date, it was in 1878 at the Congress of Berlin that their independence was recognized.

Both Montenegro and Serbia were considered in the 19th century to be Serbian states. Elements of homogeneity were the Serbian language, spoken in both countries, but also the same Orthodox church, as well as the tradition in common, dating back to the Middle Age, and above all the national feelings, existing in those times.

However, the two societies were somewhat different, owing mostly to the fact that a sort of clan and tribal organization persisted for a long time in Montenegro. This was partly the case because of geographical conditions, which were reflected in the economic life.

The agriculture was more developed in Serbia, while Montenegro had to stick to sheep and goats breeding in mountain areas. Further on, industry made easer its first steps in Serbia than in Montenegro. This led to an almost constant emigration from Montenegro, for the sake of economic reasons. In most cases families immigrated to Serbia, where some parts of the country still to this day keep visible traces of the immigration process.[1]

Serbia has always been a larger, and Montenegro a smaller country. For the sake of illustration, one could put forward figures concerning territory in 1878. Montenegro had some 10.000 km^2, and Serbia 48.000.[2] Figures on population showed that Montenegro had approximately ten times less inhabitants than Serbia.

In spite of the elements of homogeneity the development of the two countries as independent states for a rather long time led to some elements of diversity. Both states developed as monarchies, with indigenous dynasties on their thrones. The two dynasties entered into familial relations, by way of marriage, but nonetheless they represented a splitting element.

Political parties in Montenegro developed as two camps. Towards the end of World War I they were named the white, and the green. Those camps were to some extent connected with clans, because whole clans and regions of the country belonged to one or another. At the same time this was intermingled with an attitude towards the ruling dynasty of the country. The camp of the green was mostly sympathetic to the Montenegrin dynasty of the Petrović. On the other hand, at the decisive moment of unification with Serbia and other Yugoslav territories in 1918

---

1 For example in the southwest, near the city of Užice, where a district used to be called Montenegrin, for a long time, until the second half of the 20th century. The trace is also visible in the name of the small city of Kosjerić, in Western Serbia, reminding of the Montenegrin clan of the Kosijer. It spreads to Negotin Krajina in Eastern Serbia, the region close to the Romanian border, where families to this day remember the fact that their ancestors had once upon a time come from Montenegro. The same sort of memory exists in the south, near the city of Prokuplje.

2 Today the figures are different. Montenegro has 13 800 km^2, and Serbia 88 300. For Serbia this figure includes the province of Kosovo and Metohija, being under an international protection, and having a surfice of 10 900 km^2.

the white camp opted for the Serbian dynasty of Karadjordjević.[3] The peculiarity of the situation then was that the pretenders to the throne were a father in law and a son in law, for the king of Serbia had married a daughter of the king of Montenegro. The king of Montenegro, who passed over in exile in the twenties of the last century, was at the same time a poet, praising and heralding the all-Serbian solidarity.[4]

The Yugoslav monarchy failed to create a melting pot for different groups and ethnies. The communists, opposing the monarchy, as well as the whole social system, developed a doctrine according to which the Serbs were stigmatized as an ethnie oppressing others in Yugoslavia. The effort of communists aimed at supporting all other ethnies, groups and identities in order to oppose what they labeled as Serbian hegemony. Due to such a political course they were also supporting elements of Montenegrin separate identity.

During World War II a civil war between the legitimists and revolutionary communists took place all over Yugoslavia. It was extremely severe in Montenegro and provoked an enormous bloodshed. The victorious communists could after the war apply their own patterns of revolutionary government. They favoured the elements of diversity between Montenegrins and Serbs and from the very beginning of their regime they recognized Montenegrins as a nation, together with Slovenes, Croats, Macedonians and Serbs.[5]

---

3 On the two political camps and their opinions on unification of Yugoslavia, cf. in Serbian language PAVLOVIĆ M., *Jugoslovenska država i pravo 1914-1941*, Kragujevac 2000, pp. 72-73.

4 He wrote a poem on liberating the cradle of Serbdom, Kosovo, which remained under the Turkish rule until 1912, considering it the main goal of the Serbian nation. Its title is Onamo namo, after its beginning verse: Onamo namo, za brda ona… (There, there over the mountains…). Still to this day the poem is considered by many to be the national anthem of Montenegro. Following the manner of romanticism the king-poet says in the last verse, speaking of Kosovo: There shall I find my soul's rest, when Serb will no more be a slave.

5 Bosnian Muslims, or as they for the most part call themselves today, Boshniyaks, were recognized later; cf. my article published under the title *Le fédéralisme de l'ancienne Yougoslavie revisité. Qu'est-ce qui n'a pas fonctionné?*, in : Rev. Int. Pol. Comp. vol 10, N°1, 2003, p. 44.

The idea that stood behind the communist settlement, as far as ethnies and their relations in ex-Yugoslavia were concerned, was the one of enabling the enforcement of a revolutionary dictatorship. The more ethnies and groups confronted to each other, the easier the life of those holding power. One should bear in mind the fact that the whole government was illegitimate and a product of a revolutionary violence.

The communists introduced a system one could label as a moderate and controlled separate nationalism in Montenegro. The feelings of the people remained mixed and to some instant vague. There has always been some percentage of the autochthonous population in Montenegro who declared themselves as Serbs. Their number was decreasing and went down to 9% in the census of 1981. However, the identity of many in Montenegro remained twofold. Many people felt as Montenegrins in the first line, but to some extent as Serbs as well, or even as Yugoslavs.

The controlled separate nationalism in Montenegro used to be mild and mostly folkloric in character. It has never been aggressive. Yet it seemed to be crucial that the republic of Montenegro was considered to be a Montenegrin nation-state in the ex-Yugoslav sense of the term.[6]

At that stage of development came the end of socialist Yugoslavia and the installation of the Milošević regime in Serbia. The purpose of the Milošević government was primarily to match the rising nationalisms in Slovenia and Croatia. However, during the twilight of their regime the communists could not overcome their own scope of mind. In Serbia they were dreaming of a revival of the USSR.[7] On the other hand, both in Serbia and Croatia the nationalist regimes, succeeding communism,

---

6 The situation resembled to the one of Macedonia in those days. The Macedonians have always been tolerant towards minorities, but at the same time jealous to preserve their Macedonian nation-state in the form of a communist republic. The proclamation of independence brought problems to the agenda. The ethnic Albanians in Macedonia now contest the very foundations and the character of the state, in spite of Macedonian tolerance.

7 The case of Mihailo Marković, the vice president of Milošević's party is quite illustrative in this respect. Although a former communist dissident, and in spite of being considered to some extent liberal, at least in a communist sense of the word, he welcomed the government of the coup d'état in Moscow when the government of Gorbachev had been renversed.

were aiming at preserving a dominant party system. The difference consisted of introducing a mixture of nationalism and communism in Serbia, while the Tudjman regime in Croatia used to be purely nationalist in character.

The nationalism in Serbia was combined with remnants of communst ideas. Little by little, it somehow emerged into a greater Serbian nationalism, aiming to put all ethnic Serbs, who lived all over Yugoslavia, under one government.

The political development in Montenegro was rather complex at that time. Serbian sentiments, that had previously been neglected, or even suppressed in communist Yugoslavia, came to a daylight. A new generation of communist rulers in Montenegro came to power enjoying Milošević's support. They were following him, both politically and in matters of ethnicity. Milošević himself has origins in Montenegro, in the northeast of the country, where the white camp is prevailing, in the region of the Vasojević tribe.[8]

The separate nationalism of Montenegrins had to start competing with the Serbian nationalism. Montenegro was the only republic to remain in a federation with Serbia and that fact was based on two main factors. One was the task of the rulers, the so called young lions of Montenegro, coming out of the communist nomenclatura and supported by Milošević, to preserve power. The second factor was more profound. It resided in the sentiments of the people, who felt inclined to share the same destiny with Serbia and the Serbs.

Further development was connected with political processes. A split in the ruling party of Montenegro occured. The party was called the Democratic Party of Socialists, as ex-communists rebaptised themselves. This led to a split of one political camp with Milošević. As that camp managed to remain in power, its members started taking more and more

8 It is worth noting that Slobodan Milošević and his brother, in spite of the fact that they descend from the same parents, belong to two different ethnies. As it was important in the communist nomenclatura to declare ethnicity, Slobodan Milošević declared himself as a Serb, while his brother, Borislav, was and probably still is, a Montenegrin.

separatist stand. It should be said that the forrunners of such a policy did not insist too much on the Montenegrin ethnic nationalism, because they had to calculate a support of the minorities. Still the idea was there – proclaiming independence and consequently the nation-state of Montenegro.

This led to a sort of answer of the sentiments resisting separatism, that defined themselves as Serbian. The outcome of the 2003 census is therefore quite significant in this respect. The Serbian population in Montenegro now amounts to 30%. This is not a result of immigration or any similar process. On the contrary, the analysts speak of what they named ethnic transfer. As the situation is today, there are 40% of Montenegrins in the ethnic sense of the word, 30% Serbs, and 30% others in Montenegro. That is the shape of the problem currently existing.

2. TECHNIQUES OF APPROACH

If we were to ask ourselves what techniques were used to approach the problem, that has just been exposed, three of those come to our mind. Those are dictatorship, nationalism and a sophisticated international intervention. The last of the three has not been mentioned so far. Therefore, let us examine the other two.

Dictatorship as a technique of approach to the problem has been used by the communists during their regime. It was a totalitarian system designed to sacrify the liberty for the sake of a proclaimed equality and an ideal of a pure communism in future.[9] The communist dictatorship in Yugoslavia used to be fully characterized by the main features of such a political regime. The political power was monopolized by the leadership of the ruling Communist party, the opposition and pluralism were

---

9 Among the scholars who insist on sacrificing the liberty in a communist dictatorship cf. COHENDET M.A., *Droit constitutionnel*, Paris 2002, pp. 106-107. Others are inclined to put a stress on the totalitarian character of such a regime and its revolutionary violence ; cf. TURPIN D., *Droit constitutionnel*, Paris 2003, pp. 214-215.

not admitted, nor was there the rule of law, and the due process of law.[10]

The communists of Yugoslavia have constantly been trying to legitimize their regime by way of proclaiming they achieved the final settlement and soothing of ethnic tensions the country suffered of. Stimulating a mild version of the separate Montenegrin nationalism was a part of that image.[11] It was not mild only for the sake of the attitude towards others in Yugoslavia, but also because of its basic Yugoslav roots. It was separate, but never separatist.[12]

Dictatorship as a technique of approach to the problem used to be applied for decades. It only put the problem under the carpet, for dictatorships are never able to deal profoundly with social problems and thoroughly solve them. At the same time the dictatorship technique could not quite get rid of nationalism, at least in its specific and milder form.

On the other hand, nationalism as a technique, for the sake of historical circumstances, has never been fully applied as an aproach to the problem, representing the subject of this little study. Creating a Serbian state in which most of the Serbs would live under the same government has always led to a creation of a multiethnic state, because the Serbs, as well as the Montenegrins, live for the most part together with other ethnic groups. That is why the Serbian nationalism has usually had a cer-

---

10 At this point I fully agree with R.O. SCHULTZE; cf. his article *Diktatur* in : D. Nohlen (Hrsg.), Kleines Lexikon der Politik, München 2001, pp. 65-66.

11 What I call separate in this context should be properly understood. It is comparable to the notion of *inklusiver Nationalismus*, used by Gisela RIESCHER in her article *Nationalismus*, in : D. Nohlen (Hrsg.) Kleines Lexikon der Politik, München 2001, p. 314. In the old Yugoslav context it represented a cultivation of sentiments of belonging to a certain group, mostly ethnic in character, recognized by the regime, which made an individual feel separate from other such groups, but still integrated into the communist network, because of the recognition of such a group.

12 At this point there is again a parallel with the Macedonian nationalism, which also was separate, but not separatist in the times of Yugoslavia. This applies to Boshnyaks as well. Their separatist movement emerged in times of crisis and had a twofold shaping. Firstly it aimed at the separation of the whole of Bosnia and Herzegovina from Yugoslavia. Secondly, it showed tendencies to a creation of an exclusively Muslim state on some parts of the territory of Bosnia and Herzegovina.

tain feature of what one might call yugoslavism. In other words, the Serbian unity was a road leading to Yugoslavia.

It is interesting to note at this stage that the situation of Croats, the second largest ethnic group in Yugoslavia, used to be similar, but not exactly the same. The Croats also live together with other groups, but their tendency was only partly Yugoslav. It is probably because of different historical experiences. The Croats had once upon a time lived under one sovereign. It was in the monarchy of the house of Habsburg. Therefore, they had a feeling Yugoslavia was not their only option, as it was in the case of Serbs.

Here it is interesting to pose a question on the attitude of Boshnyaks and Slovenes. The former had at first an ideal of a revival of Turkey in the form of Empire and Caliphate, as it existed until 1919. In the course of time they had to face the reality and remnants of such dreams ceased to be visible. The latter on the other hand, had a feeling comparable to the one of Croats, but to an even stronger degree.[13]

Nationalism came to the agenda towards the end of the communist regime, when the communists, monopolizing political power, started seeking for a new foundation of legitimacy of their rule. Although it seemed to be replacing it, the nationalism was indeed only the last stage of communism.[14] At that stage the communists were trying to convince people they were to create all over ex-Yugoslavia nation-states of all previously recognized nations in the Yugoslav communist sense of the word.[15]

---

13 For the attitude of Slovenes toward other ethnic groups in Yugoslavia cf. VODOPIVEC P., *Le miroir brisé : les Serbes, les Croates et les Musulmans vus par les Slovènes, hier et aujourd'hui*, in : M.E. Ducreux et A. Marès (eds.) Enjeux de l'histoire en Europe centrale, Paris - Budapest -Torino 2002, pp. 77-87.

14 I agree with Lidija Basta-Fleiner in this respect; cf. FLEINER Th. and BASTA-FLEINER L.R., *Federalism, Federal States and decentralization*, in : L.R. Basta-Fleiner and Th. Fleiner (eds.), Federalism and Multiethnic States – the Case of Switzerland, Bâle - Genève - Munich 2001, p. 14. See another article of L. BASTA quoted in the footnote 25 on that page.

15 This time it was *exklusiver Nationalismus*, to use an expression of Gisela Riescher, again. Cf. G. RIESCHER, *op. cit.* eodem loco. The feature this scholar insists on was

Nationalism, as implemented by the communists, suffered from some confusion if we consider the case of Serbia and Montenegro. The communists of Milošević have never been ready to put forward a clear formula of what their opinion on Serb-Montenegrin relations really was.[16] As a matter of fact the national-socialist regime of Serbia was fairly pursuing the ideas of a mild and separate Montenegrin nationalism. This was possible because of the twofold feelings of the Montenegrins. They simply started feeling a bit more Serbian than before. The federation persisted, although with two federal units only. At the beginning the ideas were not pushed to extremes.

Achieving extremes took place later, when the rulers of Montenegro and Serbia split. Djukanović opposed the policy of the Milošević regime and started seeking support in the West. Milošević for his part, continued communist dreams of a revival of a rival power in the East, thus sliding into isolation. The latter could not pose a question on Serbian feelings, because he was loosing support in Montenegro. The former, on the other hand, accentuated Montenegrin sentiments in order to promote his new policy of a sovereign Montenegrin state.

It is curious to note that the change of regime in Serbia in the year 2000 did not put an end to the independentist policy in Montenegro. The question was open, and as it could have provoked trouble on a broader scale, the international community intervened in order to find a solution acceptable to both sides. Montenegro, as well as Serbia, had declared a wish to approach the European integration process, and one day accede to the European Union. This was a good opportunity for the EU to act as a mediator. The EU had already had an experience in Balkan mediations. It was in Macedonia, where the mediation between Albanians and Macedonians had been performed together with the USA.[17]

---

clearly visible especially in the Serbian and Croatian cases. G. Riescher speaks of an *übersteigertes Wertgefühl*, as a characteristic feature of such nationalism.

16 The same somewhat paradoxical approach applies to their ideas of resolving the Kosovo problem. They have always had a mouthful of it, but without any sensible proposal of a solution.

17 The Ohrid agreement of 2001 put an end to ethnic tensions and led to the formation of a new government. Cf. on Ohrid agreement SKARIĆ S., *Macedonia – a Multi-*

This was a third technique applied in pursuit of a solution to the Serb-Montenegrin problem. The intervention of the EU was merely diplomatic. It turned out to be fruitful, for it showed an immediate political outcome in the shape of Belgrade agreement. This was followed by another document, of a legal nature – the Constitutional Charter of Serbia and Montenegro.[18] Both documents represent an outcome of the efforts of a sophisticated intervention coming from outside, in order to achieve a fair political settlement.

3. CURRENT SETTLEMENT

The Constitutional Charter of the year 2003 created a new structure for Serbia and Montenegro. The federal state of Yugoslavia, consisting of two federal units, was put an end to. The two countries now form a union of states.

The main features of the currently existing system can be displayed if we consider the decision making mechanisms of legislative and executive powers, as laid down by the Constitutional Charter.

The legislative power in the Union of Serbia and Montenegro is vested with the Assembly of Serbia and Montenegro. It is composed of 126 members, 91 of whom come from Serbia and 35 from Montenegro.[19] The over proportional representation of Montenegro is visible at first glance. Montenegro has 0,6 million inhabitants, and Serbia 9,5 million.[20] Such a representation could however hardly make equal the two components of the Union. This was achieved by the provisions on the decision making process of the Assembly.

---

ethnic and Corporative State (The Ohrid Framework Agreement of 13th August 2001), in : S. Milacic (ed.) La reinvention de l'Etat, Bruxelles 2003, pp. 157-176.

18 The text of the Constitutional Charter in English is accessible at the web site : www.mfa.gov.yu

19 Art. 20, Sec. 1 Const.Ch.

20 The figure for Montenegro is a result of the 2003 census. For Serbia it is an estimation, because the 2001 census did not include Kosovo. The population of that region is roughly estimated at 2 million.

A decision of the Assembly of Serbia and Montenegro is valid only if a motion is supported by the majority of members from Serbia, as well as by the majority of members from Montenegro.[21] In other words, to reach a decision of the Assembly a motion needs 46 votes from Serbia and 18 votes from Montenegro. This leads to an almost absolute equality of the member-states of the Union in the legislative process. There is only one parliamentary debate for a given motion, and one casting of votes. Still it occurs in a thorough analysis, that from a political standpoint such a casting of votes is inevitably twofold. The approach seems to be pragmatic, as it also was in other provisions of the Constitutional Charter.

This can be proved if we consider the executive power of the Union. It is vested with a body called Council of ministers, consisting of six members. The Council of ministers is presided by the President of Serbia and Montenegro, appointed by the Assembly. That person is given a somewhat special status, being entitled to propose to the Assembly the appointment of five ministers.[22]All ministers have their portfolios, while the President of Serbia and Montenegro hasn't got any. His main function is to preside the Council of ministers. That body is accountable to the Assembly of Serbia and Montenegro.[23]

The most significant feature is the decision making process of the Council of ministers. As it consists of six members, according to a constitutional provision, three of those must be appointed from each member-state.[24] The Council of ministers decides by the majority of votes. If the votes are even, then the one of the President has a decisive value. However, any majority of votes in the Council of ministers, making a decision, must inevitably be composed of votes of members of the Council belonging to both member-states of the Union.[25]

---

21 Art. 23. Const.Ch.

22 Cf. Art. 27 and 35 Const.Ch.

23 Art. 37 Const.Ch.

24 Art. 35, Sec. 2 Const.Ch.

25 Art. 36 Const.Ch.

It seems to be clear enough that in the presence of such a constitutional settlement the will of one component of the Union can never prevail over the interests of the other. The equality of partners in the Union seems to be fairly achieved. Therefore, one need not explain other features of the system, such as limited competence of the Union for instance, or the complex problem of its financing. The decision making process shows clearly enough the confederal character of the Union, as well as the equality of its member-states.[26]

I have pointed out on various occasions that the constitutional settlement of Serbia and Montenegro fits the definition of consociative democracy, as posed by Lijphart.[27] All four elements characterizing consociative democracy exist in the constitutional settlement of Serbia and Montenegro.

The autonomy of segments is quite obvious, because the two components of the Union are states.[28] The grand coalition in the Council of ministers is a constitutional rule, laid down by Art. 35, Sec. 2 Const.Ch. providing for a formation of the executive on a Serb-Montenegrin parity basis.

Another two elements put forward by Lijphart are also present. The proportionality, as it has been exposed, has its roots in the composition of the legislative power. As we have seen it took the shape of an over proportional representation of the junior partner of the Union. Further on, if we are to consider the composition of the executive, the proportionality even turns into parity.

Finally, what Lijphart names the veto of minority is inherent to the Serb-Montenegrin system, both at the levels of legislature and the executive. The respective decision making processes fairly prove this.

---

26 Cf. my texts on the subject – an article prepared for a colloquim in Lausanne, under the title *Le nouvel ordre constitutionnel de la Serbie et Monténégro*, currently under press and a book in Serbian, Osnovi ustavnog prava, Beograd 2004, pp. 135-136.

27 For Lijphart's opinion cf. LIJPHART A., *Changement et continuité dans la théorie consociative*, Rev. Int. Pol. Comp. Vol. 4 N° 3 – 1997, pp. 679-699

28 Cf. Art. 2 Const.Ch. in regard of equal status of member-states and Art. 5 regarding territories.

However, the founding fathers of the Constitutional Charter were merely pragmatic. Lijphart's theory has probably had no influence on their work. Politicians were trying to formulate practical provisions and they inevitably created an example of power sharing that could satisfy the interests they were representing. It is therefore interesting to try to evaluate the outcome of their efforts and put a forecast from the standpoint of its sustainability.

4. EVALUATION AND FORECAST

In order to evaluate the current Serb-Montenegrin settlement one should pose a question whether it fits the problem in general. Is there enough conformity between the problem and its solution?

One might say the conformity is lacking, because creating such a loose union of two countries, possessing so many features in common, does not seem to be justified by logic. Those who are homogenious should be able to form a closer union.

On the other hand, a fact emerging from the world of figures should not be neglected. The two entities differ so much in regard of population and territory, that if we are to recognize any special interest to one of the partners it should inevitably lead to some sort of special relations in order to preserve such interest.

Proposals tending to create a regional state on the whole territory of Serbia and Montenegro, have never really had an echo in Montenegro. Such proposals regarded Montenegro as a region, and they simply did not seem to be satisfactory.[29]

Towards the end of the Milošević regime, a group of experts headed by Prof. Lidija Basta, in which I was participating, assumed the task to draft a constitution for Serbia. The idea was to prepare a constitutional transition for the "day after".Our group then left the door open for both

---

29 Cf. the proposal of Prof. Miodrag Jovičić; JOVIČIĆ M., *L'Etat régional*, Belgrade – Fribourg 2003, pp. 116-125. The proposal dates back to 1996, when the book appeared in Serbian, in Belgrade.

federal and confederal settlements of relations between Montenegro and Serbia.[30] It is essential that we felt we could not draft a constitution for Serbia without throroughly discussing the problem of its relations with Montenegro.

In the light of the considerations I have just put forward one must admit that the confederal character of the current settlement does not collide with the main features of the problem. It could however be contested. It certainly is not the only possible way of settling relations between Montenegro and Serbia. One could imagine others. However it is not an inappropriate one.[31]

Another question arises at this stage. If a confederal settlement is found fitting the Serb-Montenegrin problem, could such a settlement then apply to some similar situations at least in the same region? Two topics come to our mind in this respect. One is Kosovo and the other Bosnia and Herzegovina.

A question has been put forward by many, although sometimes in a way which is not coherent enough, whether Kosovo might become one day a third partner in the Union of Serbia and Montenegro?

It is not at all easy to answer such a question. One should first define a method of approaching an answer. If we speculate in a purely academic way, we might come to conclusions that hardly correspond with the reality. It should therefore be pointed out that the Kosovo Albanians have never made any sign they might be willing to accept such a set-

---

30 Cf. BASTA-FLEINER L. e.a., *Constitutional Reform in Serbia and Yugoslavia / Proposals by an independent group of experts*, Belgrade 2001, pp. 83-101. Our work was achieved after the fall of the “ancien régime”.

31 At this point I should quote a French regionalist, who blames the phenomenon he calls “structural incapacity” of a state to respond to revendications of difference. It’s Périco Légasse who says, “lorsque le problème se pose, le fédéralisme ou le confédéralisme constituent les seuls remèdes institutionnels capables d’éviter une fracture nationale”. Cf. SALLENAVE D. / LÉGASSE P., *Nos amours de la France – République, identités, régions*, Paris 2002, p. 22. It is obvious that the Serbs and Montenegrins have opted for a confederal solution. Besides, I like the picture of a centralized state this author, slightly exaggerating, makes of France at the same spot: “un fief qui se nomme la France, dirigé depuis un chateau fort qui s’appelle Paris, par un suzerain: le gouvernement central”.

tlement. The Kosovo Serbs for their part do not find it satisfactory either. Implementing a solution which does not have almost any support on the grounds would probably lead to a failure. Still the idea should not be put aside, and the reason for this is quite simple. The two communities of Kosovo could probably never agree on any solution proposal. That is why they will both have to accept something which is not going to be the first and best option for any of the two.

The case of Bosnia and Herzegovina is different. The current constitution of the country has already introduced elements of power sharing in a rather specific manner. I simply do not think that Bosnia and Herzegovina, as a country, needs another model. In spite of some justified criticism addressed to it, the model implemented in Bosnia and Herzegovina is working. It might need some adjustments, but certainly not reshaping. In other words, the model applied should be made more sophisticated, but it should not be altered.

Finally we come to the most important question, regarding destiny of the settlement currently applied to Serb-Montenegrin relations. The question has often been raised by many whether the current constitutional system, and the Union of two countries are going to last?

Elements of uncertainty arise both from the Belgrade agreement and the Constitutional Charter. The two documents provide on a three year period of suspension for taking a final decision on the destiny of the Union on a referendum.[32]

It has been remarked such provisions inevitably bring a temporary character to the Union and its foundations. To this one should argue, such a remark implies a separatist decision on a referendum.[33] In case there might be a free and thorough debate before a referendum and campaigning for both options one can never be sure what the outcome of it may be. Let me underline at this point that both Provision on Reconsideration and Art. 60 Const.Ch. demand in case of a referendum, it

32 cf. Art. 60 Const.Ch. and the heading "Provision on Reconsideration" in the Belgrade agreement.

33 A valuable counter-argument to this is the fact that the referenda in previous Yugoslavia have usually brought a separatist decision.

should take place according to "internationally recognized democratic standards".

Besides, even without such provisions the two countries would have probably been considered authorized either to maintain the Union or dissolve it. The provisions I have just spoken of can therefore only be regarded as procedural, and not substancial.

If we start from those facts, two elements seem to be decisive, as far as the destiny of the Union of Serbia and Montenegro is considered. The first is the mentality, and the second the international influence.

The mentality of political classes, both in Montenegro and Serbia, has been shaped during the long period of dictatorship. It bears certain traces of such an origin. Politicians are sometimes inclined to the patterns of majoritarian democracy. However, this does not inevitably mean they can not get used to a system of power sharing. It might be difficult to some extent, but one can not judge such a development impossible.[34]

The influence of the international community has sometimes been overestimated. This is especially the case of those who take a critical stand toward its interventions. The influence to intervene is however rationally limited. The international community, and especially the European Union as its front runner in the Balkans, can perform a great deal of influence but they are not omnipotent.

The case of Serbia and Montenegro and their relations is not one of those in which violence might occur. Any settlement will be reached in a peaceful way. Therefore, the main issue is what values will be prevailing in case of another diplomatic intervention coming from European institutions? The peace and human rights first come to our mind. Those however remain beyound any doubt. What other values might then provide guidelines for a sophisticated intervention sympathetic to both partners of the Union? Will there be a fear of a precedent which

34 Ultra nationalist Serbian radicals are a good illustration of the complexity of situation in this respect. They are probably the most majoritarian of all on the political scene, but at the same time, for the sake of other reasons, they are not against the Union of Serbia and Montenegro.

should not be followed in case the two partners decide to dissolve the Union? This can not be excluded, but it is not likely to prevail.

For the sake of such considerations the destiny of the Union of Serbia and Montenegro seems to remain with its citizens. If they manage to adapt themselves to a system of power sharing there is no reason why the Union should not be able to adopt the European values and reach its main goal by acceding to the European integration.

From Conflict to Peace : Procedures to Enhance Peaceful Transition

From Conflict to Peace Procedures to Enhance Peaceful Transition : The Role of the International Community

Julian Thomas HOTTINGER

> *"The nature of war determines the nature of peace. This means that the factors which produce and sustain the conflict will directly impact the ensuing peace settlement".*
>
> KOSTNER, Markus & al. From Civil War to Civil Society, 1997

The attacks of September 11, 2001 in New York set in motion a series of events that we are still feeling today. In response, the Bush administration declared war against Al-Qaeda, invaded Afghanistan and overthrew the Taliban regime, and then attacked Iraq with the intention of eliminating the threat of nuclear, biological, and chemical weapons. Arms, which still remain partially to be found today.

The US administration has also invoked another claim: that these military operations were the first steps of a new policy to bring about peace to the entire Middle East. But it is just about impossible for Arabs and Muslims to take this claim seriously due to the longstanding American support for Israel. Another reason that might explain why so little has been done to resolve the Israeli-Palestinian conflict within the Bush administration is strongly linked to a series of misunderstanding following the failure of the Oslo peace process under President Bill Clinton. There is a profound belief, amongst some American opinion-makers, that the

Palestinians were "(...) either unready or unwilling to help themselves, and only wished to perpetuate the conflict", as Clayton E. Swisher illustrates in his book on "The Truth About Camp David"[1].

However, when talking about the Middle East in general, couldn't there be another problem? That we are just confronted with a case where the international community cannot make up its mind about what to do and how to go about solving the conflict in the Middle East? What adds up to exposing another myth that is strongly linked to enhancing a peaceful transition: the international community has no common thought, vision, or insight of what could be a solution to the Middle East conflict. Said differently, there is no common bottom line, so how can the international community be expected to help the parties in conflict find a solution? So the conflict just goes on.

Nevertheless, one has to be careful and not deny certain successes within the region. Very often-major peace projects at a state level might fail, but this does not mean that at different levels there is not some success and hope for the future. You can't just throw everything out with the bathwater, as we say in French. For example, it is important when deconstructing peace processes to clarify what analytical phase we are talking about as well as at what level – often called tracks[2] – is the work being done on. Why? Well simply because grass root projects have worked in various occasion but without taking into account the above mentioned analytical factors for a lot of people there is still some confusion about what is being talked about as they might have difficulties in identifying what a peace process exactly is and how it works.

WHEN DO PEACE NEGOTIATIONS START?

Quite often public opinion only perceives the final act of a peace agreement. They see on their TV screens the heads of state, ministers, or

1 SWISHER Clayton E., *The Truth About Camp David: The untold story about the collapse of the Middle East Peace Process*, Nation Books, New York, 2004.

2 DIAMOND Louise, MCDONALD John, *Multi-Track Diplomacy: A systems Approach to Peace*, Kumarian Press, Connecticut, (Third Edition) 1996.

even rebel leaders, sitting down together to sign an agreement. There will be handshakes and smiles, while the talk is already about the future implementation of the agreement. But rarely does the public realise how difficult, complex and time taking negotiations have been just to obtain an agreement on paper. And the public is often even less conscious of the price paid to gain peace and what energy will be needed to enhance a peaceful transition.

My personal aim within this paper is not to go into all the knots and bolts of peace negotiations at the beginning of this 21st Century, but to look at some of the major trends peacemakers are confronted with today, and what role and tools the international community has to enhance a peaceful transition. That is, a peace-making process that can take years to establish due to its complexity, as more and more often it is very demanding job. Why? Well most often today actual peace-agreements demand a total layout from "a to z" of what is expected in the near future.

In the last ten to twelve years, more and more often peace agreements have become complex documents that must look into all of the details – of what would be seen as a project of society – before one or the other of the parties are willing to sign. Rarely in modern peace negotiations do you agree to only exchange prisoners, or do you only agree on a cease-fire, or a cessation of hostilities, and build up from there. No! This is, by far, not considered enough. You are forced to look into the mistakes of the past, try to find ways of correcting them, before looking at the future and establishing in what way communities – divided by years of bitter hatred – can envisage reconciliation tomorrow[3].

But before even getting that far, one cannot help wondering how you foresee future negotiations, which are often, at an analytic level, presented as pre-negotiations, the negotiations to obtain an agreement, and finally, the post-agreement phase or implementation phases.

3 PAGE FORTNA Virginia, *Peace Time: Cease-Fire Agreements and the Durability of Peace*, Princeton University Press, Princeton & Oxford, 2004.

The common denominator of the three analytical phases is the need of establishing a creative process, a precarious and slippery journey of discovery. This means that the final outcome can never be foreseen from the beginning of the process. Clearly, the parties will have their own views on what they want to achieve, their own "models" of desirable settlement, but only those in a privileged or extremely powerful position will be able to pre-define their objectives and get, in some areas, what they want. This, of course, is a daunting prospect for a negotiator or process designer. Consequently, while the parameters of the process need a careful design, the course of action has to be flexible enough to cope with the unforeseen.

As for the international community, what role is it expected to fulfil and how can its task be enhanced in these very complex negotiations?

THE INTERNATIONAL COMMUNITY RESPONSE TO CONFLICT : ACTORS AND ORGANIZATIONS

As already mentioned in the introduction, there are quite often major myths that accompany peace processes, the implementation of a peace agreements and the will to stop a conflict, or at least transform it. One of these myths, and the biggest, is without doubt this foggy structure of an international community, in singular, homogenous. Rarely in any conflict, and especially in the Middle East, has the international community been so divided, engaged in favour of one side or the other. The international community usually responds to urgency and manages in the best of cases to agree on a minimal threshold and on short-term objectives. It is extremely rare that mid-term or long-term aims can be agreed upon and, to a certain extent, implemented. Interests, which can be political, economical or social, are just divergent and when working on a conflict, neutrality remains more of an ideal hope than a reality.

Of course, it would not be fair to generalise and I have personally known some cases when, even though the international community did not manage to agree upon what was supposed to be done, the result was successful. But one has to be careful, as the international community, quite often is only help to find or implement the solution, but not necessarily the principal bearer: the parties engaged in a conflict are those responsible for finding an adequate solution. Only they can decide which are the solutions, how they can be implemented and what society would expect as a result of negotiations. In other words, what can society and the conflicting parties live with.

The international community might help by bringing the conflicting parties together, organising the negotiations, talking to the parties, financing the process, by organizing parallel meetings or helping the actors find solutions and contribute financially to the implementation of the agreement, but in no way can you expect it to solve the problem. Even though members of the international community might be tempted to try.

Over the last few years, the international community has been accused, in various conflicts, of wanting to impose a solution. In some cases, out of pure desperation, the international community has been tempted to want to solve the conflict, by using force, getting involved in the substance, and imposing visions or ideas that will definitely not "stick on the ground" for a whole series of reasons. Maybe this is due to the fact that since the end of the Second World War, there has been a will to intervene within conflicts at different levels, with the hope of solving them. At an analytical level there is a three-tier system with an intervention, at the first level, within the United Nations (UN). The second tier would be the regional organizations and the third tier is known as the Non-Governmental Organizations.

THE FIRST TIER : THE UNITED NATIONS

The UN, until quite recently, has been developing its vision of what would be a proposed agenda for peace. The principal agency of the UN in this area is the Office of the Secretary-General, the Department of Political Affairs. As for the Department of Peacekeeping Operations, it oversees the operational side of peacekeeping. Special representatives and envoys frequently play an important role in the UN practical conflict-resolution activities and assist the Secretary-General. Rarely though does the UN itself, as a sole international body, run a process as the UN remains "the only existing framework for building the institutions of a global society" and thus the only institution which holds the expression of the international community. And to fulfil such a task unanimity amongst its members is required. The UN therefore tends to only take part, as a supplementary actor in the resolution of a conflict, be it for example, in peacekeeping or be it in guaranteeing the implementation of an agreement.

THE REGIONAL ORGANIZATIONS : A HETEROGENEOUS RESPONSE

Regional organizations, up to now, have played a key role in organising and running peace negotiations. They are not the only actors representing the international community but they have played a substantive role in various resolutions of conflicts. In some cases, it is believed that regional actors, due to their proximity, due to their knowledge of the conflict and due to the fact they suffer the indirect consequences of the conflict, would tend to want to find a durable solution. In other cases, the regional actors have been accused of being too involved in a conflict; to be looking after their own interests and to be too strongly linked to the conflicting parties.

Whatever the case might be, for the last ten to twelve years, a lot of processes have been put up, organised and directed by regional structures, such as the Organization for Security and Cooperation in Europe (OSCE), the collapsed Organization of African Unity (OAU), which in the meantime has become the African Union (AU) and the Association of South-East Asian Nations (ASEAN). The ASEAN initially didn't want to get involved in member states' internal affairs, but has been active in implementing the Memorandum of Understanding within the Aceh Peace Negotiations, which was negotiated in Helsinki in 2005[4].

One region, which strikingly lacks a comprehensive regional organization, which could help in resolving conflicts, is the Middle East. Not that regional organizations do not exist, there is, for example, the Arab

---

4 KINGSBURY Damien, *Peace in Aceh: A Personal Account of the Helsinki Peace Process*, Equinox, Jakarta & Singapore, 2006.

League and the Gulf Cooperation Council. Both represent interests of their members but, unfortunately, they are not regional organizations that span beyond the regions' political fault lines. As far as conflict resolution goes, with the exception of the Arab League's experience in Somalia at the end of the 1990's till the beginning of the 2000's and some active negotiations in Khartoum between the Somali Islamic Union of Courts and the Transitional Federal Government, in 2006, very little has been done.

Right now the Arab League is building some capacity to deal with conflicts to help mediate but its activities will remain marginal as long as it does not itself with the fault lines that divide the Middle East in general

If it is true that regional organizations have the major advantage of being near the conflict and they know the main actors, the cultural setting and the institutional settings, there are major disadvantages too. Regional organizations or neighbouring states are considered quite often to be part of the conflict itself or not necessarily considered to be neutral within the conflict. This was the case for the Burundi, where the Tanzanian Government heavily invested in peace talks to obtain an agreement for it's small neighbour, Burundi, while various party in the conflict didn't perceive their big neighbour as being the most neutral of actors. Julius K. Nyerere together with Yoweri Museveni had imposed a regional embargo on all goods being imported into Burundi and Tanzania backed one of the main Hutu parties within the negotiations[5].

THE WORLD OF NON-GOVERNMENTAL ORGANIZATIONS

The third tier covers a heterogeneous group best known as Non Governmental Organizations (NGOs). The spectre covers humanitarian agencies, such as the International Comity of the Red Cross (ICRC) right up to different academic centres, such as the European Centre for Conflict Prevention (ECCP). All NGOs, even the most specialised, are involved in some activity which has to do with conflict, negotiating an

5 MATHE Sérgio, *Negociando Identidades: Uma Leitura das Negociaçoes de Paz para o Burundi 1998 – 2000*, PADRIGU, Göteberg, 2001.

agreement, implementing an agreement or taking part in what is known as conflict transformation. Quite often, the distinction that is made in the NGO world goes along the lines of those NGOs that are financed by governments and those that depend on public donations. Nevertheless, it is exceptionally rare that any NGO today depends on one form of financing and limits itself to precise tasks. Though some cases might still exist.

As negotiations have grown more and more complicated so has the involvement of NGOs[6].

THE ROLE OF THE INTERNATIONAL COMMUNITY WHEN ENHANCING PEACE?

As we have tried to explain throughout this paper, the international community is called upon more and more often to fulfil a task when trying to resolve a conflict. The international community, through the explanation of the three-tier system, has tried to respond to theses demands or requests for help. But is it enough? The tools are there. A complex network of different institutions, organizations and, in some cases, political personalities, are put at disposition of a process. But is this enough?

Over the years, the Middle East has had its share of negotiations with some phases of success and other fragments of failure. As long as there is an ongoing conflict, there is usually an ongoing peace process. In very few cases can one say that a process starts with an initial phase of "talks about the talks", the corpus of negotiations and ends with the implementation of what is agreed upon. It is not a road on which you walk from point A to point B and it is not a path that is always visible and within the comprehension of the public. Every process has its ups and downs. All processes do a few steps forward and a few steps backwards. Some processes get to a phase such as the negotiations and then stagnate while others get pinned down within their implementation.

---

6 HUBER Konrad, *The HDC in Aceh: Promises and Pitfalls of NGO Mediation and Implementation*, East-West Center, Policy Studies 9, Washington 2004.

Public opinion is convinced that a peace agreement, once it is signed, should bring peace and tend to not understand the difficult phase of implementation, known by professional mediators to be a real back-breaker.

Nevertheless, where a misjudgement is often made, is in believing that the international community, by itself, can bring about peace. The fundamental pressure, decision taking and structuring element within a peace agreement can only come from the conflicting parties. The international community can help and can bring in expertise, finance the process, create the necessary venues and apply some political clout by talking to different actors when necessary. But what it cannot do is solve the conflict.

This is why there is a need of talking, studying and analysing how the international community can help to enhance peace but not impose "peace".

Since the UN Boutros Boutros-Ghali proposed Agenda for Peace, on-going debates on how peace could be obtained more efficiently has been organized[7]. However, so far though there is "no one size that fits all" when it comes to working on conflicts, as the nature of the conflict is bound to condition the negotiation of a solution.

WHAT ROLE DOES THE INTERNATIONAL COMMUNITY FULFIL IN A PEACE PROCESS?

Beyond the institutional and organizational set up that has been put together these last few years, it would be interesting to turn the question around and try to imagine what the international community can do, or does, to enhance peace at an informal level. Said differently, what concretely can be done within different phases of the conflict and it's resolution, so as to make some progress in resolving the issues at stake?

---

7 TARDY Thierry, *The Brahimi Report: Four Years On*, Geneva Centre for Security Policy, Geneva 2004.

It would be worth looking at some concrete ways in which the members of the international community can help enhance peace.

Initial contact with the Parties – There is nothing more dangerous than to isolate a party in the midst of a conflict and let it feed on its own logic. It the recipe for creating extremism, consolidating hardliners, and at the same time the party just becomes a group that will just impossible to follow, understand and work with. Therefore, the international community, or some of its members, will try to establish contact with the party at the very early stage. Maybe the initial contacts will not necessarily be with the leadership of the party but with a circle of intellectuals that gravitates around the nucleus. The idea is to follow the party, understand exactly what is happening and, at the same time, if such a party does ever decide to negotiate, that they do have some external people with whom they can talk to and get them to address their adversaries. In some cases, you follow parties for years, without getting anywhere near a negotiation stage.

When following such a group, you'll notice that their programme changes, leaders appear and disappear, members fall in disgrace but, at least, there is an external contact, which helps the party communicate. One of the worse cases that has actually been addressed and illustrates perfectly this problem is the Ugandan Lord's Resistance Army (LRA). This armed group has been fighting the Ugandan government for over twenty years in the name of the northern Acholi communities[8]. The political agenda of the LRA has never been very clear and its leader, Joseph Kony, is more of a religious leader who bases his believes on the Ten Commandments, than a political leader. Due to the total isolation this armed group has been living in, when the option of negotiating an agreement with the Government of Uganda (GoU) was looked into, we hit a serious obstacle. The LRA had been feeding itself its own thoughts in isolation, while being equipped by the Khartoum regime, which was using them to fight John Garang's Sudan People's Liberation Movement/Army (SPLM/A) in Southern Sudan. In such a case, the hope to

---

8 Armed group refers to groups that are armed, and could use force to achieve their goals. They are not under state control in comparison with paramilitary bodies that the state usually controls.

be able to establish a venue, negotiate a political agenda and at the same time deal with the indictments of the International Criminal Court (ICC) was just too much for such a rebel group. They were forced to call upon Milton Obote's Diaspora to help them negotiate, but with the risk that this Diaspora did not necessarily represent the fighters on the ground and they tend to defend a totally different political agenda. This has been partially the cause for various breakdowns within the negotiations.

Levelling the ground – If the isolation of a group in itself is a problem, the issue that always comes about is how can you level the ground amongst the parties and prepare them for negotiations. In most negotiations, the government delegation is quite at ease with the negotiation techniques and the content linked to the conflict, while other parties, having invested their energy in fighting and surviving in the bush, find it hard to understand the mechanisms used within negotiations and feel a certain unease at having to sit at the table.

Therefore, there is a strong need for the international community to help prepare all sides, and the most common technique is to organize seminars or workshops. The idea is to run a series of workshops, at an informal level, in such a way that topics that do contain issues close to – or in common with – the conflict can be dealt with. This does not necessarily mean that you deal with the issues from the country in conflict, but you will address similar problems that flourished elsewhere and explain what solutions were found. The aim is not to say that a solution found in a country "A" is necessarily the solution for country "Z". What you do is, by explaining what was done elsewhere, you enlarge the spectre of thought of your future negotiators while getting them to exchange with their enemies on a neutral ground and issues for which there should be no passion or personal involvement.

Sometimes, workshops are organised years before any party decides to negotiate, though by doing so it has the advantage of already creating some common ground on foreign issues amongst enemies while getting all parties used to the idea of orally exchanging instead of shooting at each other on the ground.

Indirectly, the fact that these workshops work well quite often sets the mind of some of the leaders of the conflicting parties to the idea that they could think of negotiating instead of fighting. This does not mean that they will automatically change their logic and quit fighting and honestly start talking. According to the circumstances on the ground, they might be tempted to try and negotiate, or better said, fight across the table with the hope of obtaining gains that they are probably not achieving in the fields.

Human Rights – No matter what stage your conflict is at, it is always important to address as early as possible, Human Rights. The aim is not to render one side or the other guilty for having violated Human Rights, that is an issue that will have to be addressed at a latter stage. The aim, when addressing Human Rights, is to try to convince the parties to respect some fundamental rules while giving the humanitarian aid organisations a possibility of having access to the civilian population, which is suffering from the conflict[9].

The fact that Human Rights, Humanitarian corridors, agreements on basic rules, are so important is that they can make a major difference for the civilian population suffering from the conflict while trying to obtain a minimal consent among fighting parties so that the international community can help fulfil the humanitarian task. Quite often, when negotiating Human Rights standards, you get to know the commanders, leaders, and members of a fighting groups or parties. From the parties perspective, there is quite often a will to try to do better in what concerns humanitarian violations while the parties hope that the international community would take more interest in what the conflict is all about.

Of course, violations are committed, and whatever is negotiated is not always respected. Some parties might even take advantage of what was being negotiated, but in general, when Human Rights have been negotiated with armed groups or parties, there is quite often a sense that the international community is following the conflict, worried about the

---

9 Mc Hugh Gerard, Bessler Manuel, *Humanitarian Negotiations with Armed Groups: A Manual for Practitioners*, United Nations, New York, 2006.

conflict and, at the same time, watching all actors. Now one has to be careful, as Human Rights are not always negotiated exclusively by the international community. It is usually an area in which NGOs, regional structures and some departments of the UN are very present. As for the fighters on the ground, sometimes the negotiations of Human Rights the very first encounter is made with representatives of the international community, especially if training courses are given on the topic.

There are exceptions to what is said here above. Sometimes the mere fact of wanting to address Human Rights issues can relight the conflict and make the situation worse for its victims. So one has to be very careful when deciding on how and when such negotiations can take place, as the main outcome is for the negotiated content to make a positive difference instead of rendering the situation worse.

Confidence-Building Measures – Confidence-building measures are considered to be a problem, or better said, a constant worry. The international community hopes to build confidence between parties as it is seen as a positive step before negotiations. The problem is that each party wants their enemy to make concessions but does not necessarily want to do it themselves. One must also be careful that the measures you are using for building confidence gradually grow and do not become overblown or excessive for one side or the other when being implemented.

Confidence-building measures can start by something very simple, like letting fighting forces use an area for a short time or period to feed them and then move on. In other cases, the simple fact that mail can be exchanged with the fighters' families is already a positive step, and seen as an important confidence-building mechanism. One can also create areas of "non engagement" at the military level. Nevertheless, the aim behind all of this is not to make life more comfortable for one side or the other but to prove to each side that there can be a certain amount of trust and that at a basic level there can be some tolerance and understanding.

The international community usually measures the armed groups goodwill to negotiate according to their acceptability of confidence-building measures and to that they respect their engagements. For years, especially in the military field, confidence-building measures were the first steps taken before a cessation of hostilities or a cease-fire could be negotiated. If the confidence-building measures were respected and some basic agreement could be obtained, it was considered that, with the necessary political engagement, a cease-fire could be looked into and initially negotiated, following a cessation of hostilities that held on the ground.

Dealing with pre-requisites – Dealing with pre-requisites is often a major task for the international community. Parties will start by saying that they might envisage negotiating if their enemy makes a major concession. It can be a declaration of surrender, liberation of prisoners or for the army to evaluate an area or a certain percentage of the national territory. The problem that remains though is how do you start pre-negotiations with prerequisites on the table?

There are basically two schools of thought as far as this issue goes. There is a group which refuses to discuss prerequisites and state that it there are prerequisites that can't be dropped it is an evident sign that the parties don't want to negotiate in good faith. There is a second school of thought, that believes that prerequisites can be looked into, but not necessarily negotiated, and that if the parties want to negotiate them, they are to be put in the agenda of the talks, and negotiate them together with the rest of the content. There is not much use in trying to negotiate prerequisites with a facilitation team as only your adversary can agree or disagree.

This issue remains a key element within pre-negotiations and an important task for the international community. It is rare, not to say exceptional, that parties will not condition their taking part in negotiations to a series of prerequisite which their enemies have to comply with.

Ushering the parties to the talks - Substantive efforts have to be made to convince a party about the benefits of negotiating an agreement. Years are usually invested in this task by members of the international community, in trying to convince or "push" the parties so that they will envisage a negotiated solution to their problems. Each case is quite different, but in general you do find common steps being taken throughout this ushering phase or this phase of persuasion. Sometimes strong tactics can be used by certain nations while in other cases even economical sanctions will be used to wear down the most recalcitrant parties[10].

Feed in Expertise – Expertise is vital in any process. Surprisingly it is not the content or details of the expertise that is important, but breaking of a frame of mind. If parties are forced to look into other examples, other cases, while understanding the logic prevailing in solutions obtained, the delegates will tend to start seeing some of their problems not as necessarily unsolvable.

Within the negotiations between the North and South Sudan, the fact that in the wealth sharing we were able to address highly complicated issues dealing with the petrol revenue was of great help, as everybody had to learn and long discussions took place until the content was understood. Quite often the delegates found themselves debating issues together with the international experts brought on board to help them figure out how a petroleum economy work. And in this precise process the entire facilitation team was dependent on the expertise and knowledge the international community could obtain and put at disposition of the negotiators.

A continuing search for lessons, insights from other cases of conflict management and resolution in conflicts are equally important when parties are not able to mend their own torn fence and need help to do so.

Others areas in which the international community can make the difference are: in helping to build up the mediation team, by looking for experts and in some cases like Switzerland does, making experts available for a facilitator during the process, while covering her/his expenses. There sometimes is a need to reassure the parties through informal channels and by letting them know that the members of the international community are there to help them. In other cases this means helping to go as far helping the parties to find middle ground and drop their hard-line positions.

---

10 KREMENYUK Victor A. (ed), *International Negotiation: Analysis, Approaches, Issues*, Jossey-Bass, San Francisco (Second Edition), 2002.

Another way of marking the international community's interest is by nominating observers to the process. Their task is to follow the discussions taking place, help the facilitation and brief their capitals on what is happening. In some processes where the United Nations is not represented, or not necessarily following the negotiations, it is quite often up to the observers together with the Facilitator to brief the United Nations so as to help prepare the next steps. Especially when the implementation phase comes about.

One area in which the international community has a heavy hand is in the financing of a peace process. Rarely are the budgets of peace negotiations over-following with cash. There are a lot of unexpected expenses, such as flying the delegations to the venue, covering expenses for experts, and paying hotels and security. There is also a need for a stable and running secretariat, as the quantity of paper work in any negotiation is astronomical. Furthermore, if obtaining of an agreement just on paper is expensive, the implementation phase, which is nothing else but the application of what was decided in the agreement, usually can explode the budget.

However, the price of peace is relative low in comparison to a conflict. One way of reducing expenses is to well prepare the implementation phase by creating a Joint Assessment Mission (JAM) that will prepare for the pledging of funds to cover implementing expenses according to needs.

Finally, the last two stages which are important and should be mentioned are the need of having the implementation monitored, and closely linked to this, having the international community helping the parties to stick to their engagements. Both tasks can be qualified as demanding and risky as parties will accept with difficulties the fact that they are finger pointed when violating and agreement or accused of not respecting the arrangements they signed to. When it comes to the monitoring of implementation there are probably as many models as there are negotiated agreements, but most commonly a core group of countries, usually with strong political clout, due to their role in past history or because of their importance within the international community, will be responsible for the monitoring and following up of the signed agreement.

Of course exceptions do exist, and Norway is the best example of this as shown in the role this country has been fulfilling within the peace process in Sri-Lanka.

CONCLUSION

Describing a negotiation process in all its complexity is just about impossible. We have opted in the present case to show how the international community can help to enhance peace, through its institutional structures and various techniques. Of course not all techniques are specific to the international community, but they do tend to give a concrete vision of how things are put in place and work. Nevertheless, one must never forget that in negotiations there is no "one size fits all". Each case is unique.

In sum, when reflecting on the Middle East, there are probably two ways in which the international community can help, as two urgent needs can be fulfilled without necessarily a huge economical investment or with much controversy. First of all, more content analysis has to be used to evaluate the effects of techniques intended to facilitate agreements. This research could be carried out through various research centres throughout the region. Nevertheless, it would be important that participants from all sides take part in such a task. Secondly, insights into the process of negotiations such as those negotiated within the Middle East, have to be studies. Information is still rare. Little is known about how the Peace Treaty Between Israel and Egypt in 1979 was dealt with, or the 1994 Treaty of Peace Between the State of Israel and the Hashemite Kingdom of Jordan, or the Israel's Peace Initiative of May 1989. There is a strong need to provide political actors with in-depth knowledge on past negotiations with the hope that this acquaintance will help facilitate future negotiations through a process-oriented problem solving approach.

From Negotiations to Democratic Legitimacy : Lessons from the South African Transition

Nicolas HAYSOM

INTRODUCTION

This article concerns the democratic legitimation of the outcome of a negotiated settlement. To be more precise the type of "negotiated settlement" with which this presentation is concerned is a negotiated settlement in a situation of intra-state political conflict and violence. It needs to be clarified that the concerns the paper addresses deal primarily with the processes by which the settlements are actually achieved, concluded and implemented rather than the substantive provisions of such a negotiated settlement. There is however an obvious linkage, a common thread, between both process and substance in negotiated peace settlements. It is the process questions however that are most commonly neglected by analysts of such settlements.

In a world in which ever sharper intra-state tensions are evident there has been an unprecedented constitutional interest in creating political frameworks which capture and hold the loyalty of all citizens. This is especially so in regard to nation states driven by fault lines running along cleavages of religion, race, ethnicity, language or region.[1] This interest has been expressed in the concern to develop a notion of nationhood which admits diversity, and an understanding of national

---

1 HAYSOM N., *Constitution Making and Nation Building*, in : Raul Blindenbacher and Arnold Koller (eds), Federalism in a changing world, MQUP, 2003.

identity which is compatible with the assertion of sub-national identities. For the same reason there has been greater interest in systems of power sharing in, political systems which ameliorate some of the features of a 'winner-takes-all' liberal democracy, which promote a wider 'buy-in' or stake holding in the system especially by minorities. Such systems typically focus on establishing a fairer distribution of political power, entrenching fair economic opportunity across the group fault lines, acknowledge a new imperative for inter-group tolerance, protecting and asserting minority rights promoting wider participation in and ownership of state structures, and insist on (at least) proportional representation in political decision-making.[2]

What animates the new debate on the substance of constitutions now animates considerations of process. The substantive elements of an inclusive nation-building social compact, for example federalism, are designed precisely to offer wider stakeholding, responsive and accountable government within an integrated national framework. Yet an imposed solution to a divisive political conflict, for example a federal framework, will not be a solution if it is an imposed framework. This point was recently made clear to the author during an engagement with political actors in the Philippines on federalism as a solution to the problem of Moro Mindanao. In short, the right answer through the wrong process will not usually yield an acceptable solution. Indeed, the very reason for preferring a negotiated settlement to a military one is that, as Fischer and Ury pointed out a decade ago,[3] voluntarily agreed outcomes are more stable and more lasting than imposed ones. What is true for the political elite who negotiate an end to internal strife is true for the ordinary citizen. They need to consent voluntarily to the deal.

The call for democratic legitimation of a negotiated settlement is not so much rooted in the grand theories of Hobbes Locke Hume or Rosseau. It is rooted in the practical imperative to make negotiated solutions popular and hence, durable and lasting. There are good reasons why democratic legitimation is crucial to the durability of a negotiated solu-

---

2 ibid pp.

3 FISCHER and URY, *Getting to Yes*.

tion particularly because negotiated solutions usually, at least at the outset, take the form of elite pacting. It is critical that the settlement and its core values should eventually take root in the political culture of a post conflict society. Negotiated settlements are an attempt to embark on a new social contract, not only between citizens *inter se* but also (in cases of inter-community conflict) between groups within a nation state. The product of the negotiations may eventually take the form of constitutional principles or even a new constitutional framework.[4] It may also embrace a diverse set of new political arrangement emanating from a long process of negotiations.[5] These may include international guarantees and the involvement of international actors; cease-fire provisions including the establishment of a new set of security institutions; the development and entrenchment of new political and minority rights; the rebuilding of a democratic state; and guarantees relating to amnesty and reconciliation.[6] It is obvious that this compact requires legitimation if it is to be viable and respected.

There is another reason why democratic legitimation is an important element for the successful implementation of negotiated settlement. A negotiated solution or settlement to a deep-rooted conflict frequently enshrines new social mores like inter community tolerance, a respect for fundamental rights hitherto neglected and a de-demonisation of members of the antagonist parties. If these new values are to be absorbed into the political culture, then it is critical that they be embraced by ordinary men and women – the citizenry at large. Democratic legitimation is the key to this process.

---

4 As in South Africa see HAYSOM, *Negotiating the Political Settlement in South Africa – Are there Lessons for other Countries*, Track Two/CCR Cape Town 2002 p 51-63.

5 As in the Sudan or Sri Lanka where the solution, it is agreed, lies in a federal framework, a framework which had been rejected by the dominant group for decades.

6 Amnesty provisions particularly may stick in the throat of the populace if granted by an erstwhile regime to itself. Thus in both Chile and Argentina the extent or even the existence of the amnesty for members of the former regime are being challenged.

In this presentation I will be canvassing the South African experience. While the presentation tends to simplify the South African model, it is necessary to point out that in reality, the road to a negotiated settlement was more bumpy and precarious than is often recognized. Those of us who participated in it referred to it as a 'rollercoaster of hope and despair'. The dividing line between success and failure is a thin one. South Africa, nonetheless, offers examples from which the interested comparative scholar can draw lessons and learn from our mistakes.

AN INTRODUCTION TO THE SOUTH AFRICAN NEGOTIATED SETTLEMENT

Extracting key lessons from the South African negotiated settlement is best done thematically rather than through a chronological narrative. However, in order to engage in a thematic treatment of the South African experience, it is necessary to set out briefly the sequence of events between the beginning of the negotiations in 1990 and the adoption of the South African final constitution in early 1997.

Although there had been an engagement between leading members of the then South African Government and Nelson Mandela prior to 1990,[7] for present purposes we will take the beginning of the process of negotiating a peaceful solution to the South African conflict as starting in February, 1990 when President F.W. De Klerk repealed the proscription on the African National Congress and other liberation movements, and released Nelson Mandela. Between 1990 and the end of 1991 there followed a protracted set of negotiations over political preconditions for negotiations. These ostensibly sought to effect a "level political playing field" between the principal protagonists (that is the National Party Government supported principally by white South Africans and the African National Congress supported principally by black South Africans). It was characterized by sporadic incidents of violence, which threatened to overwhelm the main peace process. This was so

7 SPARKS Alistair, *Tomorrow is another Country: The inside story of South Africas Negotiated Revolution*, London Heinemann 1995.

particularly because formal inter party talks on a final political solution had not as yet commenced. During this period there was a process of normalizing South Africa's security and public law landscape by repealing racially inspired and repressive legislation. In addition political prisoners were released' and political exiles allowed to return to the country.

During mid 1991 and in order to protect the main political process, the two major parties as well as the Kwa-Zulu based Inkatha Freedom Party, a wide range of civil society groupings, other interested political parties, churches and businesses embarked on an initiative to curb the growing levels of violence and to facilitate the participation of even a wider group of stakeholders in the process of peacemaking. This initiative came to be known as the National Peace Accord, and would eventually see the establishment of district level peace committee led by civil society stakeholders.

At the end of 1991, the first formal attempt at an all-party convention to broker a settlement collapsed amidst mutual recrimination. The government had challenged the ANC to decommission its fighters. The ANC accused the government of supporting a violent third force as part of a double agenda. The process of reaching a comprehensive solution would flounder until agreement on the process a road map by which a negotiated solution would be achieved. That road map was agreed in 1992 in a 'Record of Understanding'. That process envisaged the adoption of a two phase negotiated solution.[8] In the first phase, a multi party process operating on the basis of 'sufficient' consensus, or consensus would adopt constitutional principles, which would guarantee basic rights and structures of government in any final settlement. These constitutional principles constituted a confidence-building measure, guaranteeing the outcome of the second part of the constitution making

8 See generally MOSS G. and OBERY I. (eds), *From "Red Friday" to CODESA*, Ravan Johannesburg 1992. FRIEDMAN S. and ATKINSON D., *South African Review 7 : The Small Miracle – South Africas Negotiated Settlement*, Ravan Press Johannesburg 1994. FRIEDMAN S. (ed), *The Long Journey – South Africas Quest for a Negotiated Settlement*, Ravan 1993. See EBRAHIM Hassan, *Seal of a Nation – Constitution making in South Africa*, Cape Town Dud 1998.

process, which would be a majoritarian, democratically elected constitutional assembly, whose mandate would be to draft a final constitution for South Africa.

The multi-party talks got underway under the name of CODESA but it too broke down because of its clumsy way in which the talks were engineered and in which the negotiations were carried out. In due course a second all party convention was convened which essentially met throughout 1993. The multi-party negotiating process was a re-crafted negotiating process, which allowed a single text to be produced for the plenary committee of all the participating political parties. This single text process allowed for the more rapid development of consensus on: the text of an interim constitution; the framework under which elections would be held for a constituent assembly (which would also serve as a democratically constituted interim government); and the binding constitutional principles, which would have to be enshrined in the final constitution. It was in this manner that the South African process was able to unlock the gridlock created by the need for an inclusive process guaranteeing the rights of political minorities, while at the same time giving effect to the need for a majoritarian constitution making body.

The first democratic elections were held in 1994. Between 1994 and 1996, the Constitutional Assembly (which was simultaneously the National Assembly) drafted a final constitution. The first draft text was adopted in 1996 and submitted to the Constitutional Court for certification of compliance with the constitutional principles. The Constitutional Court rejected the first draft but accepted the subsequent second draft as being in compliance with the constitutional principles.[9] The final constitution came into being in February 1997.

KEY ELEMENTS IN THE DEMOCRATIC LEGITIMATION OF THE SOUTH AFRICAN NEGOTIATED SETTLEMENT

In this presentation it is argued that democratic legitimation of the settlement involves much more than a plebiscite or referendum on a new

---

9 See EBRAHIM op cit. The Judgements themselves make interesting reading.

constitutional text. There are vital elements to the way the negotiations are conducted, environmental and structural elements, that serve to legitimize the peace process as a whole, and ensure that its character and results are inclusive. It is the absence of some of these elements that has eroded other peace processes with which the author has had first hand experience: Burundi, Sri Lanka and Sudan.

From Bi-lateralism to Multi-lateralism

The South African process was fortunate in having two prominent parties take responsibility for the success of the project of securing a negotiated settlement yet both sides and especially their leaders, were insistent on an approach, which would see the broadest range of stakeholders implicated in the project. This shift from bi-lateralism to multi-lateralism is evident most conspicuously in the negotiation and conclusion of the National Peace Accord. The National Peace Accord took the form not only of a deliberate inclusion of (or at least an invitation to) all significant political players but also the presence of churches, businesses and civil society organizations in its deliberations and its implementation.

In the critical CODESA and multi-party processes, the two pre-eminent parties, the National Government and the African National Congress, were insistent on including as broad a range of political parties and political view points (in the form of traditional leaders for example) as was feasible. This inclusivity in approach was a significant step in broadening the stakeholding and ownership of the process as a whole. The South African process was governed by the repeated invocation that it was better to have potential deal breakers inside the process than confront them afterwards outside the process intent on sabotaging the fruits of the negotiations.

To be sure, multi-lateral processes are more difficult to manage than bi-lateral ones,[10] and the South African process succeeded because at the

---

[10] Compare for example the immobility of the Burundian peace negotiations in which 19 parties of equal voting weights participated, and also the Congo peace talks at which more than 300 groups claimed a right to participate.

heart of the process stood the two principal parties, led by uncontested leaders, both confident enough to take risks. The device of 'sufficient consensus' was also a key factor in ensuring the manageability and hence success of the multiparty talks.[11]

The need for manifest advantages for all sides participating in the process

The South African process recognized at the outset that for the principal protagonist players it was necessary that their participation in a negotiated settlement should be manifestly justifiable and bring rewards not only to the party but also to its supporters. In this regard the South African negotiations followed an elaborate "tit for tat" dance in which each party agreed to reciprocal compromises and concessions. These allowed the other side to produce evidence for its supporters of the advantages of a negotiated settlement. This process significantly aided both parties in justifying their participation in the talks as well as the compromises that they themselves were then required to make in order to achieve a settlement. Thus the release of political prisoners was matched by a unilateral cease-fire by the ANC. The repeal of legislation by the government was matched by the ANC's lead in the lifting of a sporting and cultural boycott on South Africa. An agreement to the road map of negotiations together with definite timeframes by the government was met with a call for the lifting of economic sanctions by the ANC.[12]

What is true for the principal parties is true for the ordinary citizens. Recent events in Sri Lanka have suggested that if there is rising unemployment and economic hardship during the negotiation of a peace process popular frustration will be deflected towards the peace process itself.[13] In short it is necessary for the broader legitimacy of the peace

---

11 The notion of 'sufficient consensus' was subsequently adopted in the Northern Ireland assembly on the means to accomplish broad consensus, short of unanimity, for binding political decisions.

12 HAYSOM N., *Negotiating the Political Settlement in South Africa – Are these lessons for other countries*, Cape Town CCR 2002 p.17

13 Sri Lanka is a recent example of where broad support for a peace process was undermined by popular discontent at the prevailing governments economic policies.

process, that ordinary people see an improved quality of life. It needs to be emphasized that peace (the mere absence of violence) is itself a bread and butter issue for the people living in a conflict zone. There is an immediate improvement in the texture of everyday life in war-torn societies once a cease-fire or a cessation of hostilities comes into being. It is necessary, however, to back such a development with the necessary humanitarian and development aid to secure popular approval for the outcome of the process.

The importance of legal continuity

Democratic legitimation should not be reduced to legal legitimation or the need to meet the demands of legal continuity and legal certainty of the post-settlement administration. However, this is an aspect, which should not be minimized. The absence of formal legal legitimacy and statutory/constitutional authority for the arrangements as agreed to in a peace settlement can provide legal confusion at the outset. At the worst, there may be debilitating legal and judicial confrontations, and an erosion of popular legitimacy flowing from the absence of legal legitimacy. Thus in South Africa (and in Burundi) steps have been taken to ensure that the arrangements agreed to in peace talks also find effect in a seamless and necessary legal legitimacy.[14] This is so even if one of the contending parties denies the legitimacy of the governing regime. In Sri Lanka and in Sudan the forces of the rebellion have been reluctant to concede weight to the imperative of legal continuity and formal legal legitimacy. In part this is a realistic apprehension of being held hostage by their opponents legal and constitutional process requirements. In general however, it is far better to respect the need for legal continuity and to found at the outset a respect for the rule of law rather than to establish new institutions on the basis of power relations alone.[15]

---

14 In both South Africa and Burundi, sitting parliament have been required to approve the texts of agreements, or the consequential constitutional instruments that substantially displaced sitting members.

15 Professor Ghai, on the other hand, in a discussion with the author has proposed a more robust approach. Where de facto the old order has been displaced one should

Balancing transparency and confidentiality

Negotiated transitions inevitably or usually commence with confidential exploratory behind-the-scene discussions. In many cases this is necessary. Without such confidentiality some negotiations would simply not take place. Indeed the absence of confidentiality in political negotiations can and does lead to allegations of bad faith, double agendas or opportunism. This occurs particularly when negotiations are carried out in the glare of the media spotlight and in which the contending parties talk not to their negotiating partners but to the media. They prefer to address their own constituency in the guise of talking up their position to their enemy rather than in seeking compromises. However, there comes a time in the negotiations when the absence of transparency leads to a loss of faith in the negotiations and accusations that private deals are being brokered. It is necessary then to balance the need for transparency and confidentiality in a negotiation process. As the negotiation process unfolds, there is an increasing demand for transparency both in regard to the road map – the way forward – as well as the substance or outcome of the negotiations. Negotiations in deeply divided societies take place in a corrosive atmosphere of uncertainty and insecurity.

The need for the leaders to bring their supporters to the table

Indeed mature negotiations require more than transparency. Mature negotiations require a constant inter play between public and negotiators, between constituencies and leadership. It is precisely this relationship that vests the negotiations with a degree of democratic legitimacy and encourages the rank and file to better understand both the deals that are being done, the compromises that must be affected, as well as the strategic thinking which underlines such negotiations. If the product of the negotiations is later to be taken to the populace for endorsement, the environment for such endorsement will be soured if the negotiators have kept everyone in the dark during the talks. It would be of little use for

not cling to a legalistic approach. The evidently unconstitutional displacement of herident estrada in the Phillipines would support such an approach.

negotiators to sign off on a deal only to have it rejected by their supporters. In South Africa the negotiations were structured to allow for report backs and consultations especially between the ANC and its allies and supporters. On the National Party's side F.W. de Klerk insisted on a prior mandate to negotiate from the white community and for this purpose successfully conducted a referendum confined to the white community. In retrospect, even through the ANC had reservations about a referendum, (which would allow whites a veto over the continuation of the negotiations); the referendum was an important element in securing the legitimacy of both the process and the outcome amongst white South Africans who had the most to lose in the process.

The necessity for depth of support: a democratic underpinning to a negotiated settlement

It was a pre-condition for a successful outcome to the talks that the final constitution, the product of the peace process should be one endorsed directly by and reflect the aspirations of the majority of South Africans. This was particularly so in South Africa because of the long history of white minority rule. Any constitution developed and sanctified without the approval of the black majority, would lack the necessary legitimacy. It is for this reason that the ANC insisted on an elected or mandated democratic forum for the drafting debate and adoption of a final constitution. While such popular endorsement of constitutions can take place through mechanisms such as plebiscites and referenda, these are blunt and clumsy instruments for endorsing complex proposals on the structures of the state and the formulations of fundamental rights. They are in any event post facto devices for testing support. They would not allow for the weighting of popular support in the exercise of constitutional choice. The necessity for depth of support in South Africa required a forum in which democratically elected representatives could give effect to a popular mandate and allow, the weight of popular support to be reflected in the final text. A simple and absolute minority veto would have entrenched white power and minority interests.

The Constitutional Assembly thus became the single most important mechanism of securing the democratic legitimacy of the negotiated settlement. This is not to suggest that other mechanisms cannot achieve a similar result. Of particular currency in certain recent national constitutional reforms is the 'Constitutional Commission' – partly or wholly appointed by the government (Kenya, Thailand, Philippines, Zimbabwe). In some cases the support for this otherwise ambiguous route to democracy has arisen in contexts where there exists a pervasive distrust of opaque parliamentary wheeling and dealing[16] (Kenya).

The need for breath of support

It is also true however that depth of support or majoritarian support alone may not be enough to firmly found a modern constitution or for the adoption of a new set of political arrangements. Minorities in particular will have little faith in majoritarian goodwill and will be loath to enter a process in which the majority can simply ignore or dominate other linguistic, religious, ethnic and other minorities. Indeed it is precisely for this reason that decision-making majorities and procedures for amendments to a constitution are universally required to be exceptional and special. This notion of 'breath' of support serves to distinguish this distinctive and additional requirement for adopting constitutional reforms as opposed to merely majority support. In South Africa the reluctance of minorities to accept the ANC's insistence of a majoritarian constitution-making process became manifest in intense violent conflict in Kwazulu Natal between 1990 and 1994. This impasse was only broken through the device of the binding constitutional principles' by which minority fears could be allayed through a process, which would guarantee that political minority concerns would be addressed regardless of the majoritarian nature of the process.[17]

The general imperative of inclusivity found effect in the South African case through the CODESA forums, the Multi-party process, and the

---

16 In Kenya there is good reason to believe that the partly elected Constitutional Commission enjoyed (and enjoys) more support than a Parliament that was seen to be self-interested in its approach to constitutional issues. The legitimacy of the commission relied on extensive civil society participation as well as an exhaustive process of popular consultation.

17 See note 2

adoption of the constitution of the 'binding constitutional principles'. The requirement that the constitutional assembly adopt certain central provisions by exceptional majorities (75%) as well as the subsequent political compromises undertaken by the ANC to ensure that the constitutions eventual adoption should be by an even greater consensus indicates the importance with which 'breadth of support' was viewed by the principal parties.

The notion of inclusivity however finds much broader expression than in the decision-making requirements of the various fora. It is also to be found in the openness of the process to all parties including civil society and the encouragement, support and opportunity granted to them to participate.

Direct participation

In South Africa, notwithstanding the emphasis on inclusivity in regard to participation in the main decision-making forums and the emphasis on an elected constitutional assembly, it was felt that there should be maximum opportunity for direct participation of ordinary citizens during the constitution-making process in addition.[18] This took the form of ensuring that the media reported on the deliberations and decisions of the various committees of the assembly. It also took the form of village, town and community meetings in which members of the constitutional assembly were required to listen to – not address – ordinary villagers. It took the form of soliciting written submissions from the people at large on the content of the new constitution. Even if many of these submissions were not, on the face of it, constitutional in nature the initiative allowed an opportunity for ordinary people to participate in the process and to raise issues important to them. These – such as spousal abuse – on closer inspection do indeed relate to constitutional values and questions of responsive government even if they appeared to some to be symptomatic of the frustrations of daily life. To the surprise and astonishment of the management of the Constitutional Assembly, a full two million South Africans contributed their views on the content of the

18 See EBRAHIM op cit.

constitution. These contributions were collated, summarized, published and responded.[19] To without the Assembly being seen to process these submissions the exercise will be viewed as a public relations stunt. This process had a significant impact in giving ordinary men and women a sense of participation and ownership of the constitution-making project.

No place for triumphalism

It is clear that there is no place for triumphalism in a negotiated settlement which seeks as an outcome ownership of it which traverses political ethnic or cultural fault lines. Upon the adoption of the South African constitution President Nelson Mandela could quite correctly claim that each and every party had contributed parts to the constitutional text. The negotiators took care to allow formulations into the draft, which had emanated from the parties raising particular anxieties. This ensured it reflected the concerns raised by them in their own words. This promotes a document which no one party can claim as its own and in which all parties can legitimately claim to have played (to a lesser or greater degree) some part in creating. What is true for the text is also true for the conduct of the negotiators. The negotiators in the South African case tried not to claim individual clauses as a partisan victory or that they had "won" the negotiations. Self evidently such an approach excludes the other parties from a sense of ownership and hence responsibility for the product.

In general it is important for all parties to recognise that its statements during settlement negotiations/constitutional negotiations reach not one audience but several: their own constituency; the other sides negotiating team; the other sides constituency; third parties and their supporters. These statement sometimes have to address the anxieties and concerns of them all.

---

19 In the Nepalese constitutional reform process of 1990, there was also some astonishment at the scale and number of responses that a general call for submissions elicited. The response however were not treated or processed – and this is one of the reasons that the product, the 1990 Nepal constitution, does not enjoy the legitimacy it might.

Drafting style

The approach to the drafting of the constitution by South Africa's founding mothers and fathers was that the text should be as lucid and as readable as possible. It should also be seen to address the ordinary concerns of men and women. That latter was done through the express project of addressing economic cultural and social rights in the text. The former was achieved through the engagement of experts capable of reducing complex constitutional jargon to simple text. Although the 'plain language' advocates had their detractors the eventual product contributed to a constitution which is in general more accessible than most. Upon adoption, the constitution was translated into the 11 official languages, and over 2 million copies distributed to the public.

If there is a need for plain language, this does not mean there is no space for poetry. The language of the preamble and other analogous provisions needs more than the dry tone of the constitutional lawyer. For example, the ringing call of the US Declaration of Independence is an indispensable and continuing element of the popular appeal of the US Constitution.

Dealing with the Past

Just as there are process elements or features of a negotiated settlement that enhance its popular acceptance and democratic legitimation, so there are elements that undermine its legitimacy. One such aspect is the way in which the treatment of past human rights violations and other abuses are treated. In post-conflict situations there are usually victims and perpetrators of such abuses on both sides. Zealous punishment of only one side's fighters can jeopardize the agreement. Yet a failure to do anything can lead to charges that the negotiated settlement contributes to a culture of impunity and will leave lingering resentments amongst ordinary people. In South Africa the treatment of this question through a Truth and Reconciliation Commission has been much publicized. The Commission was able to grant amnesty only via truth telling process.[20] It was also able to hear victims and to propose compensation for them. Although the latter promise has not been fulfilled and although there were accusations of bias against the former regime, TRC played no small part in laying a foundation for reconciliation in South Africa. It is not a model that is necessarily exportable. East Timor accepted it only in small parts, and Burundi not at all.

Reconciliation

Apart from human rights violations, one of the inevitable consequences of inter group conflict is the mutual demonisation and stereotyping by antagonistic communities. This legacy of inter-community hatred must also be dealt with if an environment is to be created that is conducive to the acceptance of a negotiated settlement and, beyond that long-term reconciliation. Although the respect and admiration Nelson Mandela attracted by his conduct and stature has put South Africa in good stead, there is still insufficient inter group socialization outside educational institutions. In other Conflict situations such as the Balkans, the Middle East and the Great Lakes Region of Africa, NGO's have done pioneering work in promoting people to people contacts, especially amongst children. These are important initiatives in building understanding between members of rival communities. It is unthinkable that any national reconstruction can take place in post conflict situation, such as Rwanda, without such reconciliation. I would single out the Sri Lankan NGO. 'Mothers of soldiers missing in Action' as a bipartisan women's initiative that has brought women of the south into contact with their Tamil counterparts.

Continuing Constitutional Education

Every year South Africa celebrates 'Constitution Day' as a public holiday. On this day, public lectures are held and festivals are organized around themes connected to the constitution. It is argued that constitu-

---

20 The Truth and Reconciliation Commission 1998, *The Truth and Reconciliation Commission of South Africa Report*, Cape Town.

tional education, the grounding and popularization of the values of the constitution are part of an on-going project whose aim is to create a political and civic culture based on the need for tolerance, respect for human rights, and an appreciation of a hard won democracy. It is ordinary men and women, it is argued, who are the beneficiaries of the constitution, its surest guardians and its most reliable defenders. It is for this reason that it is said that a constitutions safest and surest home is in the hearts of ordinary men and women.

SHORT BIBLIOGRAPHY

ANDREWS P., ELLMAN S. (eds), *The Post Apartheid Constitutions*, WUP Johannesburg 2001 (see especially chapters by Leon Wessels, Roelf Meyer, Cyril Ramaphosa, and Hassan Ebrahim).

EBRAHIM H., *Soul of a Nation – Constitution-making in South Africa*, Cape Town DUP 1998.

FRIEDMAN S., ATKINSON D. (eds), South African Review 7: *The Small Miracle – South Africa's Negotiated Settlement*, Johannesburg Ravan Press 1994.

FRIEDMAN S. (ed.), *The Long Journey: South Africa's Quest for a Negotiated Settlement*, Johannesburg Ravan Press 1993.

HAYSOM N., *Negotiating the Political Settlement in South Africa – Are there lessons for other countries*, Cape Town, Centre for conflict Resolution, Track Two Occasional Paper 2002.

HAYSOM N., *Constitution-making and Nation Building*, in : Raoul Blindenbacher and Arnold Koller (eds), Federalism in a Changing World, MQUP, 2003.

HARRIS P., REILLY B. (eds), *Democracy and Deep-rooted Conflict: Options for Negotiators*, International IDEA, Stockholm, 1998.

Trust and Tolerance as State Making Values in Multicultural Societies

(Paradoxes and Chances of Federalism as a Conflict-Management Tool)

Lidija R. BASTA FLEINER

INTRODUCTION : MAPPING THE ISSUES

Any discourse on federalism as a conflict-management device for segmented societies that aims at identifying major paradoxes and viable chances of this case of "political use of federalism", ends with the irksome/troublesome task of explaining why multicultural federalism[1] can hardly work. Federalism in general and federation in particular are about responding to societal demands for group liberty.[2] Since multicultural federalism (at least in a normative sense) is based on the recognition of existing ethnic, religious, or linguistic diversities as legitimate,

---

1 By "multicultural federalism" I shall understand all federal arrangements for the societies with major cultural cleavages, be it of ethnic, religious, linguistic nature, designated and designed to accommodate given multicultural differences.

2 I shall understand federalism in a very general sense, as an eminently *anti-majoritarian device*, structurally linked to the constitutionalist argument of legally established limits and control for power-holders (shared-rule and self-rule). It is precisely this power balance which makes of federalism an institutional pillar of vertical separation of powers, aimed at providing mutual control between different levels of government in particular, and of political system in general When translated into the terms of federal polity, these institutional requirements imply contractual arrangement and partnership as a socio-political underpinning of a non-centralised state organisation.

as well as on the desirability of maintaining these legitimate diversities, that goes against a modern democratic principle of political liberty as an absolute political equality, and against majority as a sole legitimate representative expression of popular government. Federalism has at the same time correlated to the modern statehood and remained an immanent challenge to this statehood as that of democratic republic. The very idea of "group liberty" as a virtue of itself also principally questions individualist underpinning of human rights as another major pillar of liberal constitutional democracy. On the other side, a structural tension between democracy and human rights will remain immanent to modern polity despite a familiar argument that democratic rights are justified only to the extent that they safeguard others, more fundamental rights. Moreover, both individual liberty and democracy are structurally related to two major civic virtues or values – those of tolerance and trust respectively. Together with solidarity, these two moral resources, sometimes referred to as a "political culture", are viable only against a powerful background of citizenship/nationhood that is constitutive to political community.[3]

These eminently liberal virtues either are absent or not forceful enough in the cases of segmented multicultural societies. Mistrust and intolerance are inherent in identity conflicts; and federalism, as part and parcel of conflict transformation, should be instrumental in building up trust and tolerance that are a sine qua non for solidarity. In consequence, an important point to investigate is whether federal arrangements at all, and if so, under what conditions (liberal or others), can address structural causes for mistrust and intolerance in a given multicultural environment and thus critically contribute both to state making and nation building?

---

3 More OFFE C., *Political Liberalism, Group Rights, and the Politics of Fear and Trust*, in : Basta Fleiner L.R., Swiderski E. (eds.), Democratic Transition and Consolidation in Central and Eastern Europe, PIFF, Helbing & Lichtenhahn, Basel, Geneva, Munich, 2001, pp. 8-9. For W. Kymlicka, besides certain virtues needed in virtually any political order (courage and law-abidingness, as well as economic virtues), there are the virtues distinctive to liberal democracy: public spiritedness, sense of justice, civility and tolerance, and a shared sense of solidarity and loyalty. (KYMLICKA W., *Politics in the Vernacular. Nationalism, Multiculturalism and Citizenship*, Oxford University Press 2001, pp. 295-296.)

This paper will argue that a major paradox of multicultural federalism lies in the fact that it should create trust and tolerance, which in fact are its own preconditions! Indeed, multicultural federalism can work only if it succeeds in democratically commanding a loyalty that transcends cultural cleavages, i.e., if it democratically reconciles cultural and political pluralism. The paper will also argue that such reconciliation is structurally unfeasible within a consequently liberal democratic set up.

The paper will address structural causes for the lack of trust and tolerance in the cases where a federal design of some kind is expected to mitigate cultural cleavages, especially as a part of conflict transformation strategy in state building and nation making processes.

PARADOXES OF MULTICULTURAL FEDERALISM : TRUST AND TOLERANCE AS CROSS-CUTTING ISSUES

A trusting and tolerant citizen, and a government that is trustworthy due to its acceptance by the majority of its people and due to its effective protection of human rights - this is what liberal democracy is about. So defined, a sine qua non testifies of a structural ambivalence within both liberty and democracy. A legally guaranteed liberty of an individual protects an individual from state power, but leaves her/him nonetheless exposed to the liberty of others. These "others" he/she need not necessarily accept as persons, but remains principally confident that their liberty – although limiting his/her own - will not basically bring it in danger. She/he is prepared to *tolerate* other's liberty because the values and identity principles that they all commonly share prevail. On the contrary, if a common denominator lacks, which as is often the case with segmented multicultural societies, no tolerance is viable in terms of a major pattern of behaviour. Claus Offe rightly says that "the step from liberty to democratic rights follows the same ambivalence", which made the entire early history of democratic political thought – from Rousseau to John S. Mill – advocate democracy while at the same time preventing its destructive potentials.[4] This immanent tension between

4 Ibidem, p. 9.

desirable and frightening aspects of popular sovereignty is resolved by trust. The fact that majority decisions are principally accepted also by those who disagree, is due to trust in the reasonableness and good intention of fellow citizens. It means that someone accepts some amount of risk for potential harm in exchange for the benefit of co-operation.

In the end, it is trust, which fundamentally matters, since tolerance is also contingent upon the presence of trust. However, it is a well-known argument that trust has a paradoxical place within democracy given that politics as such would seem to throw the very conditions of trust into question. *Political* relationships are about conflicts over goods and power. This is why trust complements and supports deliberative resolutions of political conflicts. At the same time a deliberative approach to political conflict can generate trust, both among individuals and among groups, as well as between individuals and groups and the institutions.[5]

Such an interrelationship between democracy and trust has "altered an ethos of democratic theory", moving it away from strictly egalitarian concepts of the responsibilities of individual citizens and towards a "pluralized egalitarianism". In consequence, trust raises the question as to the means and mechanisms through which such a pluralized concept might become more operative. This argument of Mark Warren[6] seems to me more than pertinent for the topic of the paper. The process of deliberation and opinion formation that precedes voting is critically important for building up trust within multicultural societies. A "vote-centric" majoritarian democracy has proven to be one of the decisive reasons for mistrust between majority and minority, where the cleavages run along ethnic, religious or linguistic lines. Violent elections and refusal to accept the results coming out of democratic procedure, or even a refusal to take part in the elections, remains one of the major paradoxes of majoritarian democracies in multicultural societies. Without entering into the debate whether a community driven multiculturalism, once accommodated within public sphere as well, still remains

---

5 More: WARREN M.E., *Democratic Theory and Trust*, in : Warren M. E. (Ed.), *Democracy and Trust*, Cambridge University Press 1999, pp. 311-360.

6 Ibidem, p. 337.

faithful to authentic liberalism, hardly anyone today would doubt a form of consensual democracy as critically instrumental and supportive of imbibing trust in segmented multicultural societies.

Paradoxically enough trust can also be broken by power-sharing federal arrangements that provide a veto possibility for each group against policies that it would find particularly harmful for its interest. Impartial institutions, including those to protect minorities without unduly offending majority concepts of fairness, are a necessary but not sufficient condition for the perception of fairness. Consensus-driven democracy is based on a premise that the functioning of society depends not only on justice of its institutions or constitution, but also on the virtues, identities, and practices of its citizens, including their ability to co-operate, deliberate, and feel solidarity with those who belong to different ethnic and religious groups.[7]

Here, it is worth reminding ourselves of what Will Kymlicka sees as major fears about citizenship in the face of minority rights, namely: loss of equal citizenship status, fragmentation or weakening of citizenship identities, erosion of civic virtues and participation, as well as weakening of social cohesion and political unity. He also shows where to look for the reasons.[8] In fact, these convincingly show that the inclusiveness of liberal state relies indeed on a "thin" conception of nationhood. In other words, a normative basis of liberal theory of justice is too "tight" to include minorities as a state building element without at the same time putting into question the promotion of responsible democratic citizenship *under liberal terms*. This is of course the conclusion Kymlicka himself would never draw out of his own arguments.[9] I would nonetheless claim that any plausible nation building within segmented multicultural societies has to redefine the very fundamentals of liberal nationhood, in order to provide a proper framework for building trust and tolerance. A negative value standing towards ethnic concepts of nation-

---

7 Also LEVI M., *A State of Trust*, European Institute Florence, Working Paper RSC 96/23, p. 14.

8 KYMLICKA W., NORMAN W. (eds.), *Citizenship in Diverse Societies*, Oxford University Press, 2000, pp. 30-41.

9 KYMLICKA W., *Multicultural Citizenship*, Oxford University Press, 1995.

hood is consequently liberal and, as such, immanent.[10] Understandably enough, it remains stuck in its narrow normative basis. Liberal tolerance is that of individual freedom, absolute formal equality and justice as equal distribution of rights. On the other hand, federalism as a conflict management device for multicultural cleavages can work only if tolerance as part of responsible citizenship goes much further, beyond co-existence and even beyond respect, and takes the shape of a value-driven tolerance, which would accept major cultural diversities (ethnic, religious and linguistic) as intrinsic value.[11]

One of the first and major questions in this context would be what role federal arrangements could play (multicultural federalism). As I have already said at the outset, I argue that the major paradox of multicultural federalism lies in the fact that it should create trust and tolerance, which in fact should make this same federal design viable. I also related this paradox to constitutive features of liberal democracy which have always been challenged by federalism and since two decades have also been challenged by multiculturalism. Now I shall explain how I under-

---

10 Though he is aware of the fact that, in terms of logic, ethnic nationhood is not causally linked to the phenomenon of intolerance and hatred toward "others", Ignatieff, nevertheless, draws a conclusion that there is much greater probability that a society of a civic nationalist type i.e. "a society anchored in a culture of individual rights and liberties", even if it ran, for the moment, off the road of tolerance, "is more easily returned to the practice of toleration than one where social allegiance is invested in ethnicity. See e.g, IGNATIEFF Michael, *Nationalism and Toleration*, in : Caplan Richard and Feffer John (eds.), Europe's New Nationalism – States and Minorities in Conflict, Oxford University Press, New York, Oxford, 1996, p. 219. In his other book *Blood and Belonging*, he is, however, much more explicit in stating that only a civic nation, which is "a community of equal, rights-bearing citizens, united in patriotic attachment to a shared set of political practices and values", is compatible with Enlightement`s values of rationalism and individualism, since this sort of community is created by choice and rational attachment of its members. On the other hand, what constitutes ethnic nation is the inherited belonging, or more precisely, "it is the national community that defines the individual, not the individuals who define the national community." IGNATIEFF Michael, *Blood and Belonging – Journeys into the New Nationalism*, Vintage, London, 1994, pp. 7-8. (JOVANOVIC M., *From Ethnic Nationhood to Multicultural Citizenship*, in : Eriksonas Linas and Müller Leos (eds.), Statehood Before and Beyond Ethnicity, P.I.E. - Peter Lang Publishers, Brussels, 2005, pp. 319-339.

11 More on various types of tolerance in FROST R., *Vier Konzeptionen der Toleranz*, in : Kaufmann M. (Hg.), Integration oder Toleranz, Verlag Karl Alber Freiburg/ München 2001, S. 106-117.

stand these challenges (1) and what would be major reasons that federal arrangements cannot work as conflict transformation strategy in all those cases where (new) state building and nation making are supposed to take place (2).

MULTICULTURAL FEDERALISM : MAJOR CHALLENGES

As already said, federalism puts in question and aims at redefining the absolute political equality as political liberty – the latter being a consequence of the liberal principle of formal equality, which reduces justice to equal distribution of rights. Federalism has always questioned the two pillars of the modern liberal state – those of democratic sovereignty and procedural legitimacy: First. Federalism denies to the national majority the claim to be the (only) legitimate expression of the sovereignty of the people. Besides, federation replaces sovereignty with more diffuse sovereign powers of the federal state, on the one hand, and of its constitutive entities, on the other. In other words, by its inherent response to group liberty, federalism redefines democratic sovereignty both as a legitimacy basis and as *suprema potestas*. Secondly. Multicultural federalism also substantialises a modern procedural legitimacy formula in all those cases in which the federal institutional set-up represents a strategy of diversity accommodation through public recognition of the latter within a given multiethnic/multicultural society. A procedural design of secession of three northern Catholic and French speaking districts from the canton of Bern and the creation of the new canton of Jury in 1978 can be indeed invoked as a paradigmatic example for the substantialisation of the modern procedural legitimacy formula.[12]

---

12 A cascade system of popular votes within the Jura region, composed of three downward levels – the Jura region, districts, communes – transparently testifies of the basic element to give validity to the Swiss federation: /cultural/ *minorities cannot be overruled on constitutive issues, because these affect state legitimacy itself.* Had the procedure been strictly majoritarian, it would have complied with the procedural democracy formula. Under the principles of procedural legitimacy, strictly taken, the separation process would have been valid by the very fact that the Bernese authorities decided first to establish a constitutional framework and the procedure under which the majority – at the level of the whole canton of Bern only! – could have arrived at a consensus. However, the Bernese people did not vote on

Federalism emerged as a possible conflict-management device of inter-ethnic conflicts precisely because of its "illiberal" underpinnings. In many cases until now, however, it radicalised the problem to which it was supposed to be a solution. Why? Because the major challenge of multicultural federalism could be summed up as follows: *How to provide political solutions to cultural conflicts?* Ethnic, religious, linguistic demands should instead be translated into *multicultural civic principles and designs*. Again, multicultural citizenship in liberal terms is, structurally speaking, a contradiction in adiecto.

Like federalism, multiculturalism persists as an endemic, anti-liberal challenge to constitutional democracy. Together with federalism, it calls for the revision of the major liberal democratic principle, namely, that majority as such is the legitimate expression of the sovereign will of the people. This has been done in a two-fold manner: First. Multiculturalism questions the intrinsic premise behind the modern nation state, which is that only a society homogenized in (one) identity can lead to political consensus as democratic consensus. Second. The communitarian demand that ethnic, religious, cultural dientities should *publicly* matter makes an epochal departure from the constitutive principle of modern politics, that of neutrality of public sphere against ethnic, cultural and religious group identities.[13]

secession procedure merely to make secession procedurally legitimate. i. e. valid for the majority. The procedure simultaneously took into consideration the founding tenet of Swiss federalist political culture – that of a decentralised loyalty: minority issue was addressed as the issue of political integration already at the constitutive phase of the new canton. By being given the possibility to decide against majority, *minority also democratically legitimised the creation of the new canton.* The Protestant French speaking population, who wanted to stay within the canton of Bern, were themselves vested with the same right to territorial self-determination as the separatist majority.

13 The break-through from the demand of equal individual rights to the rights of peoples to be respected as equal in their diversities is the main tune of the communtarian debate, which sometimes tries, not always convincingly, to argue with liberal arguments. (More in : TAYLOR Ch., *The Politics of Recognition*, and HABERMAS J., *Struggles for Recognition in the Democratic Constitutional State*, in : Gutmann A. (Ed.), *Multiculturalism*, Princeton University Press, Princeton, New Jersey, 1994, pp. 25-73 and pp. 107-148. See also: KYMLICKA W., *Multinational Citizenship: A Liberal Theory of Minority Rights*, Oxford University Press, Oxford, 1995.

The case multiculturalism makes for positive collective freedom also contests constitutional democracy on the issue of how far the "politics of differences" should be placed on state-building level. Given the individualist and majoritarian underpinning of liberal constitutional democracy, the latter cannot of itself accept the politics of group differences on a state-building level and therefore is structurally incapable of meeting the multiculturalism claims on the values of diversities and collective rights as such. It remains defensive towards the multiculturalism argument that formal equal rights alone cannot guarantee equality, as long as they are not accompanied by the rights to be equal in respective differences. The liberal democratic defence of diversity is based upon a universalistic rather than a particularistic perspective. This explains why some teleological reinterpretations of modern constitution, which try to re-legitimise the political symbolism of human rights, principally question the very liberal leitmotiv of the French Revolution of (merely) Liberté – Egalité – Fraternité (Liberty – Equality – Fraternity), and articulate instead an alternative syntagm of Sécurité – Diversité – Solidarité (Security – Diversity – Solidarity).[14]

Given that multiculturalism understands equality as the right to diversity, it logically implies that the formalism of the liberal equality, based upon ontological individualism, is to be transcended. To put it in a more straight forward manner: There has emerged a need for *substantialization* of human rights based *also* upon ethnic, religious and cultural diversities. This appears to be a clear-cut consequence of putting forward the thesis that man's dignity has to be regarded as an open concept.[15] Accordingly, pluralism introduces a new reading of the constitutionally spelled out principle of tollerance. As already said, the latter cannot be reduced to the receptiveness of diversities merely on the individual level, but has to do with diversities on group level, too. The common good starts to be pursued along co-existence of differences, where also group identity is immanently imbedded into the constitu

---

14 DENNINGER E., *Vielfalt, Sicherheit und Solidarität: Ein neues Paradigma für Verfassungsgebung und Menschenrechtsentwicklung*, in : (derselb.) Menschenrechte und Grundgesetz, Beltz, Athenäum, Weinheim, 1994, pp. 13-72.

15 DENNINGER E., op. cit., pp. 33-36.

tional identity of a given society. When so interpreted, the principle of tolerance renounces "eurocentrism" which underlies modernity as such. At the same time it makes democratic principles of constitution of a given polity more receptive for basically community-driven, as opposed to individual, social organisation and nation building.

Kymlicka highlights nine differences between liberal and illiberal nation building, and claims these are a matter of "degree", in order to argue that, "what distinguishes liberal nation-building from illiberal nationalism is not the absence of any concern with language, culture, and national identity, but rather the content, scope, and inclusiveness of this national culture, and the modes of incorporation into it."[16]

However, there are convincing empirical arguments to claim that an authentically liberal nation-state has principally failed to accommodate cultural diversities and has proven a fallacy for national minorities, be it constituted upon ethnic or civic understanding of nationhood as citizenship. Modern concepts of nation were precisely the attempt to answer the question on the legitimate bearer of the constitution-making power. At the same time, they all, with different underlying principles in mind, tried to cover-up one and the same thing, namely that citizenship, as the major founding principle of the modern state, symbolises the *universality* of a democratic political community within a *particular* nation-state. The problem arose once the given concept of nation became no more inclusive and "universal" but rather exclusive within one and the same nation-state, more particularly when (eth*no)-nation* and *demos* no more coincided.

Minority rights as individual rights (and other rights) have cast a new light on citizenship as the principle to symbolize universality within a particular nation-state. Minorities do not fit in the constitutive principles of modern polity as (through majority defined) democratic polity.

---

16 KYMLICKA W., *Western Political Theory and Ethnic Relations in Eastern Europe*, in : Kymlicka W., Opalski M. (eds.), Can Liberal Pluralism be Exported, Oxford 2001, p. 59.

The two basically different concepts of nation[17], which underlie the citizenship of contemporary Western constitutional democracies, could be qualified as those of *democratic civism without/against multiculturality* (American and French respectively) and *democratic civism out of monoculturality* (the German model). Both concepts fall short of bringing viable solutions to ethnic, religious, linguistic and the like minorities. In both cases minorities *as groups* – principally – have nothing to say on fundamental constitutional issues. In consequence, minorities cannot participate in the citizenship they have not consented to. They have been sending the message that universality of the modern polity does not work for them, since, for them, it is "exclusive" universality.

Put differently, structural tenets of liberally grounded universality have to be reconsidered and redefined. In terms of constitution making and nation building, this means that the problems of design of *pouvoir constituant* and of citizenship have to be revisited. A new answer is needed for a critical question on legitimacy foundations: *Whose* is the state? A democratic integration of multicultural societies as a new type of corporative societies is a structural pre-condition for the viability of a human rights policy.[18] This is why the major questions are: *W*hat would be the sources of democratic unity in a multinational state? What role can constitution making/constitutional consensus play in a democratic inclusion of cultural diversities? Is "citizenship out of democratically

---

17 More on the differences between the two main concepts of nation, in : BRUBAKER R., *Citizenship and Nationhood in France and Germany*, Harvard University Press, Cambridge, London, 1992. Cf. also, GREENFELD L., *Nationalism. Five Roads to Modernity*, Harvard University Press, Cambridge, Mass., 1992.

18 For example, a communitarian concept of citizenship, which prevails in the new constitutions of Central and Eastern Europe, certainly testifies to a deficit in the identity and homogeneity of the new polities *in statu nascendi*. The fact that this concept is much more concerned with civic duties turns it into a promising integrative force. However, the major underlying principle, namely, that it is the community which is constitutive of the individual's identity, ran counter real-existing communit*ies* within what is constitutionally laid down, i. e. positivated as a (supposedly one) community. This is what "ethnification" of polities and politics in Eastern Europe is about: communitarian concept of citizenship *as* in fact *ethnicity* remains an intrinsic obstacle for an authentic communitarianism. The protective state policy vis-à-vis all its citizens gives way to a systematically invasive state policy against certain ethnic groups of citizens.

integrated ethnicities" possible, and if so, within which constitutive and constitutional framework?

Only if multicultural federalism succeeds in answering these questions positively, it can prove instrumental to building trust and tolerance. Swiss multicultural federalism is a proof that it is possible, however, at the cost of liberal principles. The Swiss federal polity is first of all a democracy of institutionalised cultural differences and its nationhood is that of democratically integrated cultural diversities.[19] Here, federalism has been introduced as a structural principle of democracy. In other words, unlike United States and Canada, which represent *democratic federations*, Switzerland is to be seen as a *federalized democracy.* Here, communal civism has embraced *participatory democracy as a federalist element* to protect interests of structural minorities within a given multicultural society. Swiss consensus-driven democracy has made the abstract principle of people's sovereignty more concrete and operational through traditional Swiss instruments of democratic decentralisation, those of municipal self-government and of direct democracy.

FEDERALISM AS A CONFLICT-TRANSFORMATION STRATEGY?

Unfortunately, there are hardly better examples to sustain the argument on structural paradoxes of multicultural federalism as a conflict management device than those related to state reconstruction and nation-building after ethnic or religious wars. The involvement of the international community, however legitimate it may be in terms of peace-keeping or even peace-enforcement, opens new dilemmas, especially in the cases where the international community facilitates constitution-making. The "transfer" of pouvoir constitutiant from a polity in statu nascendi to international major players cannot but make a legitimacy paradox of multiculural federalism even more complicated.

---

19 More in BASTA L.R., *The Nation-State Federalism and European Integration*, in : Jyränki A. (Ed.), National Constitutions in the Era of Integration, Kluwer, London 1999, pp. 151-172.

All major federal arrangements in general, and federations in particular, share something in common. In order to be legitimate, a consensus underlying such arrangements need not only democratic support but also a federal consensus, a federal compact, which would in form of a constitution, define the terms of federal loyalty – the terms of federal trust. The interrelationship of constitution making and nation building, thus, shows that state building is at stake.

This is why the constitution-making process is so important. For example, all three ex-communist federations inevitably dissolved because federal trust in particular was missing; the truth of the matter is that it could not be viable within constitutive foundations of communist politics, which used constitutions as a means to simulate legitimacy foundations and provide party decisions with the image of constitutionality.[20]

In post-conflict situations an absence of tolerance and trust as necessary conditions for peaceful and democratic society is evident already at a symbolic level. A profoundly different reading of key causes of a conflict as well as a fully contradicting assessment of present situation is often at hand. In consequence, it is almost impossible to reach agreement on the constitutive nature of the future common state framework. There is not enough political will to understand the other side, however critically important it may be. The role of the elite is in this sense critical, and the paradox of the situation lies in the fact that the positions of the elites cannot be democratically verified. Besides, given that the international community has to negotiate with elites, it offers the latter a comfortable position in which they often trade constitutional solutions for own political survival. This is how – instead of state building – a real politics in its dirtiest meaning is taking place.

More in particular, in cases of territorial accommodation, it is minorities that focus on external rights for their territorial entities. This shows that they take negotiated solutions as somehow "transitory". In the "in-

---

20 More BASTA FLEINER L., *El papel de la Constitucion en la disolucioin de la Federacion Yugoslava*, in : Gonzales Enriques C., Minoras nacionales y conflictos étnicos en Europa del Este, UNED Ediciones, Madrid, 2004, pp. 123-140.

ternationalisation" of their position they see a "manoeuvring space" to sometimes again open up their issue. Moreover, although territorially based federal solutions would be in many cases desirable, it is exactly the conflict over territory, which makes ethnic demands end up as irreversible and thus categorical. Again, the case of ex-communist federations show that a crucial paradox of federalism as a conflict-management device for multiethnic societies lies in "hidden potentials" of the correlation between territory on one side, and ethnic-driven constitutional solutions in a given multiethnic federation, on the other. The major challenge that any multicultural federalism has to face in such a situation, moreover the "trap" with sometimes-fatal consequences for inner peace remains as to how to avoid that – due to constitutional foundations and established decision-making process at a federal level – every constitutional conflict turns into ethnic conflict. What is equally indispensable is that, whatever institutional designs may be pursued, they do not leave space for "re-opening" and re-negotiating constitutive foundations of the common state on an almost day-to-day basis, when differences occur between the elites representing different communities.

A far-reaching ambivalence of the involvement of the international community in designing federal solutions as part and parcel of conflict transformation strategy also has to do with the following reasons:

First and foremost, there is a principal shift in the objective of constitution making which of itself makes an authentic constitutional consensus obsolete. The international community operates under geo-strategic terms of reference, and these usually have nothing to do with internal viability, i.e., inside legitimacy of the proposed solution. Not common identity, but geo-strategic stability in the region is the matter of major concern, and internationally negotiated, in a way imposed framework for the solutions remains in principle non-negotiable. (Bosnia, the former Serbia and Montenegro, Cyprus, East Timor…)

Not surprisingly, the results until now have not been very convincing. To start with, negative effects for the nation building process have been demonstrated. Namely, nation-building processes form power relations from the inside, which the foreign interventions can only distort. In addition, this is also the reason why foreign pressure usually proves ineffective: power relations are distorted and there remain no reliable actors to respond to the pressure. Moreover, internationally facilitated or negotiated constitutional arrangements have failed to fulfil three important conditions for constitution -making and nation-building in multicultural societies: a/ the process should ensure that the constitution is legitimate and legal; b/ it should guarantee inclusion as a proof of the respect for diversity; and c/ the process should promote a direct participation of the public in constitution making.[21]

Last but not least, "international constitution making", which often imposes unviable solutions, and the lack of effective guarantees for international rule of law, inherently challenge the credibility also of federal arrangements in such cases, since – in the end – federalism *is* about constitutionally defined and respected rules of the game. Unlike post conflict societies, Western democracies build upon the inherent identity between legality and legitimacy. More importantly for democratic constitutionalism, legality as such is immanently legitimate only under two, equally indispensable conditions: a/ that legality relies upon a consensus of those concerned (government by consent), and b/ that it is "universalisible", i.e. generally applied (legal security and equality before the law). I have tried to show why these conditions have not been fully accommodated in the cases of "international constitution making".

In relation to the international rule of law, the following comments are in order. New models of peacekeeping and peace-enforcement rely more and more upon *some* nation states as global and regional actors, mainly but not always under the authorisation of the United Nations. Here, international rule of law in the sense of *international legitimacy* for human rights protection has been often more than seriously challenged. The problem becomes even worse if the actors are international financial institutions. Here, the mechanisms for judicial review in order to ensure that there is no violation of human rights are "sadly lacking". Such global actors "operate outside the established international human

21 Cf. HAYSOM N., *Constitution Making and Nation Building*, in : Federalism in a Changing World – Learning from Each Other, Federalism Conference Reader, St. Gallen 2002, pp. 261-298.

rights law framework" and "no particular judicial or other instance can hold them accountable."[22] As a result, the credibility of the role of the international community in the transition from negotiation to democratic legitimacy has been principally put in question.

22 CLAPHAM A., *Globalisation and the Rule of Law*, in : ICJ Review, 1999, N° 1, pp. 20-21.

Lessons Learned

Thomas FLEINER

INTRODUCTION

A conference on federalism in the Near East has to address two very different issues. Some would understand that federalism may be a tool to bring peace to the area by convincing politicians that they should seek federal solutions as a magic formula for peace in the Near East. Some might even expect that federalism should be the basic constitutional construction for the internal reorganisation of countries facing violence and aggression. On the other hand some may even think that federalism should be the key issue in order to establish democracy and rule of law not only in the Near East but in the entire area of the Middle East. In fact the aim of the conference was not to establish concrete proposals for any of those noble goals.

The conference was limited to scientific expertise in constitutional law and political science. Although each of the experts was personally concerned for a peaceful solution of the conflict, clear political statements were not expressed in the conference. The main aim of all participants was to share common ideas among scholars coming from different backgrounds and exploring in a scientific discourse some basic principles of federalism and to analyse to what extend those principles might help or inspire politicians in their endeavour to seek peace in the troubled area. Thoughts on federal principles expressed in the conference or inspired by the conference however may be useful, if in a hopefully near future the environment will allow a peaceful settlement of the conflict. As soon as serious negotiations would focus on the international and domestic solutions a constitutional construction will be necessary to bring or hold different societies together. At least in this period any serious thought on tools of conflict management will be helpful, as there was a common understanding, that only innovative ideas would enable politicians to find solutions acceptable for the people's of the area.

The participants were not asked to represent a specific community or political party. In contrary they were exploring basic issues and principles which might realistically have an impact for a long term solution in the area. Being integrated into their own historical community they of course were often more aware of principles which might be rejected, misused or even steer up emotions and violence instead of promoting procedures and a rational discourse on justice and a common future.

Federalism was explored as a general principle first to hold or bring peoples together. Federalism may be within an existing state a constitutional structure based on some principles to accommodate diversity. If those major federal principles such as taking diversity serious, trust, tolerance, reconciliation, rule of law, self-rule, shared rule, conflict management tools and democratic participation of citizens not only to produce majorities but to implement self-determination for individuals and groups would be implemented within each existing state in the entire area, it would certainly enhance peaceful solution and in particular strengthen cooperation by confederal or federal tools. In short: implementation of all or some of such principles could turn enemies into adversaries.

Basic principles underlying federalist concepts contain today probably the most promising instruments and values which could enable communities destroyed by emotional nationalism to overcome their differences in order to accommodate their diversities and to maintain their different identities. Federalism accommodating diversity enables new constitutional concepts which are built up on new legitimacy principles that are: a new view of the principle of rule of law, of self rule, additional dimensions of individual liberty and democracy. Federalism is by principle a compromise and thus only viable if the communities involved in state activities are prepared to sacrifice some of their strongest interests for the sake of peace.

Although this optimism may be supported by the fact that more than 40% of the world population is living in federal countries and that several of these countries have established federalism as a hope to overcome peacefully their inner conflicts and that in several cases such as Canada, Belgium, India, Ethiopia, Switzerland, Malaysia and not to forget the European Union which represents actually "federalism in the making" this hope at least up to now was realistic, we have also to be aware, that federalism may not always be the magic formula for peace.

In contrary it can even stir up conflicts and split societies. It can even enhance to stir up ethnic cleansing if it is shaped over territories with dispersed minorities, which are overruled by a majority and thus feel offended within their dignity. Neither in the middle east, nor in Cyprus, Sri Lanka, Chechnya, and many other conflicting areas in today's world it was possible to use federalism as a promising tool to bring or hold fragmented societies peacefully together. In all these cases, it is the majority which does not trust the minorities, once they will be able to participate on central decision through the shared rule principle on one side and rule themselves on the other side not to misuse federalism for their final unilateral secession. In these cases of major mistrust the power-holders of the majority are obviously able to convince their constituency to prefer the burden and risks of conflict to a constitutional peace, which would overrule vested interest and dignity of the majority.

In this conference we thus did analyse first the different existing constitutional concepts facing diversity and multiculturality such as territorial federalism, personal federalism, the multicultural society of immigration states such as the US and the Nation concept of the French tradition.

From the introduction of Ronald Watts who developed the entire map of different federal systems participants could learn, that among the 25 minus Serbia – Montenegro now 24 federal countries, there are great varieties of structural differences with regard to history, political systems and aims federalism was conceived to achieve. The status of the federal units and even the composition of the federations differ from one federation to the other. Ronald Watts gave an impressive picture of the flexibility federalism is able to cope with including asymmetric federal constructions to be to be adaptable to very different, complex and even conflicting situations.

On the other hand Ronald Watts gave also the warning, that federalism can not be the panacea for the solution of all different kind of conflicts. Federalism is only a hope for conflict resolution major preconditions such as rule of law, democracy and the readiness to accept compromises for the sake of belonging to a union with common values are fulfilled. In addition one has not only to analyse the structure of federal constitutions, one has also to seek the underlying principles. It may well be that a federal structure may not be the solution, but the underlying principles may very well give some guidance for peaceful settlements of conflict.

The principles which we discussed during the conference were based on new views of the problem of the legitimacy of a multicultural state, of the rule of law and of democratic self-determination. A very special solution for a new legitimacy concept can be found in structures based on personal federalism. Claude Klein did open the debate on the theoretical concept of personal federalism rooted in the Austrian Hungarian Empire and promoted within ideological concepts of socialist ideas by Brunner and Renner in the beginning of the 20th century. Ideals of personal federalism although had no big political impact in the last century most probably, because the struggle for full sovereignty and democracy based on territory did not allow any real development of a federalism based on territorially dispersed communities which are not linked to a homogeneous territory.

It was Antoine Messarra coming from Lebanon who endorsed personal federalism as the solution for the entire area of the Middle East. His arguments, that personal federalism allows a more efficient unitary state concept which does not enhance secessionist movements within a territory controlled by nationalism was confronted with the need of any unitary state to have some basic communality in values which would hold the state together.

A total different concept of union was then brought on the table by Gasha Popovic who explained the recently established Union between Montenegro and Serbia which in the mean time already did fall a part. This quasi confederal union influenced or even imposed by the European Union and its concept of a Union to build a common market with quasi sovereign members as motor to unite different sovereignties is with regard to Serbia and Montenegro constantly threatened by the possibility of secession.

Such threat does of course not induce private investments within this region. The very fact, that the final territory of the state and thus its democracy and guarantee to implement the rule of law remains still uncertain, impedes any promising economic and legal development. Realistically one has though still to admit, that this solution has strongly been influenced by the international community which unfortunately often prefers a temporary peace settlement to a long lasting solution.

In earlier times the old classical confederations such as the American Colonies seceding from the United Kingdom and the Swiss Confederation defending democracy against neighbouring monarchies were hold together by the common interest of defence. Based on this communality the confederations later on did turn into stronger federations. It seems however unlikely that a the establishment of a confederation with the aim to hold two disintegrating Republics together with the only communality of a common market can not be a promising solution as globalisation in any case promotes the common market but on a much larger scale.

In today's globalised market economy the common aim to establish a common market is not a sufficient communality to hold a conflicting region together. Unfortunately history in the mean time since the conference has shown that the pessimistic view on the strength of the confederation to hold both republics together das been realistic.

Can the Swiss experience be of help for ideas to bring the conflicting communities together? Switzerland has established its institutions through a long specific history. They are embedded the culture of the different religious and language communities and the borderline of the nation building middle European states. These institutions can not be copied for peace settlements in other regions. However the basic principles of the Swiss example may give some guidance for other solutions.

Switzerland is not "owned" by one nation, but by the peoples of the cantons. The people of Switzerland as a composed nation based on specific communalities such as a specific concept of democracy, federalism and rule of law was able to be brought and hold together by accepting diversity as a necessary principle not only to be tolerated but even to be promoted. Its legitimacy is based on the fact, that the identity of the country is based on its diversities. United by its diversities it has to take differences serious. Thus it integrates its diversity into its political reality. The different communities are through their cantonal sovereignty part of the nation. They participate in the constitution making and by this also nation making process.

The Swiss understanding of individual liberty is connected with its concept of local democracy guaranteeing freedom in the sense of self-determination on the local level. Democracy thus is not only limited to the production of efficient majorities. Democracy is not reduced to a 51% of the winner takes all system. The lessons learned from the Swiss experience rooted in the specific history are not institutional but much more principle and value oriented. They ask us not to reduce liberty and freedom to the only negative dimension but to see all four dimensions which are liberty from the state (liberal concept), liberty to the state (collective rights), liberty by the state (social rights) and liberty within the state (self-determination by the peoples through democratic participation adopting the legislation approved to limit personal freedom).

Taking diversity serious required the Swiss to implement the self-rule principle not only on the cantonal but also on the municipal level. Dispersed minorities and small language and religious communities in particular in the trilingual and bilingual cantons required a bottom up construction of federal principles starting at the municipal level. Cantons however are required to organise themselves as unitary state, which can decentralise at their own decision. Thus they can introduce self-rule but the shared rule principle they can only introduce through the electoral system. In exploring cantonal systems however the interested researcher will find that those confronted with diversity did take diversity serious through various different tools.

Belgium federalism presented by André Alen taught us the difficulties of the combination of personal and territorial federalism. In fact, the constitutional court seems to be very reluctant to implement elements of personal federalism which would go beyond the already constitutionally provided guarantees of personal federalism. It seems that the territories are strongly opposed to be limited within their language policies by elements of personal federalism guaranteed to persons under their jurisdiction but belonging to the other language community. The Belgium federalism is a most convincing case of a federal system, which has been introduced in order to accommodate diversities. It teaches us however, that once the system has been implemented conflicts will still continue and it the question is, whether the combination of personal and territorial federalism did soften or stir up the conflicts.

The Swiss and the Belgium case in addition give evidence, that a federal state does not necessarily depend on one nation, but that states can also be viable based on different nation or that the nation holding the state together can very well be a composed nation.

Liah Greenfeld explained the system of the individual civic nation principle, implemented in the United States. She convincingly argued that the United States can neither be qualified as a melting pot system nor as a nation in the traditional French or German concept. The basic concept of the American System is rooted in the Anglo-Saxon nation principle, which holds a nation together as a people having equal rights as individual citizens with individual responsibility. This nation concept holds individuals together, since their cultural roots are irrelevant and this is the reason different cultures can integrate in the American nation concept. Liah Greenfeld however insisted, that one can not impose a nation concept to other nations, thus it would not be possible with whatever political decisions to impose this nation concept in the area of the Middle East.

Didier Maus introduced the very different concept of the French nation born in the French revolution. This nation concept based on the sovereignty of the citizens united by their common values has influenced different constitutions and nations. If citizens are prepared to form a political union only based on universal values expressed in the declaration of human rights, the French nation concept can be a model. The French nation concept teaches us the importance of political values which can even ignore or deny the political reality of cultural values. It was however very clear, that the French nation concept although it has historically influenced other nation concepts cannot be taken as a model. It has its specific historical roots in the French revolution and can only be a valid model, if minorities accept to be ruled finally by majorities, which politically ignore their cultural importance. The most important lesson however the French nation concept teaches us is thus certainly, that a nation can only hold together, if there are common values generally accepted as universal values to be implemented for all peoples living within the territory of the respective nation.

On the background of the flexibility of different federal systems and taking into account the different nation concepts we continued discussion on the conflicting state and nation concepts in the near east. Israel is a state which considers itself as a secular political unit on one side and on the other as a homeland for the Jewish population dispersed in the diaspora all around the world. Thus the secular state concept is influenced by the old traditional Jewish philosophy and the basic beliefs in Jewish values expressed in the halakhah and in the Thorah may become the fundament for common values acceptable for the great bulk of the society actually totally split as Ilan Greilsamer pointed out between the orthodox religious and the liberal capitalists.

With this regard the different interventions aimed to examine and to analyse the diversities splitting societies in the Near East such as religion, language, identity and nationalism and to explore to what extent and what principles might in the long range be helpful for the seek of peaceful solutions.

As the conference was dedicated to the memory of Jean Nordmann it took of course always into account the living experiences of the Nordmann family living in a mainly catholic and bilingual environment in Fribourg. The very fact, that the late Jean Nordmann himself and his

Wife Bluette present at the conference were always promoting common understanding, compromise and tolerance in every day life was guiding the participants in all their interventions.

IS FEDERALISM A PROMISING OR UNPROMISING CONCEPT

Already in his introduction Ronald Watts was putting this crucial question on the table. It is not astonishing that his answer was neither only promising nor only unpromising. There are many factors which may help federalism to become a promising tool for conflict management. Ronald Watts mentioned in particular a democratic environment based on the principles of rule of law. Only based on these principles federalism may enable to bring or to hold fragmented societies together. In addition one has to be aware of the fact, that there is and there should not be a strict concept or definition of federalism. In fact, federal countries have developed a great variety of differences of federalism. Some countries have federalised by centralization such as the US and Switzerland and to a certain extend the European Union. Some countries have federalised by decentralisation such as Belgium, Canada and India. Some countries have developed out of a colonial system some did establish federalism on their proper decision as sovereign countries such as Belgium. Federalism has been very different according to its aim. Some countries introduced federalism as an additional tool to guarantee the rule of law and individual liberty such as the US and Germany. Some countries have established federalism in order to accommodate diversity such as Switzerland, Canada, Ethiopia, India, Malaysia and Nigeria. Some federal countries had to accommodate minorities with asymmetric solutions such as Russia or Spain. But also with regard to the institutional set up, some federal countries (USA, Argentina etc.) have chosen presidential systems; some have introduced federalism based on the Westminster type parliamentary system such as Canada and Germany. Switzerland did set up its institutions based on the old directorial system of the French Revolution. Great differences are to be seen, whether a federal country is integrated into the common law or civil law system, whether it is a twofold federalism or a federalism with multiple federal units.

Federalism has shown to be a concept of statehood which is in it self very flexible. Federalism has its own dynamics and thus is able to adapt to different developments and different needs and purposes. Federalism as such however is always the result of a compromise based on the conviction of all parties involved, that the different entities have to be respected and none of the entities can put into question the basic understanding to pursue a common state policy.

However we have to be aware of the fact, that federalism is often also seen as an unpromising state concept. Often politicians fear, that federal solutions are just the first step to secession. Unitary states claim that equality of citizens can only be guaranteed in a state, which provides for a general and unrestricted implementation of the same laws. Those who promote the democracy as principle to produce efficient majorities as the main legitimacy of the state see in federalism a basic limitation of the majority principle and claim that although the majority principle may lead to the tyranny of the majority federalism may lead to the tyranny of minorities.

Often federalism is also seen as a concept of decentralisation, which is not transparent, inefficient and it may also lead to corruption on the local level. Today's politics depend on the capacity to adapt to the needs of an ever changing world controlled by the sovereignty of the global market.

In many cases one can not celebrate federalism as the reason for peaceful solutions. Often these solutions depend just as much on the quality of the leadership. The question one has also to ask, as Prof. Lidija Basta put it, is, whether federalism will really attenuate the conflicts and not in contrary stir up conflicts. The breaking up of former Yugoslavia has certainly been caused by the fact, that the country has once been ruled not by a constitution but by the communist party, which used the constitution as an alibi to legitimate the leadership of the party. If the former Yugoslavia would have remained federal with a multi-party system however, and in if the new borderlines of the republics would have been drawn along ethnic lines, the ethnic conflict might have become so vigorous that no federal system would have been able to lead to peaceful conflict management. Thus, one might even think that ethnic federalism may stir up the conflicts. Ethopia is the only country known based only on ethnicity. Today however it is hold together by a strong one party leadership as South Africa. How would they develop in a multi-party system with changing majorities?

MAIN ISSUES OF THE CONFERENCE

As part from the discussion on the different cases of Federalism including the issue of personal federalism the main issues of the conferences were the different perspectives of the state in the legitimacy sense: Who – that is – what people or nation owns the state? What is the relationship of the state and religion? Can a nation be fragmented or composed? What are the conditions of a peaceful transition to come from A to B? What are the different perspectives of the State? The most important issues have been discussed as follows.

Idea of Federalism itself is based on different principles such as to take diversity serious, to accept compromise not as weakness but as an asset, to consider that liberty and freedom have not only one but several different dimensions in the sense that it guarantees liberty from the state (individual liberty), liberty by the state (protection of liberty and affirmative action), liberty within the state (democratic and participatory liberty) and liberty to the state (collective rights and self-determination through democracy). The main aim finally has to be, that each community can feel at home within its federal unit and through the federal unit within the federation. This aim however can only be achieved if all communities have the feeling that they own not all but part of the federation they are living in. Only based on a shared rule principle, which gives communities

The priorities of those different principles and the way of implementing might be very different from one federal solution to another. This extraordinary flexibility of different federal solution enables the federal communities, to explore solutions which can take into account those principles on one side and adopt a solution which takes into account the historic, economic, social, cultural specificities and integrates their federal solution into the international community.

In his intervention on the combination of personal and territorial Federalism André Alen focused on the possibilities of even combining personal and territorial federalism according to the Belgium experience, which – as he pointed out – has in practice been much more been developing along territorial and not personal lines.

Mr. Antoine Nasri Messara – influenced by the Lebanese experiences – endorsed the personal federalism as the ideal solution for the entire Middle East based on the history of the Ottoman Empire. Most interventions however were sceptical as to bring the totally different societies of the Near East together into one state. Personal federalism most participants claimed would even require much more communalities as a territorial federalism would. Nobody excluded however some kind of combination in particular with regard to communities which would overlap specific territories.

In a most challenging intervention Avieze Ravitzky unveiled the real roots of the Jewish religion which is in accordance to all actual basic principles of the rule of law including tolerance, understanding respect for other religions and human rights.

A federalism based on an individualistic concept of the nation as in United States can not be based on ethnic communities. It is in principle individualistic and conflicts do in general not depend on ethnicities but on conflicts of superiority, of rational or irrational choices. The American society, which mainly has developed out of the history of immigration, is totally different from traditional communities historically rooted in their territory. "America is based on a fundamental consensus regarding all the important existential questions". Such concept of nation cannot be imposed by decree. However one can learn from its experiences lessons which should be avoided.

LEGITIMACY

As general principle everybody stressed that one can only federalise if there is a clear will to federalise. Such a will of course depends to a great extent also on common values. Without any communality a real will to federalise can not develop. What would however be those values a part from democracy, rule of law and compromise. The most difficult issue of course is to find communalities among different societies, which are conflicting. Taking into account Israel one would have to find communalities bringing together at least conceptually very different religions, several languages several histories different ways of life and different political convictions. On what communalities would it be possible e.g. based on the preamble of the South African Constitution to reconcile Palestinians and Jews in a federal state composed of the two nations? Ilan Greilsammer pointed out, that even the traditional Jewish society is now totally split and that there is a real threat of implosion of the state of Israel as soon as the only communality: its common enemy would fade away.

Nobody could finally give any convincing answer on this crucial question. Of course everybody would agree that the basic principles and universal values should be the bases for any federation. However a federal state would need additional communalities which would bring different communities together within the universal values.

It may be that for the time being communalities could not be found. But there may be a peace- and constitution making process, which could establish through negotiation among the different communities some communality. How should however the procedure to elaborate and decide on a common constitution be established and organised, when it should aim at bringing communities together? Both communities are strongly committed to their religion. Legitimacy of the Israeli state is based on the Halakhah and the Torah. Legitimacy of the Palestinians is based on the Koran and for some on the Christian Bible. Can a secularised concept provide legitimacy?

On the other hand, one has to admit, that what ever solution will have to be found any peace will not be legitimate without some communalities even if it is established on two sovereign states. Compromises on the most difficult conflicts with regard to Jerusalem and to the refugees will only be possible on some communality, which will have to be found. One can also imagine as Prof. Ravitzky pointed out, that the common values may just be to accept each others different values. And this can in particular be promising, because even very diverse communities with different religious values may very well have some basic values in common. Why should then all values be the same, why could one not imagine, that not only language and religion are different but also that values may be different and that only the necessary common decisions one would have to base them on the common or universal values? Is a common state based on the Torah and on the Sharia inconceivable if both would accept the common value of the rule of Law?

SHARED RULE

For Ronald Watts the shared rule principle is part of the essentials of a federal system. One can see this principle from two sides: First shared rule means, that a part from the federation as a state there are also federal units with state qualities and thus to be involved at least as part of the constituent power. Second the shared rule principle has also to be implemented in the sense that federal units should somehow be integrated in the decision making process in particular with regard to legislative decisions of the federation.

In a con-federal system the federal units can in essential issues block the confederation with their veto-power. For this reason a con-federal system might only be achieved if it is considered as first step towards a more integrated federation. A con-federal system with important veto-powers from of the federal units is not a sustainable system. Since either the majority or the minority is in the position to tyrannize the federation it will either break up into different independent states or it will improve towards more institutionalized integration as we can see with the European Union.

An important issue is in particular with regard to the Near East the emergency power. Who is the holder of the emergency power can break up the entire system. In a situation such volatile as the situation in the Near East one will have carefully to design the organization, the powers and the fundamental protection of the citizens in cases of emergency. No community should have the feeling, that it may become the target of the war against terrorism. On the other side the fear of terrorism has to be taken serious and thus the aim to achieve security for the people a priority on the same level as the guarantee of their fundamental rights.

If a federal solution is found, this solution might specially focus on conflict management and on tools to provide procedures for peaceful conflict management. Thus in particular the procedures would have to focus on the shared rule issue and introduce a culture of negotiation and democratic procedure.

To introduce a shared rule principle into a peace-process is only possible on the bases of trust and confidence among the partners depending on their common decisions. Mistrust as Lidija Basta explains is however intrinsically linked to ethnic conflicts. Common trust is, as she points out the basic fundament of the majority principle. I accept to be in a minority, if I trust my fellow citizens that they also decide in the common interest. What is necessary in a state ruled by communities depending on their common decisions? In case a veto power would be established, this is a sign that there is no trust at all. If decisions are taken based on a culture of negotiation parties at least have to trust each other, that the information given in the negotiation, are correct ant complete. That the parties involved in negotiations are openly bargaining and that they are willing and have the capacities to implement results of negotiations. This is the bases of trust and confidence in international negotiations. In internal negotiations additional communalities are required. Such communalities may find their bases on the preparedness of all parties to peaceful conflict solutions and their preparedness for compromises for the sake of peace. Peace among the communities should thus be one of the essential communality added to the principle of rule of law. There was consensus among the participants, that these preconditions for establishing a shared rule principle in a common state are not fulfilled.

SELF RULE AUTONOMY

With regard to the principle of self rule one has to consider autonomy for territorial units as well as personal autonomy. The discussion showed clearly, that only based on both of these concepts of self-rule solutions might be found, which would enable the split society to be brought together.

The case of Montenegro with a very far reaching self-rule system including its own currency was mentioned. However there was no participant who would have thought that this model of self-rule could help in the area to bring a solution.

There is no federal solution accommodating conflicts within fragmented societies without an important self-rule factor. Crucial with regard to this factor is defence, police and inner security, education and culture, criminal and family law. To accept self-rule in these fields is only possible if the federal community takes diversity serious and if there is major trust, that federal units do not misuse power for their purposes against the vested interests of the others. Criminal law established by the federal units may lead to severe differences with regard to universal human rights values. With regard to universal values, one has not only to seek the universality of values but also to question to what extent particularities such as capital punishment in different states of the US are universally acceptable. Here a decision of the Colombian Supreme Court with regard to corporal punishment used in territories of the native Colombians may give some guidance. In this decision the Supreme Court accepted the diversity if it is necessary for the sake of peace among the different communities. Also the Swiss federal court has considered peace among the communities the decisive factor to limit individual human rights such as liberty of religion and liberty of language and to guarantee collective rights if this is necessary for the peaceful togetherness of the communities.

Taking diversity serious will require in the last instance not only to tolerate, to reconcile (South Africa) but also to respect the communities as such to be on equal footing as Antoine Messarra pointed and one may even ask, whether it would not additionally even require to enhance diversities if they are in danger. One cannot only celebrate multiculturality on the bases of the melting pot concept accepting individual diversities. One has also to accept diversities among communities as a decisive factor to stabilise the society. Diversity has to be taken as a value and asset as such. Thus it has to be enhanced in case diversity is in danger.

RECOGNIZE CULTURAL DIVERSITY AS POLITICAL VALUE

We have to be aware of the fact, that modernity and its nation concept does principally exclude diversity. The nation as Liah Greenfeld pointed out is composed of equal individuals, which all seek their personal happiness. The only common value of such society is to enable for each its individual development within as state ruled by the principle of rule of law.

Such concept can not be adopted for a state based on exclusive community values. Is there no way to bring those contradictions together? Claude Klein evoked the principle, that in such a state the minority will have to accept to be only a minority. Messarra pointed to the principle that all minorities have to be on equal footing. Lidija Basta was seeking a concept for a community without ethnicity. The French concept of the value of the equality of the citizen within the nation was considered to be too radical. Ilan Greilsammer even pointed at the importance of different electoral systems which could enable to bring society together.

Of course the traditional state concept is based on the idea, that only a community willing to live peacefully together can finally be brought together in one state. That the state as such could become the very bases which could enable for conflict management tools is up to now inconceivable. How states ruled by whatever majority can or could become honest brokers among conflicting parties as can the international community? One may not up to now enough did seek new solutions with regard to such developments. There is at least one example which has shown that peaceful togetherness can be built up on some state-like institutions and this is the European Union, which has its roots in the early supranational communities linking the former enemies France and Germany together.

COMPOSED NATION

Federal systems may be confronted by the fact, that they are not only motherland for one nation but for several nations. Belgium for instance determines in its preamble, that it is composed of three communities. The former Swiss Constitution provided in its Article 1, that the Swiss nation is composed of the different cantonal peoples. On the other hand the basic principle of one federation is that it provides only one and exclusive citizenship. The Swiss constitution which is based on a threefold citizenship built up from the municipal to the cantonal and then to the Swiss citizenship accepts in principle some diversity even on the level of citizenship. The EU is based on the citizenship of the memberstates, but it provides also for a European Citizenship with special rights to be respected in European Countries. This issue of citizenship would be the most difficult and controversial issue as it is in particular linked with the right of free movements of the citizens and their right to participate in all democratic decisions. Could a federal solution for the Near East even include different citizenship and self-rule for each community to decide on its own citizenship? What would be the consequence for the principle of free movement?

Several interventions did not only deal with the question of a possible federal solution, but they also questioned the citizenship concept based either on inclusiveness or exclusiveness.

It is obvious that any political solution in the near East will have to provide institutional guarantees in order to enable all different communities a part from the different Jewish communities such as Arabs, Druze, Christian etc. to rule their affairs on their own. Each of those communities have long lasting traditions in the area. In middle age they could develop their special community life. In the today's state conception these interests will have to be integrated and considered as primary issue to be solved. Their might result also some asymmetric federal solutions based not only on territory but on personal belonging to a specific group. All those communities must be given the feeling, that they are not only tolerated as guests in the political state but that they contribute to this state-community which is enriched and not burdened by this diversity.

MOTHER/FATHERLAND AND MULTIPLE LOYALTY

Can any state in the Near East become the mother/fatherland for such diverse and conflicting societies? Knowing the reality of the last 50 years one would exclude such idea as a dream without any bases in reality. It was Ravitzky, who invoking the tradition of the Jewish religion insisted, that without any dream reality will never be overcome. This dream may have its roots in the old middle age society in which the three religions could live together. It must be possible, that the three monotheistic religions all born in the same area although with hundreds of years different history could find some days the dream to become reality. The question of Lidija Basta whose is the state may then get the answer: To the generations seeking peace for their future. It was clear, that there is today no answer of any example or even a model for such dream. On the other side, the hope that some times peace will have to win, gave all participants the conviction that with all their scientific effort and all collected wisdom, some day an answer might be found.

This answer may also be found in the fact, that the global migration of people may soften their concept indivisible and absolute sovereignty of a state. The concept of the sovereign state only accountable to history does not any more fit to reality. Nationalism linked to the ideology of sovereignty does not any more fit to our modern reality of global migration. Thus also the territory of the homeland for refugees and settlers may sometime loose its impact on the emotions. The country of origin may not be any more linked to sovereignty but much more to the hometown and home-area, bearing the memory and identity of peoples. Those areas may have some links to some state territory but they may also be integrated into a global market and global society of communication.

It was Ronald Watts, Ms. Dreifuss and Matthias Schyder who pointed at the principle of multiple loyalties as basic for multiethnic federations. Most states today reject the possibility of multiple citizenships. As long as citizenship is linked to defence multiple citizenships will always have difficulties. But as soon as citizenship is linked to political participation with regard to the political community responsible for its members multiple citizenships may become a post-modern concept of people belonging to different states. In such cases multiple citizenships will become also acceptable from the point of view of loyalty.

RULE OF LAW AND THE RIGHT TO BE DIFFERENT

In his introduction Ronald Watts pointed out, that there is never any federal solution than within a system which respects the basic principles of the rule of law. Only a society which is prepared to observe legal norms a complex federal constitution regulating shared rule and self-rule will have chance to be implemented into reality.

The participants of both religious communities, that is of the Jewish and of the Muslim community insisted on the very roots of their religion with regard to justice. Justice is considered to be at the core of Islamic and Jewish religion. Thus a system respecting the rule of law should be developed out of these very traditions.

How can a society split by fundamental ideologies as Greilsammer pointed out, how can communities belonging one to a religion claiming universality and the other claiming to be chosen by God accept common political authorities and recognize for each other the right to be different? Without accepting such basic principle a society will not be able to come together. The state of modernity is based on the conviction, that all human beings are basically equal. Thus it did never deal with the challenge, that even within such society some people require the right to be different from others. It will require a big step to be made for a state, which has its basic ground in the modern constitutionalism also to accept the right of some people to be different with regard to their language, religion, family tradition and community life. With regard to these rights there should be no majority principle which could be claimed to overrule such basic right. It is by evoking their group rights which must be guaranteed that those people will be protected within their rights.

God created men differently has been evoked by Mr. Ravitzki. Such religious wisdom should be transformed into political reality. Of course this difference does not mean that some are better than others. Different means in the legal sense just that they are different but to be treated on equal footing. This acceptance of the right to be different should become the bases for a political policy of inclusiveness. Nobody should be excluded from political life for reason of his own identity and these different identities should be considered by the political community as equally valid.

CULTURE OF NEGOTIATION

During the discussion often the lacking culture of negotiation has been evoked as a principle failure of the actual political culture of negotiation. The winner takes all principle is considered to be the main conflict solution tool. Either one can convince the democratic majority and then impose its ideas and solution on the minority either one has to accept to be the looser of the controversy. That solutions often could become a result out of negotiations seeking a win-win solution for all parties involved, is often to quickly rejected by the political actors as a alternative possible procedure.

Historical experiences prove however that federal solutions can only be found within a culture of negotiation and compromise. A federal system which is imposed on important looser will not become sustainable. Even in Switzerland, where the Catholics considered themselves as the looser of the civil war, federalism as solution to bring the society together was mistrusted by the minority.

It is of course much more difficult to establish a culture of negotiation if religion or religions are at stake. Religions as such seem to exclude compromises and consensus as result of political disputes. According to religious beliefs things are often either black or white. But in politics one has to accept compromises and be prepared to sacrifice sacred beliefs and concepts for the sake of peace. How can people living for their next life accept such compromise which can only safe them in this life?

Indeed compromise can only be considered as a value, if the great bulk of the society prefers decisions supported almost everybody or at least a great majority. Only in democratic systems which seek such support compromise can be considered as a value. However this needs a new view of democracy. Democracy should not only be reduced to a tool to produce majority, but as a tool to enable the society to decide in common on all issues limiting their freedom. If democracy is seen as a tool to enable as much as possible of self-determination if democracy is seen as a institutional system to guarantee liberty, then the aim should not be just to produce a simple majority but as an institution, which would enable different opinion leaders to convince the people of the value of certain decisions. Democracy then is party of the liberty concept. It guarantees liberty within the state or the political system. Finally only this type of democracy will consider compromise as a asset an value and not as a weakness of a political leader.

TRANSITION AND CONCLUSION

With regard to transition all participants agreed on the suggestion made in the paper of Nicolas Haysom and Ronald Watts, that only a step by step policy could bring the societies gradually to more rational and more peaceful solutions of their conflicts. Some interveners asked also for a clear leadership prepared to re-conciliation and integration. Without brave leaders able to convince the people and prepared to a real peace-process, there is no chance in the area.

In order to start a hopeful transitory process some major pre-conditions have to be established. Rule of Law and a democratic governmental system are by no means such pre-conditions. One was aware however, that in a situation of hatred and mistrust extremist movements take often profit in democratic elections. Thus without a certain climate of trust democracy may even not be able to produce leaders prepared to re-conciliation.

Economic development is closely linked to peace and rule of law. In an environment of poverty and shortage of labour again extreme ideologies may gain all support. How to come out of this vicious circle? The gradually and step by building up of credible institutions with political authority would certainly have to be part of a step by step policy. There was no much discussion on the issue with regard to the question whether there should be only one or two states. But it is clear, that without the acceptance that each society has to establish its own institutions one would not see any final chances.

Let us be guided by experience as reason might mislead us was the key word for the founding fathers of the American Constitution. The main result of these very fruitful discussions finally may be summarized in this one sentence. Scientific discourse and research might bring new ideas which can be helpful. In the end it will be the political leaders responsible to pursue either the road for peace or conflict. If they are willing to pursue the road for peace they should be guided by the many experiences in other conflict areas made in recent years in order to learn from the bad lessens and to follow the good lessons. One of those outstanding lessons every leader might learn from is by no means the peace process followed under the leadership of Mandela in South Africa.

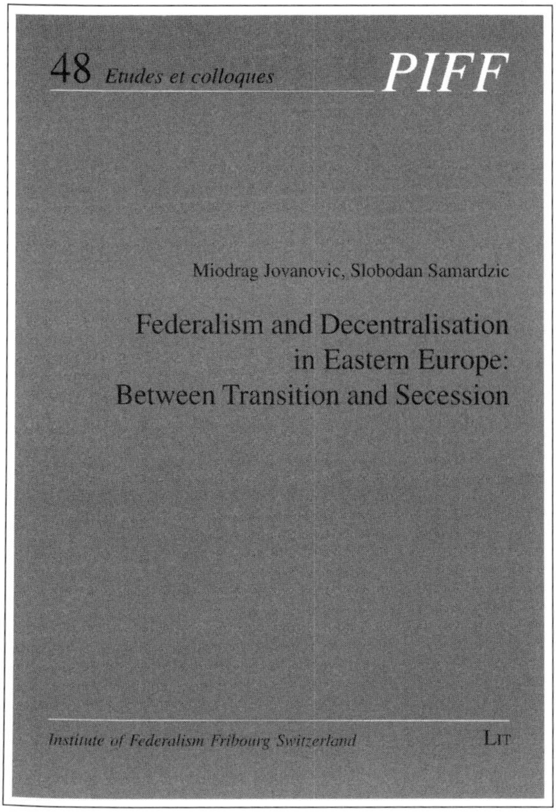

Publications of the Institute of Federalism

Miodrag Jovanović; Slobodan Samardžić
Federalism and Decentralisation in Eastern Europe: Between Transition and Secession
Although fully aware of the gravity of violent ethnic wars and challenges that multiethnic societies pose for any democratic polity, both authors endorse multicultural democracy. Jovanovic argues against territorial accommodation of ethnic demands and in favour of community-based minority rights policy. Samardzic understands territorial decentralisation as an indispensable guarantee for a fully-fledged protection of minority ethnic groups. Despite this major conceptual difference, they put forward democratic legitimacy as a fundamental condition for peaceful multiethnic societies.
Bd. 48, 2007, 240 S., 25,90 €, br., ISBN 978-3-8258-0934-8

LIT Verlag GmbH & Co. KG Wien – Zürich
Auslieferung Österreich: Medienlogistik Pichler-ÖBZ GmbH & Co KG
IZ-NÖ Süd, Straße 1, Objekt 34, A-2355 Wiener Neudorf, Postfach 133
Tel. +43 (0) 2236 / 63 535 - 236, Fax +43 (0) 2236 / 63 535 - 243, e-Mail: bestellen@medien-logistik.at
Auslieferung Deutschland: Fresnostr. 2 48159 Münster
Tel.: 0251 / 620 32 22 – Fax 0251 / 922 60 99
e-Mail: vertrieb@lit-verlag.de – http://www.lit-verlag.de

49 Etudes et colloques
PIFF
Erwin Tanner
Die muslimische Minderheit und ihre Religion
Strukturrechtliche und institutionsrechtliche Grundfragen im Bereich des Religionsrechts der Schweizerischen Eidgenossenschaft
Institute of Federalism Fribourg Switzerland
LIT